DATE DUE

OCT 17 2014	
MAR 23 2015	

HOW
TERRORISM
IS
WRONG

HOW
TERRORISM
IS
WRONG

MORALITY AND POLITICAL VIOLENCE

VIRGINIA HELD

OXFORD
UNIVERSITY PRESS
2008

OXFORD
UNIVERSITY PRESS

Oxford University Press, Inc., publishes works that further
Oxford University's objective of excellence
in research, scholarship, and education.

Oxford   New York
Auckland   Cape Town   Dar es Salaam   Hong Kong   Karachi
Kuala Lumpur   Madrid   Melbourne   Mexico City   Nairobi
New Delhi   Shanghai   Taipei   Toronto

With offices in
Argentina   Austria   Brazil   Chile   Czech Republic   France   Greece
Guatemala   Hungary   Italy   Japan   Poland   Portugal   Singapore
South Korea   Switzerland   Thailand   Turkey   Ukraine   Vietnam

Copyright © 2008 by Oxford University Press, Inc.

Published by Oxford University Press, Inc.
198 Madison Avenue, New York, New York 10016

www.oup.com

Oxford is a registered trademark of Oxford University Press

Library of Congress Cataloging-in-Publication Data
Held, Virginia.
How terrorism is wrong : morality and political violence / Virginia Held.
p. cm.
Includes bibliographical references and index.
ISBN 978-0-19-532959-9
1. Terrorism—Moral and ethical aspects.   2. Political violence.   I. Title.
HV6431.H417 2008
172'.1—dc22   2007033845

1 3 5 7 9 8 6 4 2

Printed in the United States of America
on acid-free paper

PREFACE

I gratefully acknowledge permissions to reprint in this book parts or all of works that have previously appeared. These include "Terrorism and War," *Journal of Ethics* 8 (2004): 59–75; "Legitimate Authority in Non-state Groups Using Violence," *Journal of Social Philosophy* 36(2) (Summer 2005): 175–193; "Terrorism, Rights, and Political Goals," in *Violence, Terrorism, and Justice*, ed. R. G. Frey and Christopher W. Morris (New York: Cambridge University Press, 1991); "Group Responsibility for Ethnic Conflict," *Journal of Ethics* 6 (2002): 159–181; "The Media and Political Violence," *Journal of Ethics* 1 (1997): 187–202; "Violence, Terrorism, and Moral Inquiry," *Monist* 67(4) (1984): 605–626, used in chapter 7; and "The Normative Import of Action," in *Gewirth: Critical Essays on Action, Rationality, and Community*, ed. Michael Boylan (Lanham, Md.: Rowman and Littlefield, 1999), used in chapter 8.

I am indebted to the anonymous readers at Oxford University Press for their helpful suggestions for the proposed book. I also wish to thank Peter Ohlin of Oxford University Press for his advice and encouragement.

Nearly all of the material in the book has been presented in earlier forms to various groups, and I am deeply grateful to all who gave me the benefit of their thoughts and reactions. Though I omit many names, I wish to single out a few of them for special mention.

The paper that became chapter 1, "Terrorism and War," started out as a talk on terrorism given at a session of the American Philosophical Association, Pacific Division, meeting in Seattle on March 30, 2002. It then became a paper called "Kinds of Terrorism," which I presented at the Central Division of the American Philosophical Association meeting in Chicago on April 25, 2002. It was then further developed into papers presented at a conference called "Moral and Political Aspects of Terrorism," held at the University of Arizona March 7–9, 2003; at the Conference on Value Inquiry at the University of North Dakota April 10–12, 2003; and at the annual conference of the North American Society for Social Philosophy in Boston on July 19, 2003. At these sessions I received many helpful comments on these earlier versions of the chapter. I would like to thank the organizers and participants at these conferences, as well as those who provided additional remarks, especially Sigal Ben-Porath, Susan Brison, Ed Byrne, Thomas Christiano, C. A. J. Coady, Ted Honderich, Alison Jaggar, William McBride, Angelia Means, Stephen Nathanson, Andrew Valls, and Jeremy Waldron.

Chapter 2, "Military Intervention and Terrorism," has not been previously published. It began as a talk on principled differences in the grounds for military intervention, given at a special session of the American Philosophical Association, Pacific Division, in Portland, Oregon, on March 23, 2006. I appreciate the efforts of Deen Chatterjee and Don Schied in organizing that session and the observations of the other panel members, especially Larry May. Papers that developed my thoughts on intervention were then given at Wellesley College and Hampshire College, and I thank those who arranged these talks and commented on them, especially Lester Mazor and Laura Reed. A paper that resembles this chapter was presented at a session of the Legal Theory Workshop at Yale University on February 1, 2007; I am enormously grateful to Judith Resnick for her comments on this occasion and later on and to the other participants in the discussion, especially Seyla Benhabib, Michael Doyle, Bruce Ackerman, Jules Coleman, and Joel Marks. Arguments in the chapter were further discussed at a conference at Denison University on February 22–23, 2007, where I benefited from remarks by Alison Jaggar and Fiona Robinson, then at an ethics conference at Felician College on March 17, 2007; I thank Yvonne Raley, Lisa Cassidy, and Chris Alen Sula for their contributions to this occasion.

An earlier version of chapter 3, "Legitimate Authority in Nonstate Groups Using Violence," was presented at a meeting of the American Philosophical Association's Pacific Division in Pasadena, March 26, 2004, and discussed at a colloquium at the CUNY Graduate Center, December 14, 2004. I am grateful to those who arranged these discussions and to all who commented then and later, especially Omar Dahbour, Carol Gould, Karen Kovach, John Lango, Lionel McPherson, Richard Miller, and Luis Rodríguez-Abascal.

I extend my appreciation to the many persons who made helpful comments when chapter 4, "Terrorism, Rights, and Political Goals (with Postscript)," was presented in preliminary forms at a philosophy department program at the graduate school of the City University of New York; at a conference of the Greater Philadelphia Philosophy Consortium; at a conference on violence, terrorism, and justice at Bowling Green State University; at a conference on law and the legitimization of violence at the University of Buffalo; and at presentations at Colgate University and Hampshire College. Special thanks go to Annette Baier, C. A. J. Coady, Jonathan Glover, Bart Gruzalski, Lionel McPherson, Hans Oberdiek, Joseph Raz, Peter Simpson, and Huntington Terrell. I am indebted to Igor Primoratz for including it in his collection on terrorism and for inviting the postscript that responded to a critique.

An earlier version of chapter 5, "Group Responsibility for Ethnic Conflict," was presented at a conference titled "Violence, Responsibility, and Reconciliation," sponsored by the Center for Philosophic Exchange and held at Santa Barbara City College, October 9–11, 1998. I wish to thank Aleksandar Jokić for having organized this conference and those participants who commented on the presentation. Later versions were given at philosophy colloquia at the College of William and Mary on November 12, 1999, and the Graduate Center of the City University of New York on September 5, 2001. My thanks go to those on these occasions who offered their views, especially Larry Becker, Mark Fowler, Alan Fuchs, and Paul Grieco, as well as to Ariel Colonomos, Karen Kovach, and Philip Pettit for additional suggestions.

I am grateful to Angelo Corlett for his thoughts on the paper that has become chapter 6, "The Media and Political Violence," and to John Hospers and Anita Silvers for the special issue of the *Monist* in which a paper titled "Violence, Terrorism, and Moral Inquiry," which forms part of chapter 7, originally appeared. I also thank Michael Boylan for organizing the conference on Alan Gewirth at which a paper, "The Normative Import of Action," which I have incorporated into chapter 8, was originally given, and I express my appreciation to those who commented on it.

I have approached many of the issues in this book with trepidation and even more uncertainty than I felt when addressing other philosophical issues. The most I hope for is that the book will contribute to a badly needed discussion, and I thank all those who join in this task.

CONTENTS

HOW
TERRORISM
IS
WRONG

INTRODUCTION

What questions should we ask about political violence? We are often in doubt. This book offers moral assessments of some forms of political violence. It focuses on terrorism as the most salient, current form in need of examination, analysis, and evaluation. It discusses various moral and other arguments about violent conflict and endeavors to steer future efforts of theorizing and practice in justifiable directions that will diminish the grievous suffering caused by violence and terror. The book considers conditions that promote political violence and evaluates efforts to deal with violence and with such conditions. Among the questions considered are: What makes a course of action aimed at bringing about or preventing political change morally acceptable? How, on what basis, and according to whom should political violence be evaluated?

The book compares terrorism with other kinds of violence, such as war or the maintenance and enforcement of a political and legal order that often kill far more people, including children, than do terrorist acts. It scrutinizes popular attitudes that glorify some kinds of violence and vilify others. It moves beyond the widespread but distorted picture of mystifyingly unexpected terrorist attacks that arise from nowhere, as well as of appropriate (or inappropriate) responses, and considers such events in the wider contexts of various regional and global conflicts. It looks at earlier political violence to achieve social change.

Philosophical and other academic discussions of terrorism have often been quite different from the reportage in much of the popular press and the statements of many commentators and politicians positioning themselves for advantage. Philosophers have for the most part treated the use of terrorism (and of violence to suppress it) as a topic to subject to moral analysis and critique. Political scientists have sought to understand and explain the causes of terrorism and to assess effective countermeasures. Psychologists have tried to understand the personal component of individual terrorists' violent acts. In political debates and media discussions, in contrast, all too often the assumption is made that terrorism is the epitome of evil, which suddenly and inexplicably arises to slaughter the innocent, and that the violence "we" and our friends unleash to fight against it is unquestionably righteous. Often it is even suggested that those who try to understand terrorism are thereby excusing it and thus are morally culpable. In the face of such deliberate lack of awareness, this book presents a philosophical treatment that intends to take appropriate account of findings in other academic fields, reliable reportage in the press, and responsible public discussion and does not yield to the fear of taking unpopular positions.

Over the years I have written a number of essays that assess on moral grounds the use of violence—by individuals with political motives, by groups seeking political change, and by governments. The book is based on those analyses. Three of them were written after the attack on the World Trade Center on September 11, 2001, which led to a huge resurgence of interest in terrorism and violence. Readers who believe, as I do not, that 9/11 changed everything may assume that work written earlier has automatically been superseded. My own view is that the moral issues after 9/11 are substantially similar to those that have periodically arisen surrounding violence and that the earlier essays are as relevant now as when they were written, though some have been heavily revised.

My views on moral theory have changed more than my beliefs about violence specifically. For issues of violence and ways to deal with it, I am now more persuaded than when I began these essays of the significance of the ethics of care.[1] This is illustrated briefly in chapter 2 in the discussion of international law and dealt with further in chapter 8, where I examine characteristic arguments in the ethics of care.

The ethics of care provides a comprehensive moral outlook for the evaluation of human relations generally. It can serve as a moral guide in our closest and most distant relations: in the networks that connect us as members of families and groups, as participants in civil society, and as aspirants to global civility. Traditional and dominant moral theories such as Kantian ethics and utilitarianism, with their deontological and consequentialist approaches, are still suitable for many legal and political issues when these are seen as embedded in a wider network of human relationships; however, they are less satisfactory than usually thought when expanded into comprehensive moral theories. Since in this book I am primarily concerned with violence that arises from political conflict and is dealt with in political and legal ways, the more familiar approaches often remain appropriate. However, for longer-term evaluations of political institutions and practices, of groups and the violence they often employ, and of ways to configure these domains within wider societies (including potentially a global one), the ethics of care may be more promising.[2]

In a Kantian or deontological approach to morally evaluating acts of violence, one considers the principles one deems valid that would yield judgments about particular actions. The actions are seen to have characteristics that make them wrong or right in themselves, regardless of their consequences. For instance, it is inherently wrong to lie or deceive, even if doing so may on occasion have good results. Similarly, acts of violence can often be judged to violate people's rights and thus to be inherently wrong, or they can be acts of law enforcement and thereby often justified. According to some points of view, the inherent wrongness or rightness of actions is only prima facie, and other considerations can sometimes outweigh it, but it is never unimportant.

We can contrast this with a consequentialist approach to morality, of which utilitarianism is the leading example, in which actions in themselves are neither right nor wrong but are to be judged on the basis of their consequences. From this viewpoint, violence is often considered as unfortunate but necessary to enable governing or to achieve desirable political change. Whether the good consequences of violent acts outweigh the bad depends on considerations such as what serves people's interests or diminishes their suffering. Our evaluations of these factors usually rest on empirical estimates of them that are often in doubt at the time of action but that we cannot avoid acting on.

In contrast with both of these approaches, the ethics of care especially values caring relationships, obviously at the personal level within families and among friends and less obviously at the most general level of all human relationships. It understands the importance and necessity of caring labor and the values of empathy, sensitivity, trust, and response to need. It cultivates practices such as the building of trust and responding to actual needs. In contrast to the model of the self-sufficient liberal individual, the ethics of care sees persons as interrelated. It is appropriate for the wide but shallow human relations of global interactions, as well as for the strongest and most intimate human relations of care in families. Growing out of feminist appreciations for the enormous amount of overlooked but utterly necessary labor involved in bringing up children and caring for the ill, it articulates especially the *values* involved and the guidance they provide.

The ethics of care has developed care as a value that rivals justice, and it evaluates practices of care. It is based on experience that is universal—the experience of having been cared for, since no child can survive without this—and compares favorably in this regard with contractual views only claimed to be universal. It rests not on divisive religious views but on common experience. Then, it can conceptualize that within the more distant and weak relations of care, we can develop political and legal ways to interact, and here the more familiar moral theories may be most appropriate. For the adequate moral assessment of violence and terrorism we need to consider all of these sources of moral insight.

The ethics of care can provide the grounding for the valuing of nonviolence over violence in regional and global conflicts, a concern that is relatively missing in the familiar political and moral theories designed for the interactions of citizens of a given state. The social contract tradition and the moral theories (e.g., Kantian ethics and utilitarianism) that have accompanied its development have never dealt adequately with the question of which individuals or groups are to be included in the contract. Answers to such questions have merely been assumed. In fact, violence has played an overwhelming role in establishing the boundaries and memberships of states. Nationalism and imperialism rather than contractual agreements have permeated their development and continue to dominate their situations.

When the principles deemed appropriate for citizens' relations with each other are universalized as moral theories (or even as theories of international relations), they remain abstract and nearly inapplicable to a world already carved up into thoroughly unequal states, the more powerful of which can exploit and impose their will on others—and have often done so. A moral theory such as the ethics of care is needed to ensure that we care enough about our fellow human beings to respect their rights and take appropriate account of their interests and especially that we refrain from aggressive violence. The ethics of care advises that we promote our policies and seek change and maintain order as nonviolently as possible.

At both the state and the international level, the ethics of care does not ask for justice to be *replaced* by care, either in its institutions or our moral theorizing. Within states, for instance, it recognizes the importance of law and its enforcement in protecting people from violence and in implementing their rights to equality. It asks that legal institutions be more caring than they are but maintains that justice, as a value, ought to have priority over care in the limited domain of justice, although care may be primary in the comprehensive morality within which law should guide specific interactions. The ethics of care recognizes the gross limitations of law and the superiority of other moral approaches for much of human value. Analogously at the international level, care can recommend respect for international law while contributing to more promising alternatives.

Care is obviously antithetical to violence, which damages and destroys what care takes pains to build. Care instructs us to establish the means to curb, contain, prevent, and head off the violence that characteristically leads to more violence. In bringing up children, this requires a long process of nurturing and education in order to cultivate nonviolent feelings, self-restraint, appropriate trust, and an understanding of the better alternatives to aggressive conflict. In interactions with others at some distance, the primary institutions with which to prevent and deal with violence are political and legal, and care can recommend acceptance of these institutions when appropriate even as it recognizes their limits. Moreover, it can suggest alternative ways of interacting that may prove more satisfactory. These understandings can be matched at the international level, as care recommends respect for international law and also recommends alternative methods of fostering interconnection. We should work to build interactions that are not primarily political and legal—the often nongovernmental networks of civil society, with their cultural, economic, educational, environmental, scientific, and social welfare forms of cooperative institution—and that will connect us and address our problems. We can gradually extend their reach so that we can better express our caring.[3]

It is widely understood within states (though not by every administration or official), as well as within practices of care, that those who enforce reasonable rules should not resort to the same tactics as those who break them. This point should be much better understood at the international level. Moreover, within families and in a global context, to avoid paternalistic domination, care needs to be interpreted from the perspective of *both* the recipient and the provider. Care *can* be provided in ways that are domineering, oppressive, insensitive, and ineffective, but this is not *good* care. The ethics of care provides guidance for meeting the needs of persons, including requirements for peace and security from violence, in ways that are effective, sensitive, liberating, and responsible.

There are those, of course, who will derisively protest that one cannot deal with terrorists or violent states in the same ways that parents try to deal with aggressive children, and certainly advocates of the ethics of care will agree. The point is rather that the *values* of care can provide guidance for both. Sara Ruddick has explored the way in which an ideal of nonviolence "governs the practice" of maternal care, although actual mothers are often violent.[4] She shows how relevant such practices are for those who are working to promote peace. Mothers, she observes, often "school themselves to renounce violent strategies of control and to resist the violence of others.... [They] strive to create welcoming responses to bodily life despite the disturbing willfulness" of those for whom they care. A politics of peace should be "resolutely suspicious of violence even in the best of causes." Peacemakers seldom call for an absolute renunciation of violence, but they "fix on inventing myriad forms of cooperation, reconciliation, and nonviolent resistance."[5]

Guided by the ethics of care, we would recognize that violence (or the threat of it) is an expectable aspect of human reality and that we can work successfully to contain it and decrease the damage it brings about. We would restrain rather than destroy those who become violent, we would work to prevent violence rather than wipe out violent persons, and we would inhibit violence as nonviolently as possible.

In this book I begin with the post-9/11 essays on terrorism. They consider appropriate responses and preventive measures in order to further our understanding of what terrorism is, what its likely causes are, and what we should do about it. They aim at morally assessing recent instances of terrorism and the actions, policies, and practices taken and considered to counter them.

The later chapters ask many of the same questions but focus less on terrorism. Political violence takes many forms, and considering them helps us to understand terrorism in the wider context of human conflict.

As I have already emphasized, the book assesses violence from a moral perspective. Of course, violence is morally problematic, but blanket condemnations of a simple kind are of very limited use. I make distinctions and evaluations that can be helpful to actual human beings who are living in violent societies in a brutal world. This discussion, I hope, will enable us to make more responsible decisions and to take more justifiable actions in the face of both actual and threatened violence.

The first chapter compares terrorism with war, clarifies meanings, and assesses comparative wrongs. It argues that terrorism is not uniquely atrocious but is on a continuum with many other forms of political violence, and it maintains that wars, even "good wars," are often morally far worse. It concludes with a suggestion about seeking the causes of terrorism.

The second chapter is previously unpublished. It considers the issues that surround military intervention as a response to terrorism and explores the status of international law and the extent to which morality demands respect for it. It examines the cases of genocide in Rwanda, the NATO intervention in Kosovo, and the U.S. invasion of Iraq in 2003. It investigates the idea of retroactive justification and considers its moral implications.

The third chapter considers both the standing of nonstate groups that use violence and the question of whether they can ever legitimately engage in justifiable violence. Many people assume they cannot, but liberation movements often aspire to be considered legitimate, and some have evidently succeeded.

With the fourth chapter I turn to an earlier treatment that I have recently updated. It considers how an absolutist condemnation of terrorism cannot be derived from a consequentialist evaluation and shows how it should also not be thought derivable from a deontologically based respect for human rights.

Chapter 5 was influenced by the upheavals and violent ethnic conflict in the Balkans in the 1990s. It raises questions about group responsibility that have long been of interest to me. It concludes that people can and often ought to take responsibility for the actions of groups of which they are members.

Chapter 6 considers the role of the media in responsibly dealing with terrorism. Despite changes occuring in the media since the text was written, the pressing issues today seem remarkably similar to those I have been raising for some time about the structure of media culture.

The final two chapters discuss how I believe we should conduct moral assessments of political actions. They describe the relevant factors and ways in which we can interpret their moral significance. I present guidelines for conducting moral inquiries and propose ways to improve our evaluations. Both chapters are substantially revised versions of earlier essays. The last chapter in particular contains much new material and discusses the ethics of care.

Since this book is a philosophical treatment of violence and terrorism, readers can expect it to clarify the meanings of these terms. *Terrorism* is notoriously hard to define. The word is routinely used in quite different and often contradictory ways, depending on one's interests. Philosophers have made progress in clarifying its meanings, but no single definition seems satisfactory. I discuss the reasons one can find various definitions unsatisfactory. I cannot propose a simple solution to the problem of definition, but throughout the book I attempt to improve our understanding of political violence and its various forms, including terrorism.

This book does not deal with many of the critical issues surrounding political violence. One such set of questions concerns just war theory. Since just war theory was devised to deal with the military force used by armed forces against each other, it is unclear whether and how it should influence the evaluation of such nonmilitary forms of violence as terrorism.[6] I assume that the moral imperatives central to the just war tradition (i.e., that war must have a justifiable purpose; that it must be a last resort; that, in conducting war, all sides should limit the way they use violence; and that when they do use violence, it should be proportional to the objective, thereby minimizing unnecessary casualties) are moral imperatives worthy of respect, though often indeterminate.

The concerns of just war theory to reduce the wrongs and harms of violence, even if we cannot eliminate violence from human affairs, are morally compelling regardless of the type of violence used and the type of user. Much more needs to be said, however, about the implications of just war principles. Whether war with contemporary weapons can possibly be just is a pressing question. Whether those without the means to engage in military confrontations with opposing states but with the means to cause substantial harm in other ways should be judged by the standards of just war theory is questionable, but what moral standards should be applied? Many of the moral considerations will be similar in both cases, but they may yield different recommendations from the familiar ones of just war theory. Since just war theory does not cover the violence most evident in recent years—that of resistance and liberation movements, of terrorism and guerrilla campaigns, and of the retaliation against these—even if the theory were satisfactory for states' use of military force against each other, it would be of limited use. New thinking is badly needed to help us develop evaluations that adequately address the types of violence currently taking place.

Other issues missing here are the militarization of society and its effect on the thinking of citizens, governmental policies, and states' prospects. Preparations for using violence, as well as actually using it, call for moral evaluation, but these are not discussed here. Nor do I give more than passing attention to the relative uselessness of much of the most advanced weaponry for dealing with many kinds of violence and opposition.

Other questions about which not nearly enough is said involve the enormous amount of violence perpetrated around the globe against women. When rape is used as part of a campaign of ethnic cleansing or as a wartime tactic, it is clearly political. In other cases (to the extent that violence against particular women is actually directed against women in general, as it has often been shown to be, and is part of an effort, conscious or not, to preserve men's dominance), it is political in the sense that any structure of dominance (e.g., patriarchy) has political aspects, though male dominance goes far beyond the political. Violence against homosexuals and racial minorities is comparably political, but it is more as well. Obstruction of the progress that women are making around the world and intolerance toward gender identities other than that of male heterosexuals are important components in the rise of religious extremism, with its dangerous tendencies to encourage violence and conflict. The ethics of care can be helpful in its moral recommendations for dealing with these issues.[7]

Another set of questions neglected concerns how people should try to repair the moral and human damage caused by violence. Important developments have taken place, including the establishing of international tribunals to bring to justice those who are guilty of genocidal actions and other mass violence. Much has happened to foster reconciliation and truth commissions as alternatives to trials and punishment. These are often more expressive of the values of care than their alternatives. I applaud many of these developments and inquiries but do not take account of them in this book.[8]

Urgent questions about the curtailing of civil rights in political responses to violence are also not dealt with here. These matters are obviously political in the sense in which I am using the term, and of great importance, but they are beyond the bounds of my present effort.

Much more needs to be said about how morality should guide us in dealing with violence, including its political forms. The chapters here suggest various factors and moral considerations that ought to enter into our evaluations. The issues are unusually fraught with the prospects of dreadful choices, dire consequences, and terrible failures no matter what we try to do. Efforts at philosophical understanding may nevertheless be of some use.

TERRORISM AND WAR

There are different kinds of war: world wars, small wars, civil wars, revolutions, wars of liberation. There are also guerrilla campaigns, which may become wars. In discussions of terrorism, it is a serious mistake to suppose that all terrorism is alike. Terrorism has different forms, as does war.

In the United States, the Right has been asserting that to hold anything else than that all terrorism is the same is to undermine the "moral clarity" needed to pursue the war on terrorism. Further, U.S. neoconservatives, Christian fundamentalists, and the Israeli Right are especially intent on arguing that the terrorism carried out by Palestinians is the same as that conducted by Osama bin Laden and the Al Qaeda network.[1] They agree with former Israeli prime minister Ariel Sharon that "terrorism is terrorism is terrorism anywhere in the world."[2] Asserting that Israel is battling the same enemy as the United States, Sharon has stated that "the cultured world is under a cruel attack by radical Islam. It is an enemy composed of lunatic individuals, lunatic regimes and lunatic countries."[3] Such views have found a strong echo in the United States after the attacks of September 11, 2001.

Those who maintain that all terrorism is alike also argue that the same countermeasures, such as military obliteration and preventive attack, should be used against all terrorists and that the same principles, such as "never negotiate with terrorists or with those who support them," should be applied. To U.S. Vice President Dick Cheney, with terrorists "no policy of containment or deterrence will prove effective. The only way to deal with this threat is to destroy it, completely and utterly."[4] Those who share these views are intent on rejecting any comparisons between deaths caused by terrorists and deaths caused by their opponents, on the grounds that there is "no moral equivalence" between terrorism and fighting against terrorism.

It is not only the Right, however, that seeks a simple, all-purpose moral condemnation of all terrorism. New York Times correspondent Nicholas Kristof, while acknowledging the difficulties in seeking "moral clarity," has nevertheless advocated it with respect to terrorism.[5] He has suggested that a moral revulsion against killing civilians could develop akin to that which developed after World War I and resulted in the delegitimization of the use of poison gas. But this assumes we can clearly distinguish "civilians" from "legitimate targets," which is a contested issue. Voting publics often put into power the governmental leaders—and support the policies—that terrorists oppose. If other means have failed and if violence against the members of a state's armed services is justified, it is unclear why those who bring about that state's policies and give its military forces their orders should be exempt from having violence used against them. At least such an argument could muddy the moral clarity of the revulsion against terrorism the proponents of such revulsion seek.

Furthermore, the occasions for moral revulsion are unlikely to be limited in the way those who see all terrorism as alike have suggested. Ted Honderich, for instance, shares the moral revulsion of countless others at the carnage of September 11.[6] However, he is also outraged by the fact that the United States promotes global economic policies that make many millions of people miserable in the world's poorer countries and cut their lives short. He sees enough of a connection between such misery and the appeal of terrorism to its potential recruits that he holds the United States partly responsible for the terrorism practiced against it. Moral revulsion can thus be so appropriately multiplied that the uniqueness of terrorism in provoking it is undermined, and with this goes the sought-for moral clarity. We seem to be left, then, with needing to make complex and disputable moral judgments here as everywhere else. This is not at all to suggest that persuasive judgments are impossible, but they are unlikely to plausibly focus as exclusively on terrorism as the proponents of moral clarity about it in particular wish.

Persuasive judgments should, for instance, consider how the actions of states in opposing terrorist groups have frequently killed far more

civilians than have terrorists. The Reagan administration's "War on Terror" in Central America in the 1980s killed approximately two hundred
thousand people and produced more than a million refugees.[7] States
that engage in what they call counterterrorism (but which the recipients
of their violence often consider terrorism) frequently use the argument
that they do not target civilians; an unfortunate (though foreseeable)
side effect, they claim, is that civilians may be killed. Nevertheless, their
possession of weapons capable of precisely attacking (when they choose
to) targeted persons intentionally and civilians only unintentionally is
just another way in which their superior power allows them to be dominant. It may be that such domination is what a terrorist group is resisting. It will in any case be unpersuasive to argue that such a group ought
to use means of which it is incapable. If such groups had the ability to
challenge the armed forces of the states whose domination they oppose,
they might well do so, but their lack of power is often the reason that terrorism is their weapon in the first place. As any number of commentators
have noted, terrorism is the weapon of the weak. Moreover, as conventional war is increasingly "riskless" for armed forces with overwhelming
power, who understandably try to minimize their own casualties, there
may be less and less possibility for opposing groups to attack in conventional ways the actual combatants of powerful countries.[8] To be persuasive, an argument that terrorism should never be used would have to
assume that the weapons used against it and against those who support
it are always used for morally justifiable goals and in morally justifiable
ways; however, moral clarity about such an assumption is impossible for
any reasonable person.

Those of us who are engaged year after year in slogging through arguments seeking moral clarity can reject the U.S. and Israeli Right's versions of it with respect to terrorism. But we are far from agreeing on what
terrorism is and how we can understand it, let alone how to respond to
it and how to prevent it.

My judgments in this chapter are comparative. I do not argue that
either terrorism or war can be justified, but I maintain that terrorism is
not necessarily worse than war. A great deal of recent discussion of terrorism has it that terrorism is so morally unacceptable as a means that
we do not need even to consider the political objectives of those who
engage in it. War, on the other hand, is seen as quite possibly justified.
My intent is to compare war and terrorism and to show how war can be
morally worse.

DEFINING TERRORISM

Understanding how to define terrorism is notoriously difficult. It is one of the most contested concepts and obviously complex. Governments characteristically define terrorism as something only their opponents can commit and as something only those who seek to change policies or to attack a given political system or status quo can engage in.[9] The definition used by the U.S. State Department, for instance, has included the claim that it is carried out by "subnational groups or clandestine agents."[10] And international law appears to concur.[11] This is obviously unsatisfactory. When the military rulers of Argentina caused thousands of their suspected opponents to "disappear" in order to spread fear among other potential dissidents, this was state terrorism. And as Israeli and U.S. political scientists Neve Gordon and George López, respectively, say, "Israel's practice of state-sanctioned torture also qualifies as...political terrorism. It is well known that torture is not only used to extract information or to control the victim; it is also used to control the population as a whole."[12] They conclude persuasively "that states can terrorize and can use soldiers, airplanes, and tanks to do so....Terror should not be reduced to the difference between nonstate and state action."[13]

There can also be state-sponsored terrorism when the government of one state funds and supports terrorism carried out by members of groups or states not under its control. The United States routinely lists a number of countries (e.g., Iran and Syria) that, it claims, support terrorist groups elsewhere. Furthermore, in the 1980s, U.S. support for the contras in Nicaragua, who spread fear of what would happen to people if they joined or supported the Sandinista rebels, also falls into this category. Most states recognize this kind of terrorism when their adversaries engage in it, if not when they themselves aid such terrorists.

Terrorism is certainly violence, and it is political violence. One can doubt that Al Qaeda has a *political* objective in the sense in which many people understand politics, but since it aims at the religious domination of the political, its violence is indeed political, though perhaps it is not open to the usual responses to political aims through dialogue and compromise. Its aim to expel U.S. and European forces from the Middle East is clearly political. War is also political violence on a larger scale, though if the most alarming plans of current terrorist groups were successful, they would often amount to war as currently understood. In addition, political violence can also be more limited than most terrorism, as in the assassination of a particular political leader. Terrorism usually seeks to terrorize—to spread fear among a wider group than those directly harmed or killed. And it very often attacks members of an opposing group other than those who compose its armed forces.

Two important definitional questions have to do with whether the targeting of civilians must be part of the definition of terrorism and whether such targeting turns other political violence into terrorism. Many of those who write about terrorism incorporate the targeting of civilians into their definitions (e.g., Michael Walzer,[14] Tony Coady,[15] and Igor Primoratz[16]). This is the meaning of terrorism that may be emerging in international law. Since progressives attach great importance to the development of international law, we should certainly hesitate to challenge its positions. However, international law is itself evolving and has serious limitations. As currently formulated, it is highly biased in favor of existing states and against nonstate groups. This may be a bias we should accept in a dangerous world, especially for interactions between states, but considering the moral issues involved is surely appropriate.

There are serious problems with a definition of terrorism that sees "the deliberate killing of innocent people," as Walzer puts it, to be its central characteristic or what distinguishes it from other kinds of political violence and war and makes it automatically morally unjustifiable in the same way that murder is. First, consider some of the descriptive implications. If targeting civilians must be part of terrorism, then blowing up the Marine barracks in Lebanon in 1983 and killing hundreds of marines, and blasting a hole in the U.S. destroyer *Cole* and killing seventeen sailors in Yemen in October 2000 would not be instances of terrorism, and yet they are routinely offered as examples of terrorism. Much Palestinian violence that is labeled terrorism is directed at Israeli soldiers. Although we might say that such descriptions are simply wrong, I am inclined to think they are not.

Even more awkward for the proposed definition that includes the killing of civilians as its defining characteristic is that we would have to make a very sharp distinction between the September 11 attack on the World Trade Center, which was certainly terrorism, and the attack that same day and with entirely similar means on the Pentagon, which on this definition would not be counted as terrorism (although some civilians work at the Pentagon, it is a primarily military target).[17] This seems very peculiar.

If one tries with this definition to include (rather than exclude) these cases as instances of terrorism and if one thinks that, instead of those who are technically "civilians," one simply means those who are not now shooting at one—like the Marines, when they were asleep, or the colonels at their desks in the Pentagon—and suggests that only those presently engaged in combat are legitimate targets, one will make it illegitimate for the opponents of terrorism to target terrorists when they are not actually engaged in bombings and the like. Moreover, distinguishing when members of the armed forces are actual present threats that may be targeted (as distinct from only potential threats because they are now resting) has not been part of the distinctions worked out so far, which assert that noncombatants should not be targeted. As Robert Fullinwider writes, "combatants are first of all those in a warring country's military service. They are…fair targets of lethal response…even when they are in areas to the rear of active fighting and even when they are sleeping."[18] What counts is whether they are members of the armed forces or fighting group.

An even more serious problem with a proposal to tie the definition of terrorism to the targeting of civilians but to include the attack on the Pentagon among instances of terrorism (because members of the armed forces working at the Pentagon are not currently engaged in combat) is that it puts the burden of being a "legitimate target" on the lowest levels of the military hierarchy—the ordinary soldiers, sailors, pilots, and support personnel—and exempts those who give them their orders, send them into combat, and make them instruments of violence.

Furthermore, if attacking civilians is the defining characteristic of terrorism, a great many actions that are typically *not* called terrorism would have to be considered terrorist actions: the bombings of Hiroshima, Nagasaki, Dresden, London, and all of those other places where civilians live and become targets, as well as where the aim to spread fear and demoralization among wider groups was surely present. The U.S. bombings in the Vietnam war would be prime examples. Perhaps we should just get used to calling all of these "acts of terrorism." But perhaps we should find a definition of terrorism that does not ask us to.

What many discussions of terrorism try, of course, to do is to come up with a definition such that what *they* do is terrorism and *unjustified,* whereas what *we* and our friends do is not terrorism but justified self-defense. Building the targeting of civilians into the definition is often used to accomplish this since "intentionally killing innocent people" seems by definition wrong and unjustified. However, the net then catches not only the usual miscreants of terrorism but also much of the bombing that is carried out by, for instance, the United States and its allies, bombing that proponents are very reluctant to consider unjustified. They end up with the kind of double standard that moral discussion ought to avoid. Walzer, for instance, has argued that terrorism is never justified, even in a just cause, because it deliberately kills innocents, but that the allied bombing of German cities in World War II was justified even though many innocent civilians were deliberately killed.

Of course, a great deal of discussion has centered on what "deliberately" amounts to. The claim is often made that terrorism intentionally targets civilians, while the violence of governments in seeking to suppress it only accidentally causes comparable or greater loss of life among civilians and that this makes all the moral difference. I find this a dubious assertion. David Rodin argues against the view that intention makes all the difference. He points out that noncombatants have the right to not be harmed by violence when force is used recklessly or negligently, as well as when it is used intentionally, and that the former is common in conventional warfare.[19]

Only governments with highly sophisticated weaponry can afford to be extremely selective in their targets—the Allies in World War II, for instance, could not afford to be—and we know that even "smart bombs" often make mistakes. In the wars of the 1990s, 75–90 percent of all deaths were civilian deaths, making it hard to accept that terrorism is morally far worse than war.[20] The relevant comparison with respect to civilians seems to be which side—in the pursuit of its political goals—is causing the greater loss of civilian life. Then, in a political conflict in which at least one side uses terrorism, if the deaths caused by both sides are roughly equivalent, the argument may appropriately focus especially on the justice (or lack of it) of the political goals involved.

This is not a popular point to make in the wake of September 11, but we might keep in mind that the actual loss of life caused by terrorism—in comparison with conventional warfare—remains relatively modest. It is the fear that is large rather than the actual numbers killed. Of course, this may change if terrorists come to use nuclear weapons, but the *comparative* figures might not change if the Pentagon has its way and nuclear weapons become a much more standard part of the arsenal of "defense."

Another difficulty with building the killing of civilians (or noncombatants or "the innocent") into the definition of terrorism is that, as I previously mentioned, it is not at all clear who the "innocent" are as distinct from the "legitimate" targets. We can perhaps agree that small children are innocent, but beyond this, there is little moral clarity. First of all, many members of the armed forces are draftees who have no choice but to be combatants. Many conscripts in the Israeli army, for instance, may disapprove of their government's policies. Many others of those who participate in armed conflict in the U.S. armed forces and elsewhere have been pressed into service by economic necessity and social oppression. Still others engaged in political violence around the world are themselves children, often pulled into combat at age twelve, thirteen, or fourteen. Studies by international inquiries put the number of children in combat in the hundreds of thousands.[21]

An additional complication is that many civilians may have demanded of their governments the very policies that opponents are resisting, sometimes violently. A political analyst for an Israeli newspaper, for instance, said that, even more than Sharon's inclinations, it was the Israeli public's demands that caused the violent reoccupation of Palestinian territories and massive destruction there, though Sharon may not have needed much help in deciding on these actions.[22] In January 2003 the Israeli public had an opportunity to accept or reject the policies of the Sharon government: Voters returned Sharon and his Likud party to power with double the number of parliament seats they had had before the election.[23] Unfortunately, terrorism that kills civilians to voice opposition to a government's policies does not distinguish between those who support that government and those who do not.[24] But neither does counter-terrorism that kills civilians distinguish between those who support terrorist groups and those who do not.

Especially in the case of a democracy, where citizens elect their leaders and are ultimately responsible for their government's policies, it is not clear that citizens should be exempt from the violence those policies may lead to while the members of their armed services are legitimate targets. *If* a government's policies are unjustifiable and *if* political violence to resist them is justifiable (these are very large "if's" but not at all unimaginable), then it is not clear why the political violence should not be directed at those responsible for these policies. As Angelia Means, a lawyer and political scientist asks, "In the history of modern democracy, a history that includes racial and colonial terrorism, was the use of terrorism by Others *never* justified?"[25]

We are so accustomed to associating suicide bombings with Palestinians and Al Qaeda members that it may come as a surprise to learn that suicide bombings were used extensively in the 1980s by the Liberation Tigers, who were struggling for a homeland in Sri Lanka for their Tamil ethnic minority. Prior to September 11 they had carried out about 220 suicide attacks, killing a Sri Lankan president, a former Indian prime minister, various government ministers, and mayors. Hundreds, perhaps thousands, of civilians were slain in these attacks, "though civilians were never their explicit target."[26] According to the Tigers' political leader, S. Thamilchelvam, suicide bombings were used to make up for the Tamils' numerical disadvantage; the goal was "to ensure maximum damage done with minimum loss of life."[27]

I do not mean to suggest that we can make no distinction at all between combatants and civilians or that we should abandon the restraints on the conduct of war that demand that civilians be spared to the extent possible. Rather, I am suggesting that the distinction cannot do nearly as much moral work as its advocates assign it. We should, I believe, reject the view that terrorism is inevitably and necessarily morally worse than war, which many assert because they declare that, by definition, terrorism targets civilians.

In sum, then, I decline to make the targeting of civilians a defining feature of terrorism, even though terrorism very frequently targets noncombatants. Terrorism is political violence that usually spreads fear beyond those attacked, as others recognize themselves as potential targets. This is also true of much warfare. The "shock and awe" phase of the U.S. invasion of Iraq in March 2003 is a clear example. Terrorism's political objectives distinguish it from ordinary crime. Perhaps more than anything else, terrorism resembles small-scale war. It can consist of single events, such as the Oklahoma City bombing, though it is usually part of a larger campaign, whereas war is always composed of a series of violent events. Importantly, there are many kinds of terrorism, just as there are many kinds of war.

TERRORISM AND JUSTIFICATION

Governments try hard to portray terrorist groups as those who cause violence that would otherwise not exist and to depict their own efforts to suppress that violence, however violently they do so, as a justified response to provocation. However, if the governments agreed to what the groups seek—independence for Chechnya, for instance—the terrorists' brutal acts would not take place. Thus the violence used to suppress terrorism is the price paid to maintain the status quo, just as the violence used by the dissatisfied group is the price of pursuing its goal. From a moral point of view, it is entirely appropriate to compare these levels of killing and destruction. The status quo is not in itself morally superior; it may include grievous violations of rights or denials of legitimate aims. Whether the goals of a dissatisfied group are morally defensible needs to be examined, as does whether a government's refusal to accede to these goals is morally defensible. From a moral point of view, using violent actions to bring about change is not inherently worse than doing so to prevent such change. No doubt stability has value, but its costs need to be assessed.

A more promising argument against terrorism is that it does not achieve its perpetrators' objectives and that other means are not only more justifiable but also more successful. But then the burden of making them more successful falls on governments and those with power. When nonviolent protest is met with bloodshed and consistently fails to change the offending policies even when they are unjustifiable, it is hard to argue that nonviolence works, whereas terrorism does not. Terrorist Leila Khaled said about the Palestinian hijackings of the 1970s that they "were used as a kind of struggle to put the question—who are the Palestinians—before the world. Before we were dealt with as refugees. We yelled and screamed, but the whole world answered with more tents and did nothing."[28] Terrorists often feel, mistakenly or not, that violence is the only course of action open to them that can advance their political goals. It is the responsibility of those who are able to do so to make this assessment untrue.

As many have noted, one of the most effective ways to reduce the appeal of terrorism to the disaffected is to enable them to participate in the political processes that concern them. Democracy is more effective than counterterrorism, though bringing it about can be extremely difficult, and it certainly cannot be imposed by outsiders. As Benjamin Barber writes, "violence is not the instrument of choice even under tyrannical governments because confrontations based on force usually favor the powerful....But it can become the choice of those so disempowered by a political order (or a political disorder) that they have no other options....To create a just and inclusive world in which all citizens are stakeholders is the first objective of a rational strategy against terrorism."[29]

Lloyd Dumas examines the ineffectiveness of violent counterterrorism; he states that "for decades, Israel has doggedly followed a policy of responding to any act of terrorism with violent military retaliation."[30] The result has been that "there exists today more terrorism directed against Israel than ever before....Israelis live in fear and Palestinians live in misery."[31] He concludes that "in the long run, encouraging economic and political development is the single most effective counter-terrorist approach."[32]

Claiming that all terrorism is the same and necessarily evil and that the so-called war on terrorism must stamp it out once and for all or that all responses to terrorism should be the same is worse than unrealistic and misleading. It sets the stage for those who aim to eradicate terrorism to be humiliated when they fail and to be thus provoked into even more unjustified violence.

Of course, there is no good terrorism. All terrorism is awful, just as all war is awful, and it is outrageous that human beings have not yet managed to avoid, head off, control, and put an end to war—and terrorism. Nonetheless, some wars are worse than others, and we can make moral judgments of its purposes and the way it is carried out. We are accustomed to making such judgments with respect to war; we should become accustomed to making them with respect to terrorism.

One may have grave doubts about whether the criteria offered by just war theory can *ever* be satisfied, especially in the case of conflicts fought with contemporary weaponry. But one can still agree that some wars, tactics, and purposes are *more unjustifiable* than others. Moreover, *if* war can be justified, so can some terrorism. As Andrew Valls argues, "if just war theory can justify violence committed by states, then terrorism committed by nonstate actors can also, under certain circumstances, be justified by it as well."[33] And other sources of moral assessment may offer stronger grounds than just war theory for claiming that, *if* war in all its massive horror can be justified (which most people believe even though the assertion is dubious), terrorism may also be considered justified.

Most states, as well as the United Nations, resolutely maintain that, to be legitimate, violence must be carried out by states, not nonstate groups. However, the United Nations also recognizes a fundamental right to self-determination that includes rights to resist "colonial, foreign and alien domination." As Robert Fullinwider notes, "since the United States is a country founded on violent rebellion against lawful authority, we can hardly endorse a blanket disavowal of the right by others violently to rebel against their own oppressors."[34] What is so disturbing about terrorists, he concludes, is that they appeal to morality directly without appealing to law; they rely on "private judgment." But private judgment is not only a menace when exercised by nonstate groups. When states put private judgment ahead of international law, as the United States has been doing increasingly in the George W. Bush presidency, the chances of escaping Hobbesian chaos are undermined.

It is very important for us to be able to make some relevant distinctions about terrorism. If its purpose is to impose a religious tyranny on unwilling citizens, it is worse than if it seeks a legitimate purpose. If its success would bring about the end of democratic discourse and the violation of its subjects' human rights, it is more unjustifiable than if its success created acceptable political outcomes. Judgments of its purposes are of great, though of course not conclusive, importance, as they are when applied to war. Judgments of the kinds of violence used to try to achieve or prevent political objectives are also of great significance. Terrorism that kills large numbers of children and relatively nonresponsible persons is obviously worse than terrorism that largely targets property or kills only small numbers of persons responsible for an unjustifiable policy. Terrorism that slaughters many civilians is worse than that which does not, as is war that does so. Collapsing all terrorism, even all that is carried out by those who are considered Muslim extremists, into one great inhuman barbarity perpetrated by "the enemy" or "those who hate freedom" and against whom we should fight a "war on terror" prevents the kind of thinking needed to respond appropriately to actual terrorism and to prevent its growth.

No form of violence can be justified unless other means of achieving a legitimate political objective have failed. But this is *also* a moral requirement on the governments that oppose change and seek to suppress terrorism. Additionally, those with more power have a greater obligation to avoid violence and to pursue other means of obtaining political goals.

It is not only potential terrorists who should find peaceful means to press their demands; those who resist these demands should also find nonviolent means to oppose terrorism. They should give a voice to opponents—and not just an empty voice. For instance, they should respond to legitimate calls to end an occupation, cease colonization, and stop imperialistic impositions. Governments that use violence—military and police forces, clandestine groups—to suppress their opponents are often as guilty of using unjustified violence as are those who struggle for a hearing for their legitimate grievances. Sometimes they are more at fault because alternative courses of action were more open to them.

To understand and judge terrorists (as distinct from terrorism), we must pay attention to their motives. In 1986 Benjamin Netanyahu, a former prime minister of Israel, described the terrorist as "a new breed of man which takes humanity back to prehistoric times, to the times when morality was not yet born."[35] In 2002 he repeated nearly the same words, calling terrorists "an enemy that knows no boundaries" and saying that "we are at the beginning of a war of worlds"—Israel and other democracies against "a world of fanatic murder[ers] trying to throw on us inhuman terror, to take us back to the worst days of history."[36]

According to this view there is absolutely no justification for considering terrorists' arguments; they do not function within the same realm of discourse or circle of humanity. In contrast, those who actually talk with and study terrorists are often amazed at how "normal" they seem, how articulate and rational.[37] They may be misguided, but they are not necessarily more morally depraved than many members of the armed forces of established states who speak in terms of the costs of weaponry and personnel and of the military gains they can achieve. Both sides may be characterized by a gross lack of feeling for the victims of their violence, or, if they do have some feeling, it is overridden by the calculations of necessity. Therefore, to prevent terrorism, we might often achieve much more by engaging in moral argument with its potential recruits than by declaring that terrorists and their supporters are a priori beyond the moral pale.

Many people (not only in the Bush administration and on the Right in the United States but even among liberals) equate trying to understand terrorism with excusing it. Perhaps philosophers can resist such mistakes; on some metaethical theories at least, we can persuasively distinguish between causal explanations and normative evaluations, giving us a good reason to subscribe to such theories. We are all in need of both sorts of inquiries. We need to understand terrorism in a way that includes the way terrorists think and feel and the arguments they find persuasive. This is not to excuse terrorism, but it may also well involve not excusing those who willfully fail to understand it.

THE CAUSES OF TERRORISM

Suppose we look for causes more immediate than despair, which may best be addressed in the long run by democracy and development—not imposed from outside but nurtured from within and assisted by the appropriate policies of other states. There is some agreement that the cause of terrorism is not poverty per se. The point is not that individual terrorists are not usually from impoverished families since it is well known that the leaders of revolutions and political movements are usually from the middle class. But if such leaders represent and struggle on behalf of those who are impoverished and with whom they identify, one could say that poverty was the cause of the movement. In the case of terrorism, however, we often do not seem to be able to say exactly this. Many groups in the world suffer more severe poverty than those from which numerous terrorists arise, so we must look for other causes. Religious zealotry has become primary among those suspected, but many terrorists are not religious zealots.

Certainly the factors of gender play a causal role. That masculinity is constructed in terms of the willingness to use violence and that he who does so can thereby become a hero enter fundamentally into the causal story.[38] However, these factors affect both men who do and men who do not become terrorists, and more is needed to ignite them. Some time ago, on the basis of what I had read, I ventured the suggestion that the most salient factor in causing terrorism seemed to me to be *humiliation*. Since then I have been on the lookout for supporting evidence or counterevidence, and I find much to strengthen this view.

One clear and persuasive item of support comes from an inquiry by Laura Blumenfeld, a writer for the *Washington Post,* who went to Israel seeking revenge for the wounding of her father in a terrorist attack by a Palestinian. She recounts her experiences in a book.[39] Her goal was to make the attacker see her father as a human being, and she succeeded. In an interview she said that "humiliation drives revenge more than anything else....I think for the Palestinians, they feel honor and pride are very important in their culture, and they feel utterly humiliated.... I found that feelings of humiliation and shame fuel revenge more than anything else."[40]

It is not hard to understand the humiliation that Palestinians feel: the continued and expanded settlement activity that eats up their land, the ubiquitous checkpoints, the confinement of Arafat, the destruction of one symbol after another of Palestinian self-rule, and finally the destruction of not just the symbols but also the reality of the Palestinian authority.[41] One can also understand the humiliation of Israelis, whose overwhelming military superiority is utterly unable to stop the suicide bombings and whose government engages in its own kind of terrorism in the scores of assassinations of suspected Palestinian militants, several of which have occurred *after* Palestinians refrained from violence for a period, as Israel had demanded.

Nevertheless, the reason that so much of the rest of the Islamic world feels humiliation (if it does) is much less clear. Sympathy with the Palestinians apparently plays a central role. In addition, it seems to be in part the result of the economic disadvantage that affects much of the region and the degree to which oil, by far the major source of strength there, is under the control of Western power. With its quite glorious intellectual and artistic past and substantial resources, the region's current economic weakness may well be galling. Moreover, as many have pointed out, the lack of opportunities for political expression engenders frustration. However, what seems to be the most serious source of felt humiliation is cultural. The inability of traditional Islamic patterns of life to withstand the onslaught of capitalist culture and Western images may well be experienced as humiliating. Benjamin Barber considers "the aggressively secular and shamelessly materialistic tendencies of modernity's global markets and its pervasive, privatizing attachment to consumerism."[42] Though fundamentalism is an invention of the West, he notes ("the Crusaders were the first great Jihadic warriors"), it should not be a surprise that "a handful of the children of Islam...imagine that the new global disorder [brought about by the worldwide market] spells the death of their children, their values, and their religion."[43]

What is humiliation? It has not received adequate philosophical attention, and I recommend it as a topic for further inquiry.[44] Avishai Margalit is one of the few philosophers who has written about humiliation. He sees it as "any sort of behavior or condition that constitutes a sound reason for a person to consider his or her self-respect injured."[45] He sees the decent society as one "whose institutions do not humiliate people."[46] This is a normative sense of humiliation rather than an account of how it is experienced, but he later describes it as "a loss of human dignity" and makes the interesting claim that, when we remember being humiliated, we relive the emotion.[47] I am skeptical that this is more true of humiliation than of some other strongly felt emotions, but the claim merits investigation.

Here I suggest only that humiliation is not the same as shame. One feels shame because of some felt deficiency in oneself. One feels humiliation because of what someone else has done to diminish one or to show disrespect. Certainly shame and humiliation are related; if one did not feel one had the deficiency one is ashamed of, the other would perhaps not be able to humiliate one. Nonetheless, one could have the deficiency and still not be humiliated by that other if that other were considerate, sensitive, and respectful. If, on the other hand, one *is* humiliated (and especially if one is intentionally humiliated), the result is often anger, as well as (and perhaps even more than) shame. Consequently, the response may quite easily be violent.

Some humiliation is caused intentionally. It is hard to believe that many of Israel's policies and actions toward the Palestinians have not been intentionally degrading. Many wrongly imagine that humiliating a child or a foe is the way to "teach them a lesson." The kind of humiliation Americans may be causing in the Islamic world often seems unintentional, more like the blustering of a huckster who cannot imagine that anyone does not want his touted new product or service. However, if the American cultural onslaught does produce humiliation, whether intentional or not, it behooves us all to develop more sensitivity and to be more considerate and respectful.

Feminist approaches to morality can certainly contribute here. Feminists may be especially helpful in learning to understand humiliation and how to deal with it in ways that do not lead to self-defeating spasms of violence. In men, a connection seems to exist between adopting a macho posture and feeling loss of face when that machismo is challenged or shaken. Women have had much and rich experience with humiliation but seldom respond with violence—or terrorism.[48] Understanding why could be highly relevant.

TWO

MILITARY INTERVENTION AND TERRORISM

MORALITY IN INTERNATIONAL RELATIONS

One unfortunate casualty of the foreign policies of the George W. Bush administration is the very idea of morality in relations between states. I have a long-standing interest in this topic since one of the first books I ever edited (or coedited in this case) was called *Philosophy, Morality, and International Affairs.*[1] This was during the Vietnam War, and we editors and contributors, most of us philosophers, all argued for paying *more* attention to what morality would recommend for U.S. foreign policy and for recognizing the appropriateness of the moral evaluation of states' behavior.

In reaction to the misuses of morality by the George W. Bush administration, however, a sizable number of commentators, as well as government officials, politicians, and even law professors, are calling for a return to what they think of as the "realism" of the Cold War era of foreign policy, in which morality in international affairs was discredited.[2] According to this kind of "realism," all states pursue what they take to be their national interests regardless of moral considerations; thus, any state that fails to do so is naïve and misguided. Also according to this view, the outcome of policies based on this line of thinking will be better than those that result from the pursuit of unrealistic moral ideals. A book published in 2006 by Anatol Lieven and John Hulsman has been taken (though not entirely accurately) to reject not only the "messianic commitment" to spread democracy advocated by some neoconservatives and promoted by the Bush administration but also the idea itself that moral considerations should guide foreign policy.[3] They call their book *Ethical Realism*, but their heroes are Niebuhr, Morgenthau, and Kennan, the same heroes embraced by the earlier "realism" in international relations theory. Additionally, an influential group of professors of law has argued against the view that we have moral obligations to respect international law.[4]

Of course, misguided idealism and short-sighted realism are not the only alternatives. Those of us concerned with moral issues, in international and other contexts, can continue to advocate morally justifiable policies. Morally justifiable policies should be certainly based on extensive empirical findings and accurate understandings of relevant facts and in this sense be realistic. While it is true that George W. Bush's crusade to impose democracy on Iraq through invasion and occupation has been a disaster, it has followed from a misuse of morality even minimally understood and does not constitute evidence that morality in international affairs is out of place. The Bush administration's claim that the world should do as we demand because we have "moral" motives has undoubtedly been a terrible failure, but again it has failed because of a misuse—not a reasonable use—of morality. There is simply no connection between the views that morality should guide foreign policy, and that the United States should act unilaterally, ignore the interests of other states, refuse to speak to adversaries, or use military superiority to force the world to accept U.S. hegemony—all doctrines of the neoconservative agenda bought by the Bush administration and then blamed on the "moral" position that the United States' mission is to spread democracy everywhere, by force if necessary.

To conscientious moral philosophers or citizens, moral issues are inescapable in any case. In asserting that the United States *ought* to pursue its national interests above all, the "realists" make a moral argument. They cannot escape moral questions but only disguise them, and the recommendations they offer are by no means the most persuasive. Far more promising are arguments that we *ought* to respect international law.

Most of the deplorable aspects of recent U.S. foreign policy seem to reflect a sharp turn by the administration of George W. Bush away from respect for other states and peoples of the world and toward a dangerous and indefensible unilateralism.[5] I will not speculate on whether this turn has been motivated more by religious ambitions to spread "freedom" or by economic and strategic interests related to oil. At a fundamental level the administration of George W. Bush seems to believe it *ought* to be an imperial power. It admires the Great Britain of the nineteenth century and its empire, which it sees as imposing peace and progress on the world. Whatever the motives, the aims of the administration have added up to a unilateralism in U.S. policies that deeply endangers the world and any semblance of hope we might have for global order. This unilateralism has particularly dangerous implications for U.S. decisions to engage in military intervention and to do so in ways that threaten what order has developed in the world. Unfortunately, we cannot be confident that a Democratic administration would be either fundamentally different or vastly more reasonable.[6] The public and its representatives seem to have accepted the threat of terrorism as requiring drastic unilateral measures.

The George W. Bush administration's unilateralism undoubtedly contains a strong macho element. Sometimes the masculine posturing is for strategic purposes. As Maureen Dowd captured it, "in 2000 and 2004, G.O.P. gunslingers played into the Western myth and mined images of manliness, feminizing Al Gore as a Beta Tree-Hugger, John Kerry as a Waffling War Wimp with a Hectoring Wife and John Edwards as his true bride, the Breck Girl."[7] This element often bleeds into policy itself, as in the case of the administration's energy policy. As Thomas Friedman wrote of Vice President Dick Cheney, Cheney is "so convinced that conservation is just some silly liberal hobby" that he will never seriously move the United States toward energy independence; Cheney "presents all this as a tough-guy 'realist' view of the world," although it is in Friedman's opinion "an ignorant and naïve view."[8]

In addition to the distortions of policy brought about by the tough-guy element, other distortions can be attributed to the ideology of the market that plays an excessive role in the George W. Bush administration. It leads to an exaggerated desire to compete, to dominate, and to pursue the self-interest of the United States and its citizens regardless of who gets hurt. This ideology requires the privatization of governmental functions and the promotion of business interests above all others, and it sees law as an obstacle to be circumvented. This has been especially pernicious with respect to international law.

WHY INTERNATIONAL LAW?

Morality is sometimes at odds with the law, including international law, so why should we respect international law? We should not merely presume that morality in international affairs recommends that international law be observed. When I began to look for grounds on which to distinguish between military interventions that seemed morally justified and those that did not, I was very skeptical about international law from a moral point of view. It seemed too biased in favor of existing states and against groups seeking change even when that change was morally warranted. Furthermore, international law seemed clearly constructed to promote the interests of existing states, no matter how morally dubious their standing or objectives. These reservations are very different from those of U.S. conservatives who believe the United States is so superior to other states that it should not be limited by international constraints and from those of the "realist" opponents of moral restraints in how states pursue their interests, but they are substantial nonetheless.

I also had reservations about law that result from an appreciation of the ethics of care and its values (see chapter 8). Care and justice are in many ways alternative approaches that emphasize different clusters of values, so that if one considers an issue from the perspective of care one may be expected to be skeptical of the approaches of justice and law, including international law.

Yet the further I have explored the arguments, the more I have become impressed by the potential of international law for dealing with relations between states, and I have come to the conclusion that the ethics of care would recommend respect for international law in the world as it now exists, though in the longer term it would advise less reliance on law and much more development of caring alternatives.[9] These would include a variety of efforts across state boundaries to deal with problems before they lead to violence, as well as efforts to prevent hostilities through international arrangements—some formal, some informal. Nongovernmental organizations of various kinds, efforts to alleviate economic injustices, and agencies to foster peace and head off violence can much better exemplify care than can most laws and their enforcement, but the latter may sometimes be needed to prevent or limit explosions of violence, and the ethics of care would agree. This chapter supports the position that, from the point of view of morality, international law ought to be respected; and the ethics of care would recommend this for the sort of world in which we are now living.

One reason we should respect international law is that only with cooperative respect for international norms among states with conflicting interests can we hope for the peaceful resolution of disputes that might otherwise turn murderous and calamitous, with technological advances continually exacerbating the problems of conflict. This answer may rely too uncritically on an analogy between law within states and between them. Since comparable vulnerabilities and mechanisms, especially of enforcement, are usually not present in the international arena, the arguments may need to be different. Still, relying on experience, we can conclude that norms that independent states agree to and consent to apply to themselves can facilitate progress toward a world that is less violent, destructive, threatening, and insecure and that international law is the best available source of such norms. We can acknowledge that international law should not *always* be determinative of policy and still maintain that it is deserving of a very high degree of respect.

That international law as presently constituted has been designed to serve the interests of existing states, with all their flaws, does not undermine the argument for respecting it. Many deficiencies in governing and in the international system of sovereign states are beyond the reach of (and are even protected by) international law. Nevertheless, international law is a better source of hope for keeping the world from exploding in violence than the alternative of ignoring it. That the administration of George W. Bush has so grievously dismissed international law is a ground for the moral condemnation of the Bush administration, not a criticism of foreign policy based on morality.

As a number of advocates of the importance of international law have noted, recent U.S. foreign policy has departed from its direction during a long period following World War II, in which the United States enthusiastically promoted the rule of law in international affairs. In that earlier period the United States negotiated treaties and set up institutions that indicated acceptance of international obligations and a willingness to abide by these institutions' decisions. Such policy had wide support and was thought to promote U.S. interests. As one writer observes, this "growth of international law and its influence...was a very positive development, and the United States and the world benefited enormously from the increased international cooperation it made possible."[10] The 1990s, however, began to witness a decreased willingness on the part of the United States to accept multilateral approaches, and the Bush years have pulled the United States still farther away from respecting international law.

Certainly there have been voices (and not only among legislators or commentators seeking a popular following) opposing the influence of international law on the United States.[11] Supreme Court Justice Antonin Scalia has even stated that the Court should not use "foreigners' views as part of the *reasoned* basis of its decisions," implying that U.S. courts are not even to consider valid arguments and ideas that originate elsewhere.[12] It has been suggested that those who favor an expanded role for international law (e.g., with respect to human rights) might hesitate to support U.S. entry into international conventions such as the Convention to Eliminate All Forms of Discrimination against Women (CEDAW) because the United States' hostility toward internationalism and demands for exceptions for itself could weaken rather than strengthen this development.[13] However, when the influence of international law is blocked at one level, it can enter at another, as when cities and states accept the guidance of CEDAW or the Kyoto Protocol on global warming regardless of the United States' failure to ratify them.

Despite the insularity and resistance to international cooperation by certain elements in the United States, international law had generally been deemed worthy of considerable respect by most administrations until that of George W. Bush. Thomas Franck expresses his discouragement over this development: "Emerging is [an] approach that classifies international law as a disposable tool of diplomacy... [with] no greater claim than any other policy or value preference" when deciding how to advance the national interest.[14] Such advocates of international law now make the case that the recent departure has been a grave mistake and that what is needed is a return to U.S. support of international law. As William H. Taft IV puts it, "For the same reasons we promote the rule of law within states, we need also to promote it among them. That means states must reach agreements on how they are going to conduct themselves, how they will resolve disputes, and then abide by the rules and systems they have agreed to."[15] He even thinks international laws and institutions are more important than before in meeting the threat of terrorism: "Rather than worrying about whether international law imposes excessive constraints on our flexibility, we ought to be using it" against terrorist groups that have no legitimacy in the international system.[16] International law already condemns terrorism. The United States cannot defeat terrorism alone; it requires the cooperation of other states; "their cooperation will assure that the terrorists are increasingly marginalized."[17]

Brian Urquhart, deploring the lawless world brought so much closer by the policies of the George W. Bush administration, writes that "it is nothing less than disastrous that a United States administration should have chosen to show disrespect for the international legal system and weaken it at a time when the challenges facing the planet demand more urgently than ever the discipline of a strong and respected worldwide system of law."[18] In the face of globalization, climate change, and terrorism, international law is needed now more than ever.

Additionally, while a number of law professors and practitioners, along with occupants of the White House, have been discounting the importance of international law, legal scholars outside the United States gladly acknowledge what is aptly called "law's power to pull states toward compliance."[19] Franck surmises that leaders in Washington must "harbor a grudging awareness that the rest of the world still regards the rules, however egregiously violated by a few powerful scofflaws, as legitimate and binding."[20]

THE CHALLENGE OF TERRORISM

As we think about what U.S. policy ought to be, we ought to address the obvious and serious problem of terrorism, which has arguably had a particularly noxious effect on the direction of the George W. Bush administration and its respect for law, both international and domestic. Claiming that the attacks of September 11, 2001, completely changed the world, the George W. Bush administration has promoted its unilateral policies as needed to defend the United States against the threat of terrorism. It immediately launched its "war on terrorism," which almost all unbiased observers can see is misguided. One cannot make war against a tactic, which is what terrorism is. If the war is relabeled, as it has often been, as a "war on terror," that is hardly better since a war on an emotion makes little sense. More importantly, it is misguided in collapsing very different elements of violent opposition to U.S. policies into one unified "enemy" who is evil.

Louise Richardson, the author of the best single book on terrorism that I have read, makes clear how the war on terrorism is mistaken in many substantive ways: It is a "war" that can never be "won" and that will have no end. As she observes (and as should have been obvious), "it is very difficult ever to declare victory in a war on terrorism or terror, much less evil."[21] Also, if the aim of the war, as Bush suggests, is to rid the world of terrorists, it makes it far too easy for them to thwart our aims with occasional attacks. Terrorists want to be thought of as soldiers at war; statements by Khalid Shaikh Mohammed illustrate this very clearly.[22] To grant them this status and excellent recruiting tool, Richardson argues, is self-defeating.[23] A far better goal would be to contain the threat and reduce the appeal of terrorist groups to potential recruits.

Richardson reviews the history of fighting terrorism with military force and "the lesson that has already been taught many times"—that states cannot translate overwhelming military force into victory over terrorists.[24] The Russians in Chechnya, the Israelis in Lebanon and the occupied territories, Peru against the Shining Path, and many other cases provide evidence. An exception has occurred where the military is deployed domestically and freed from democratic constraints, as in Argentina in the 1970s, when a military junta aimed to eliminate not only terrorist groups but all political opposition as well. There are not many similarities between the few successful uses of military force against terrorism and the Bush administration's wars in Afghanistan and Iraq or Israel's war in Lebanon in the summer of 2006, all purportedly to crush terrorism.

Supporting his view with a vast amount of empirical data, Robert Pape, author of another very useful book on terrorism, shows that the primary goals of nearly all terrorists are to rid the lands of the groups with which they identify of foreign military forces.[25] This should certainly be considered in weighing arguments for military responses to terrorism. That invading Iraq would produce large numbers of new recruits for terrorism was entirely foreseeable.

Richardson, who has studied terrorism as a political scientist for several decades, shows how terrorism, even religious terrorism, is not new and not especially linked with Islam. Like many others who have actually studied terrorists, she understands that terrorists are almost never the psychopaths or one-dimensional evildoers they are portrayed to be.[26] They are usually "human beings who think like we do" and have political goals they are trying to achieve.[27] They are often angry "young idealists wanting to do their part" for their country or group and "motivated by a desire to right wrongs and do their best" for what they consider a noble cause.[28] The U.S. government's failure to understand terrorism or learn from previous experience with it has been disastrous. "We cannot defeat terrorism by smashing every terrorist movement," she writes. "An effort to do so will only generate more terrorists, as has happened repeatedly in the past. We should never have declared a global war on terrorism, knowing that such a war can never be won....Rather, we should pursue the more modest and attainable goal of containing terrorist recruitment and constraining the resort to the tactic of terrorism."[29]

Some have recently argued that the terrorism of Islamic fanatics presents a new kind of challenge. They allege that whereas terrorism in the past may have been open to rational responses and capable of being deterred, participants in the "new terrorism" cannot be contained, only eliminated. Such arguments serve to promote the "war" on terror, but there is much evidence to refute them.[30]

"Terrorism" is a highly contested term, as is evident throughout this book. The definitions used are far from consistent. Many make the targeting of civilians central to the definition of terrorism. Together with a few others, I have argued against this, suggesting in the preceding chapter that terrorism most resembles small war in the ways it should be evaluated. Others contend that it should not be assimilated to war since this encourages a military response, whereas some form of "police action" would be more appropriate.[31] If one tries to think of terrorism within the framework of crime and policing, however, one may fail to appreciate its political motives. That terrorism is political violence should be part of any definition. Robert Goodin argues persuasively against viewing terrorism within the framework of just war theory and its moral conditions and assessments. He thinks that doing so puts the emphasis on the killing of noncombatants and fails to appreciate what makes terrorism distinctive from other violence: its intent to spread terror.[32] However it is defined, there is little doubt that the Bush administration has for political purposes exaggerated the threat it presents. A book called *Overblown: How Politicians and the Terrorism Industry Inflate National Security Threats and Why We Believe Them,* which presents a vast amount of empirical material, effectively makes the point.[33] Though the threat that nuclear material may become available to potential terrorists is alarming, the ways we should confront the problem are not like components of a "war on terror."[34]

The administration of George W. Bush has used the war on terror as an excuse to invade Iraq and to ignore international law. It insists on retaining the right to launch preventive wars to safeguard the United States and its citizens from "evildoers" who may engage in or aid others to commit terrorist attacks against them. The result has been an extraordinary decline in the power of the United States to gain support for and decrease opposition to its policies and interests.

MILITARY INTERVENTION

Even if the case for invading Iraq was mistaken—since the claim of a connection between Iraq's Saddam Hussein and any terrorist groups was unfounded and Iraq was found to have no weapons of mass destruction that it could transfer to terrorists—we should consider what *might* justify military intervention to prevent or to respond to terrorism. We require a better understanding of when military intervention may or may not be justifiable. This would have to show why the invasion of Iraq seems so clearly wrong when some other interventions were not wrong (or would not have been). There is no doubt that terrorism violates human rights and that "humanitarian intervention" has come to seem justifiable to many in order to prevent massive violations of human rights. Would thwarting terrorism be legitimate grounds for military intervention that is claimed to be for humanitarian reasons? Or could military intervention to avert terrorism be justified on the classic grounds of self-defense?

When arguments that Iraq was a threat to the United States persuaded almost no one, George W. Bush spoke often of how the invasion was justified to liberate Iraq from a brutal dictator, as if the United States were engaged in a humanitarian intervention to restore protection of their human rights to the Iraqi people. This argument, too, has been rejected by almost all critics, but one can well imagine a failed state with terrorist groups that prevent a responsible state from forming. Might intervention be justified to build a viable state that would not threaten other states?

The norms of international law requiring states to renounce aggression against one another and to resort to military force only on grounds of individual or collective self-defense have been fairly clearly worked out. In the period after World War II they were formulated, incorporated into the United Nations charter and subsequent Security Council resolutions, and implemented on a number of occasions. They have been modified to allow preemptive strikes in cases of imminent attack but to rule out the kind of right to launch a preventive war that the George W. Bush administration has proclaimed for itself.[35] Discussion of preventive war has also shown how unwise, as well as illegal, it would be.[36]

Starting in the 1990s, an extensive literature capable of guiding policymakers on "humanitarian intervention" was also developed, including how such intervention might be reconciled with international law.[37] One can conclude that respect for human rights became part of the requirements recognized in international law. Although remaining in much greater uncertainty than the norms for self-defense, standards concerning intervention were developed to prevent the massive violations of human rights that occur in genocide and ethnic cleansing. As Thomas Franck expresses the view from the current perspective of international law, "it has become commonplace that the international system may lawfully intervene in situations of cataclysmic civil strife and other massive violations of human rights, with or without the consent of the government of the place where the violations are occurring."[38]

What remain much less clarified are reasonable norms that could be incorporated into international law for military intervention to prevent or deal with terrorism. As Tom Farer wrote shortly after the attack of September 11, the war against terrorism could either eclipse humanitarian intervention in U.S. foreign policy altogether or lead instead to even more intervention claimed to be justifiable on humanitarian grounds, as well as on grounds of preventing terrorism, as the United States and other states engaged in efforts to reconstitute failed states.[39]

I now consider three cases of military intervention or possible intervention in this gray area of intervention on grounds other than self-defense: Rwanda, Kosovo, and Iraq. I do not discuss Afghanistan since this has generally been interpreted as a case of self-defense against attack rather than one of intervention.[40] The UN Security Council determined, in the wake of the September 11 attacks, that, when a state supports and harbors a nonstate terrorist group, it opens itself up to measures of individual or collective defense that may be taken against it, in accordance with accepted international rules, by those that such groups attack.[41] This may well not be the best interpretation of what happened, and there are good reasons to suspect that several aspects of the U.S. military response in Afghanistan were unwise and unjustifiable, but it was not the threat to international law constituted by the invasion of Iraq. Nor was it the kind of humanitarian intervention motivated by concern for the victims of rights violations rather than by states defending themselves, although that might have been considered in connection with Taliban rule. I limit the discussion here to military intervention on grounds other than UN-authorized self-defense.

Concerning Rwanda, something of a consensus has developed that the world community should have intervened to prevent the genocide that occurred there in 1994, in which perhaps a million people were slaughtered. There is much less agreement on Kosovo (and Bosnia before it), and there is considerable agreement again, by now, that the U.S. intervention in Iraq was not only unwise but also seriously illegal and morally wrong. Of course, there are many cases I am not discussing, but the apparent inconsistencies in many thoughtful judgments about intervention in Rwanda, Kosovo, and Iraq are problem enough to take up here.

I agree, though perhaps with less conviction than some others, with the widely shared view that intervention should have occurred in Rwanda. The judgment may now be fairly easy to make but was less so at the time. We now know the ghastly consequences of not intervening, but they were less clear beforehand, and we do not know what bad consequences might have resulted if we had intervened. What happened in Somalia understandably suggested caution. That international law would have accommodated itself to intervention may, however, be relatively clear.

I also believe that the United States' part in the NATO intervention in Kosovo in 1999 was defensible, even though it was not authorized by the Security Council in accordance with existing international law. It is clear, I think, that the U.S. invasion of Iraq in 2003 was morally wrong, as well as a grave violation of international law. Here I would like to clarify the principles and reasons on which such different and seemingly inconsistent judgments should be based (if they should be based on principles) and later I will consider how the ethics of care might not only be relevant in reaching these and related conclusions but also offer a number of valuable insights.

In her contribution to a useful volume for considering the justifiability of intervention, Iris Marion Young argued, following Hannah Arendt, that the justification of intervention depends entirely on its consequences.[42] I adopt a moral approach that is different from this thoroughgoing consequentialism. Decisions have to be made on the basis of what can be known at the time, and in my opinion decisions about intervention need justification as much as do overt acts and their consequences. Analytically, we can separate a decision to intervene from the historical fact of intervention and evaluate them separately; however, without going into this much detail, we can argue that we must consider more than consequences (or even anticipated consequences) in evaluating both. Although consequences should be taken into account in evaluating decisions and actions, both the relevant deontological principles of which they may be instances and the values that acts express are also important. Even though defenders of the invasion of Iraq keep saying that the decision to enter by force had to be made with the intelligence available at the time, this does not undermine the point. One problem was that those deciding did not consider the intelligence *available*, only their distorted selection of it. Another was that they ignored both international law and much else of moral relevance.

Young examines NATO's bombing of Yugoslavia in 1999, undertaken because of the killing and expulsion of Albanians in Kosovo by Serb forces. She concludes that it was not justified because, in her view, it did more harm than good. The massive ethnic cleansing of Albanians was carried out by Serbs *after* the NATO bombing, roughly ten thousand people were killed in the war, and the destruction in Kosovo and Serbia was severe. As an independent report put it, Serb forces could not hit NATO, but they could attack the Albanians, who had asked for NATO support and intervention, and they did.[43]

Chris Brown argues in the same volume that humanitarian intervention, including military intervention, to prevent grave human rights abuses such as ethnic cleansing can be justified by the norms of international law that seem to have superceded the old order of nonintervention and that the intervention in Kosovo was such a case. He acknowledges that there is much concern about the inconsistency with which intervention takes place and the misuses to which it lends itself. He believes that the failure to intervene in Rwanda was shameful but that this and other inconsistencies do not undermine the case for Kosovo. Recognizing that the self-interest of states will play some part in decisions to intervene, though it should not be the only factor on which decisions are based, he concludes that its presence among the motives of states should not be thought to render intervention unjustified.[44]

Philosopher Richard Miller offers a persuasive critique of the current major theories of justifiable intervention proposed by John Rawls, Michael Walzer, and various other philosophers and political theorists.[45] All of them, he believes, ignore both the actual realities of intergovernmental relations and the likely interests of those in a position to intervene in promoting their own geopolitical power.[46] I strongly share Miller's concern for the actual circumstances and nonideal realities that surround us. I have long tried to consider what we ought to do, politically and morally, from where we are here and now rather than from some imagined ideal position,[47] but I reach some different conclusions from Miller about intervention.

In *The Law of Peoples,* Rawls delineates normative principles of justice that would secure human rights everywhere for the mutual relations of peoples in a world already divided into sovereign but very unequal states.[48] This is a shift to a more realistic perspective than was evident in his *Theory of Justice.*[49] To Rawls, however, once the normative goal of a lawful world of peoples who are either liberal and democratic or non-liberal but "decent" has been spelled out, questions of *how* to "bring all societies to this goal" of honoring the "law of peoples" become questions of "foreign policy," to which political philosophy has little to contribute.[50] With respect to intervention, he says that "an outlaw state that violates [the human rights honored by both liberal and decent regimes] is to be condemned and in grave cases may be subjected to forceful sanctions and even to intervention."[51] He argues that "liberal and decent peoples…simply do not tolerate outlaw states….Liberal and decent peoples have the right, under the Law of Peoples, not to tolerate outlaw states….Outlaw states are aggressive and dangerous; all peoples are safer and more secure if such states change, or are forced to change, their ways."[52] Nevertheless, this leaves unconsidered questions of which ways of using which kinds of force can be justifiable and of what to do about violent groups that are not states.

I do not agree that political philosophy should have little to say on issues of how to attain an acceptable world order. As we persist in our efforts to further the goal of a lawful world, we need moral assessments at every step of the way. We require political and moral understanding of how to deal with states and groups that violate norms of human rights and standards of mutual toleration of states, and we need moral appreciation of the overwhelming wrongs of war and violence.

Miller gives examples of U.S. nonintervention in (and actual support of) states whose governments are friendly to the United States even though they suppressed minority rights and caused tens of thousands of deaths in the process (e.g., Turkey, Indonesia). He is concerned primarily that theories of justifiable intervention can provide excuses for powerful states to intervene when doing so promotes their interest, even though it is against the will of many or most of those affected. Anyone concerned with intervention needs to be well aware of this problem, but in my view it should not preclude arguments on when intervention justifiably ought to take place. Miller suggests that current documents in international law provide a better basis for debate about the justification or criticism of governments that intervene or grossly violate the human rights of whole peoples than do the leading philosophical theories of humanitarian intervention. On this point I share his appreciation of what the international law perspective can offer.

Miller asks for judgments based on the whole constellation of moral considerations relevant in particular cases. On this basis, he finds the NATO intervention in Kosovo highly questionable because the destruction and loss of life were too great and the decision process leading up to it was too flawed. But he considers the context only as far back as the decision immediately preceding the NATO bombing. For an adequate evaluation one should also take into account the prior years of Milosevic's misrule: the war against Bosnia, the shelling of Sarajevo, the ethnic cleansing that had already occurred not just in Kosovo but also in Bosnia and Croatia, the massacre of Muslims at Srebrenica, and the fanning of nationalist flames on which Milosevic had come to power. Among the consequences, one should consider that the NATO intervention made possible the overthrow of Milosevic, which was not clearly foreseeable but did occur and in all likelihood would not have happened without the intervention. That he and others were put on trial in the Hague rather than allowed to dominate a Greater Serbia cleansed of all non-Serbian groups needs to be weighed in the evaluation and may tilt the judgment toward intervention.[53]

International law may well agree, depending on the interpretation, that the NATO intervention in Kosovo, though not in compliance with the requirement of Security Council authorization, was still permissible under international law and morally justified.[54] Strong arguments for intervention have been offered by the Independent International Commission on Kosovo, which concluded that the intervention was "illegal, but legitimate." Richard Falk, himself a member of the commission, writing in the *American Journal of International Law,* says that "in Kosovo the moral and political case for intervention seemed strong: a vulnerable and long abused majority population facing an imminent prospect of ethnic cleansing by Serb rulers, a scenario for effective intervention with minimal risks of unforeseen negative effects or extensive collateral damage, and the absence of significant nonhumanitarian motivations on the intervening side. As such, the foundation for a principled departure under exceptional circumstances from a strict rendering of Charter rules on the use of force seemed present."[55] This conclusion seems to me persuasive. The intervention in Iraq, however, was very different.

THE CONTRIBUTION OF INTERNATIONAL LAW

The international law literature provides some helpful distinctions and suggestions for evaluating military interventions that philosophers might do well to consider. Contemporary international law pulls in contradictory directions. On the one hand, key principles demand nonintervention. These principles have been worked out for the rough world order in place for centuries (the so-called Westphalian system) and are expressed in the United Nations charter and many other authoritative documents. The UN charter was devised and agreed to by states insistent on protecting their own sovereignty from outside interference. The charter specifies that the only grounds on which states may use military force is self-defense, individual or collective, and it makes clear that the UN is not authorized to intervene in member states' domestic affairs. In cases of disputes between states, the Security Council is to authorize any collective military action taken to keep or restore peace. As one authority declares, "sovereignty in its modern sense is simply the demand of each territorial community however small and weak and however organized, to be permitted to govern itself without interference by larger and more powerful states and, at least in 1945, without interference by the entire organized international community. Our international legal system is scarcely imaginable without such a concept of sovereignty."[56]

On the other hand, a strong imperative *for* intervention has developed within modern international law: internationally guaranteed human rights. As UN Secretary General Kofi Annan has expressed it, "State sovereignty, in its most basic sense, is being redefined.... States are now widely understood to be instruments at the service of their peoples, and not vice versa."[57] When governments trample egregiously on the rights of those they govern or fail miserably to protect their citizens from such gross violations of rights as take place in ethnic cleansing or genocide, international law permits or even calls upon states to take action.

A related international norm seems to be developing in the wake of the upheavals in the Balkans and calls for secession there and elsewhere. It demands that, in the pursuit of self-determination, there must be restraint on the part of states resisting secession, as well as by those seeking independence.[58] Alain Pellet, president of the UN International Law Commission, assesses this development as follows: "One can infer" from the responses of the international community "a legal rule excluding the right to resort to force, either by the seceding forces or by the government of the state concerned. This constitutes a clear break with classical international law, which accords governments a monopoly on constraint over their respective territories."[59] Fairly clearly, sovereignty in international law today does not grant states complete immunity from intervention.

One might think that because of these contradictory pulls, international law would be of little help in arriving at moral evaluations of military intervention, but I do not believe this. On the contrary, it may offer measured normative recommendations for a dangerous world.

Summing up the requirements of contemporary international law, W. Michael Reisman writes that "a fundamental contradiction distinguishes the legal principles of state sovereignty and human rights. I believe that modern international law has resolved this antinomy in the following way: state sovereignty prevails in all but the most egregious instances of widespread human rights violations, in which case multilateral or, in extreme situations, unilateral action to secure an immediate remedy or even to change a regime—if need be, forcibly—may be taken."[60]

This leaves undecided when that presumption in favor of sovereignty has been overcome and when international law calls on the worldwide community for forcible intervention, through the Security Council if possible, or otherwise if not.[61] And here is where some new thinking may be most useful.

In recent years a kind of "retroactive endorsement" or "ex post facto validation" of some interventions seems to have developed.[62] For instance, even though the Security Council did not authorize NATO's intervention in Kosovo (because of the threat of a Russian veto), it subsequently took action implicitly endorsing the intervention. In this and quite a few other cases (e.g., Liberia, Sierra Leone), although international law was technically violated, it was not seriously undermined because the offending action was legitimated after the fact. However, international law is a fragile construction. If the only remaining superpower disregards it, it can be sorely threatened. This is what many defenders of international law feared from the U.S. invasion of Iraq in early 2003 in direct violation of international law and the UN charter. Not only did the invasion fail to receive Security Council authorization, but it was clearly *not* an expression of the "collective will." And it has *not* received retroactive justification.

Tom Farer summed up the road to war: "At the time of the invasion, when the United States sought the Council's authorization, it was unable to muster even the requisite nine votes, much less the acquiescence of all the permanent members. Indeed, a majority of the permanent members appeared to be opposed....In addition, before, during, and after submission of the case to the Council, the president of the United States signaled a determination to act unilaterally in the event the Council failed to authorize the use of force."[63] Farer concluded that "the invasion of Iraq has about it an aura of ominous implications for international order."[64] Evidence continues to mount that George W. Bush and former British prime minister Tony Blair were intent on proceeding with the invasion regardless of the Security Council's deliberations or decisions. International law had become to them little else than an awkward obstacle.

Shortly after the U.S. invasion of Iraq, Thomas Franck lamented that "after a decade's romance with something approximating law-abiding state behavior, the law-based system is once again being dismantled. In its place we are offered a model that makes global security wholly dependent on the supreme power and discretion of the United States and frees the sole superpower from all restraints of international law and the encumbrances of institutionalized multilateral diplomacy."[65] He implored lawyers to stand up for the rule of law.

To the Bush administration, the failure of its intervention in Iraq to receive authorization by the Security Council or even validation after the fact has been yet another sign of what is wrong with the UN and international law. But to many defenders of international law, the system's refusal to be bullied by the United States to authorize the invasion or even to accommodate itself to it by retroactive justification is a sign that the system indeed has considerable strength.[66] Franck notes that "the Security Council has been scrupulous in its resolutions pertaining to Iraq to avoid anything that could be interpreted as a retrospective validation of the invasion."[67] Shortly after the invasion, Carsten Stahn concluded that "the normativity of the principle of the non-use of force [except as provided in the charter] is still intact."[68] This may have been optimistic, but subsequent developments have strengthened rather than weakened it.

Retroactive justification is certainly not a very satisfactory expression of international legality or of global moral consensus. However, it is far better than failing to obtain even this. Moreover, it may provide a source for a tentative normative principle with which to make the necessary distinctions between different cases of military intervention. It allows us to say that *only those interventions capable of receiving at least retroactive justification in international law (if not prior Security Council authorization) should even be considered candidates for morally justifiable intervention.* Using this test, the invasion of Iraq fails, the NATO intervention in Kosovo passes, and intervention in Rwanda would have passed. These are the outcomes that in my view we would reach independently by using the version of the method of reflective equilibrium for moral justification that I have advocated.[69]

Some clarification concerning international law is needed here. As I understand it, international law is not limited to the later Security Council resolutions I have referred to since the same veto by a single state that could prevent prior authorization of an intervention, no matter how highly recommended from a moral perspective, could prevent retroactive resolutions that provide justification. International law includes the opinions of leading theorists and practitioners and customary international law, as well as the central documents of international conventions and institutions.[70] Jane Stromseth argues that a change such as I have described (i.e., accepting in some cases humanitarian intervention without prior Security Council authorization) should develop as a matter of customary international law and that it would be premature to try to codify it.[71] Her argument seems persuasive and may apply to other issues as well.

Of course, there are differing theories of international law. Admittedly, it is amorphous and hard to define, yet certainly meaningful. Morality is even more amorphous and hard to define, with even greater differences among theories, than is international law, yet it is also meaningful. One could argue that the claim that international law ought morally to be respected is even stronger than a comparable claim about domestic law since international law is more dependent for its interpretations on good moral arguments and less dependent on actual, flawed institutions than is its domestic legal counterpart.

The principle I have suggested conforms to the view expressed by Michael Reisman in the title of his article "Why Regime Change Is (Almost Always) a Bad Idea." As various writers remind us, the temptations for strong powers to use intervention in clumsy, ineffective, stupid, and self-serving ways are formidable. Nevertheless, in certain situations we ought to take responsibility for preventing even greater harms than military intervention will involve.

Relying on international law for our moral judgments in the way suggested is surely not adequate. Rosalyn Higgins wrote in an earlier treatment of intervention that international law cannot itself answer questions about what are acceptable and unacceptable levels of intrusion and that it can only assist in formulating answers when a political consensus exists.[72] Such a view may be overly modest about the independence of international law, but in any case, as moral philosophers we certainly do not take any legal opinion or political consensus as definitive. Nevertheless, they may be highly instructive on what may be possible and on the limits within which our recommendations may be relevant.

In his conclusion to the volume he edited on intervention in 1984, Hedley Bull observed that "the growing moral conviction that human rights should have a place in relations among states has been deeply corrosive of the rule of non-intervention."[73] He concluded at the same time that, although coercive interference of many kinds is an endemic feature of our international arrangements, there is no alternative to the rule of nonintervention.[74] In any case, he wrote, the idea that "a particular nation or peoples is endowed by God or history with a role or mission that entitles it to impose its will on others for their own betterment" has "no prospect of being endorsed by the prevailing consensus…and can find no place in any agreed public doctrine of the rights of intervention."[75] This judgment applies well today to the mission claimed by George W. Bush to impose freedom on those without it.

THE ETHICS OF CARE AND INTERNATIONAL LAW

I conclude that, in a world dominated by states striving to promote their own interests and threatened periodically by terrorism and war, the rule of law and thus international law clearly ought to be promoted. This can be demanded on many moral grounds, including the ethics of care (see chapter 8). On the other hand, as an advocate of the ethics of care, I do not believe that law is as much of an answer to the world's problems and conflicts as do many of the theorists I have cited with approval.[76] From the perspective of care, law is a limited approach for a limited domain of human activity. For that domain, it may be the best hope in the short run for escaping the worst impending disasters of imperialist delusions, religious fanaticism, and conflicts between states and groups. As we look ahead, however, to how the world needs to progress toward something better than an aggregate of states and groups all pursuing their own interests and ready to use violence, at best within the restraints of international law, the ethics of care offers hope of something more satisfactory and of ways to move toward it.

One can show the promise of the ethics of care for dealing with global conflict and with efforts to foster international civility. When one examines various questionable assumptions made in thinking about international relations as well as different effects of globalization in political economy, one can appreciate how the ethics of care may be fruitful for dealing with the issues involved.

Joan Tronto has suggested that peacekeeping is a kind of care work. She sees an important shift in discourse about humanitarian intervention from something like a "right to intervene" to a "responsibility to protect." She interprets this as being in line with a transition in moral discourse about international affairs from an ethic of justice to an ethic of care.[77] I am less persuaded that such a shift is taking place in a way that is more than sporadic, but I agree with Tronto that it should and that the ethics of care is a promising source of guidance for preventing resorts to violence. The ethics of care encourages states to take responsibility for protecting vulnerable populations and for promoting peaceful resolutions of conflicts. However, rather than classify law enforcement—either within states or between them—as *itself* care work, I believe it better to see it as part of the practice of justice that should be more influenced by care than it is. Moreover, it should be continually shrinking as practices of care—both within states and internationally—reduce the need for law to be *enforced* against the recalcitrant. Negotiating disputes noncoercively and addressing the problems of those politically disenfranchised or exploited can more clearly become practices of care. Properly developed, they should make the need for military intervention, for forces to keep the peace between warring groups, and for enforcement of the reasonable restraints of law (to which all can become accustomed) ever less demanded.

Lori Damrosch, in an early consideration of how the norms of international law concerning intervention were changing, suggested that "if the sense is growing that collective organs *must* do today what only yesterday was widely viewed as . . . 'unlawful,'" then lawyers might do well to look at developments relating to intervention in domestic legal systems. "There may be analogies," she noted, "in the ways that feminists have sought to revise traditional conceptions of when an outsider—a neighbor, or a professional, or an official body—not only may but must intercede to prevent life-threatening abuse within the family sphere, despite the presumption of nonintervention which would ordinarily apply."[78]

Stanley Hoffmann, who has been writing perceptively about morality in international affairs for many decades, considered the fears of some that powerful states would misuse any justifications of humanitarian intervention against weak ones. It is an understandable fear, yet nonintervention can be worse in its callousness and indifference. Hoffmann concluded that perhaps we need "to engage in more preventive action. Such action certainly would have been preferable to military action in the cases of Somalia and Bosnia. So perhaps the answer to some.... fears is more intervention rather than less—in other words, additional softer preventive actions could be taken. We cling to the notion of peace as a norm, which results in states not moving until that norm has been broken. Perhaps we should accept sickness as the norm, with actions being necessary in order to contain these sicknesses."[79]

Such views make eminent sense from the perspective of an ethics of care. Instead of focusing on rules to follow and violations to punish, the ethics of care would attend to the political, social, and economic problems that often make the rules inadequate in their protection of actual persons and groups. In addition, instead of relying on military intervention to punish violators of the norms of international law, the ethics of care would counsel preventive engagements and measures aimed at deflecting violations and undercutting the need for punishments.

A number of trends are currently challenging the world order, such as it is, of relations between sovereign states restrained by legal or quasi-legal norms. One is certainly the Bush administration's imperialism, which many argue is a dead end for the United States and the world.[80] Another is the enormous power of multinational corporations, which work around and sometimes overwhelm even powerful states. The results need often to be resisted. Another trend, however, is the development of the global networks of civil society, groups of activists, officials, and citizens who pursue a variety of goals across the divides of state boundaries.[81] This trend can be thought of as "civic and regional globalization" and contrasted with "imperial globalization."[82] It is capable of influencing the foreign policies of states.

For the normative evaluation and guidance of such groups' activities, the ethics of care could be enormously helpful. Gradually, within these networks of interaction and caring, the need for military intervention and the enforcement of international law might be reduced, even though not eliminated. This we can hope for, although changes in the direction of the world toward a caring global order will take vast, prolonged, and organized efforts. But the interest in human rights, which has transformed international law and the policies of many states in a mere half century, may come to be matched by an interest in the caring networks that sustain human beings, whose rights are to be respected, and that allow them to flourish.

THREE

Legitimate Authority in Nonstate Groups Using Violence

Can groups using violence we judge to be terrorism ever legitimately represent oppressed people? If terrorism can never be justified, those groups who use or condone it can perhaps never become the legitimate authorities of the people they claim to represent. But if struggles to attain independence can sometimes be otherwise justifiable and if terrorism is sometimes used in those that are, can this use be justifiable and its users the legitimate representatives of their groups?[1]

In 1987 British prime minister Margaret Thatcher said of the African National Congress, whose leader, Nelson Mandela, was in jail, "Anyone who thinks it is going to run the government of South Africa is living in Cloud Cuckooland."[2] In 1988 a Pentagon report called the African National Congress one of the "more notorious terrorist groups."[3] Exactly ten years after Thatcher's remark, Queen Elizabeth II greeted *President* Nelson Mandela "on his first official state visit to London."[4] Clearly it is possible for yesterday's terrorists to become tomorrow's statesmen.

Just War Theory and Legitimate Authority

In just war theory, various *jus ad bellum* requirements are suggested in order for war to have any chance of being just. Morally adequate grounds must exist for the war to be undertaken in the first place, and other requirements state that a legitimate authority must make the decision to go to war.

As Heather Wilson notes in a helpful book, very little attention has been paid to the requirement of legitimate authority in the recent just war literature.[5] "That only a sovereign state may legitimately wage war [has seemed to be] a foregone conclusion in the twentieth century," she writes.[6] Just war discussion usually assumes that it is states that are parties to a conflict and that a state's legitimate government has decided in some rightful way on going to war. However, it was not always so easy to assume this: From the middle of the twelfth century to the late thirteenth, Wilson writes, "the main problem for canon lawyers was to define who among existing political leaders had the authority to initiate war."[7] The issue is again highly relevant. As Wilson describes the changes in the contemporary period that continue to make just war theory and the question of legitimate authority controversial, they include "the rapid decolonization of much of the world, the widespread occurrence of civil conflicts, the use of extremes of violence, and the desire of identifiable peoples to join international society as independent sovereign states."[8]

Since the end of World War II, the principle of self-determination has had a profound effect in international affairs. Whether self-determination is a moral right or a right in international law, or not a right at all for groups, remain highly contested questions,[9] and I do not deal with them here. What I will try to clarify is the following question: When liberation movements pursue aims deemed justifiable, who has legitimate authority to use violence in their behalf, and how should this be decided? With the growth of national liberation movements since the Second World War and the recent expansion of terrorism carried out by nonstate groups, the questions of what—for just war theory and its implications—a requirement of legitimate authority in nonstate groups would be and whether those who use violence and especially terrorism could ever meet it become relevant.

In the liberation struggles of many former colonial territories, the leaders of the freedom movements have become the internationally recognized heads of the new national entities these struggles have created. These movements have characteristically used violence and have at first been dismissed as terrorists, murderers, and criminals. But if successful, many have gradually come to be seen as the legitimate representatives of their "people." Their use of terrorism can become accepted as a means of resistance contributing to liberation. As Robert Young writes, "terrorist acts carried out by the members of the African National Congress were surely among the factors that led to the overthrow of apartheid... and given the horrendous suffering occasioned by the way the system of apartheid operated, some of the ANC's carefully targeted terrorist actions in South Africa are surely to be numbered among the morally justified uses of political violence."[10]

Concerning the authority to use force in national liberation movements, Heather Wilson concludes that

- The right of self-determination may legitimize the recognition of a government or a provisional government which otherwise would be premature.
- National liberation movements can have international legal personality.
- A large number of States now maintain that national liberation movements may legitimately use force to secure the right of their people to self-determination. The trend in international law... since 1960 in particular has been toward the acceptance of their legitimacy. However, a powerful minority of States, including those that confront national liberation movements, do not accept their authority as a matter of international law.[11]

Elsewhere she writes that "it would be a mistake to overlook the change in ideas which has taken place.... Wars of national liberation are no longer matters where international law definitely favours the established government to promote international order and protect the status quo."[12] However, for the political decisions that may or may not be especially influenced by international law, the issues are highly clouded.

TERRORISM AND JUST WAR THEORY

Let me consider again how I am using the term "terrorism." I have argued in other chapters that it should not, as part of its definition, stipulate that its violence attacks civilians, though it often does.[13] My usage departs from the definitions accepted by many, including the U.S. government (although not consistently),[14] Michael Walzer,[15] Tony Coady,[16] Igor Primoratz,[17] and many others, but it accords with that recommended by Andrew Valls[18] and Robert Young.[19]

One good reason not discussed earlier to remove the stipulation that terrorism targets noncombatants or "the innocent" from its definition is given by Walter Laqueur, who observes that it is "certainly no longer true" that terrorism is violence perpetrated against noncombatants. "Most terrorist groups in the contemporary world," he writes, "have been attacking the military, the police, and the civilian population." Hence, he says, a definition that sees terrorists as those who randomly attack civilians "may not be very helpful in the real world."[20] Of course, this presumes we can agree on who the "terrorist groups" are without a prior definition of terrorism, but that might actually be easier. Who would doubt, for instance, that Al Qaeda is one?

I think we ought to count, as news reports inconsistently do, the blowing up of the U.S. marine barracks in Lebanon in 1983, the bombing of the USS *Cole* in Yemen in 2000, and the attack on the Pentagon on September 11, 2001, as terrorist attacks even though the targets were military ones.[21]

Contrary to my view, Shannon French thinks that terrorism does necessarily target noncombatants and that this clearly distinguishes terrorists from warriors.[22] Terrorists, in her view, are murderers, and their actions are never justified, whereas those who fight just wars may well be within their rights in doing so. Her argument depends on a sharp distinction between a person who is a direct, present, mortal threat, such as a soldier pointing a gun at one, and a noncombatant who is not such a threat. However, this interpretation is unpersuasive. What could be more of a threat to a Palestinian than those in Ariel Sharon's government who give orders to the Israeli Defense Forces to send helicopter gunships to blow up those they consider "militants" in their cars and routinely kill civilians who happen to be nearby? Compared to this, a reluctant Israeli conscript with a gun may be less of a threat.

More persuasive than French's dichotomy is Michael Walzer's additional category of legitimate political targets, though he does not extend it to his analysis of contemporary terrorists. Nineteenth and early twentieth-century revolutionaries, he notes, targeted noncombatants, but they were political officials whose governments were oppressive.[23] The revolutionaries still avoided killing "ordinary" citizens, and in this they differed from many contemporary terrorists. Since contemporary politicians are much more effectively protected, however, assassinating them may often be almost impossible. Groups who oppose them, lacking armies and sophisticated military hardware, may believe they have few means of resistance available other than terrorism. Certainly much or most terrorism involves deliberately harming civilians, but the issue is whether this should be seen as a *necessary* feature of the definition of terrorism, and there are good reasons to assert that it should not.

Michael Walzer points out that today's terrorism, which kills large numbers of civilians, did not develop until *after* the terror bombing of World War II (e.g., of Hiroshima and Dresden), which undermined the distinction between legitimate military targets and civilian populations.[24] Furthermore, one can argue (though Walzer does not) that in democratic states, where governments depend on the support of voters, responsibility for policies deemed oppressive must be shared between governmental officials and the populations who vote them into office. Thus are citizens often included among those that terrorists consider to be legitimate targets. Of course, children are not responsible and should be exempt from attack, but this holds for both sides of a violent conflict.

I also reject, as explained earlier, the view held by the U.S. government and reflected in its definition and in much of the media (though many political theorists reject it) that terrorism is always carried out by nonstate groups, not by governments.[25] This simply contributes to biases in our discussions of violence. As James Sterba observes, "most of the clear cases of terrorism directed at innocents are cases of terrorism as practiced by states, such as France under the Jacobins [who originated the term 'terrorism' for the actions of the revolutionary government], Italy under Mussolini, Germany under Hitler, and Chile under Pinochet, rather than terrorism as practiced by substate groups or individuals."[26] We should continually remind ourselves, he argues, that "the most significant terrorist problem is that of state terrorism or state-supported terrorism."[27] The United States does recognize state-supported terrorism, but only that carried out by states of which it disapproves, never that by those it has supported, as in Central America during the Reagan administration.

In her analysis of the uses and abuses of the term "terrorism," Alison Jaggar concludes that "since terrorism is widely condemned, current usage thus tends to delegitimate struggles by the weak while legitimating repression by the strong."[28] Surely it is implausible to think that the only legitimate uses of violence are by the strong.

We should also avoid saying (as established states have done) that all use of violence by nonstate groups is automatically unjust. The 1977

United Nations International Convention for the Suppression of Terrorist Bombings asserted that "No cause however good warrants a violent response if the actor is an individual or group, not a state."[29] We have already seen how the acceptance of national liberation movements has changed this attitude among many states. Shannon French notes that "if we rule that any fighters who belong to a militant organization that does not represent a state do not qualify as legitimate combatants, we may...delegitimize all rebels and insurgents, regardless of the merits of their cause, the human rights abuses they may have suffered, or the oppressive and unrepresentative nature of the governments targeted by their rebellions."[30] That surely would be unreasonable.

The argument that I make in this book is that terrorism is not uniquely atrocious. All violence is atrocious, and methods should have been developed to deal with conflict in nonviolent ways. War is especially heinous, and so is terrorism, but in actual circumstances some uses of violence may be justified, and terrorism may not be more unjustifiable than war.

Instead of considering terrorism always and inevitably unjustifiable because it targets civilians, we should consider the aims of terrorists and of those who use violence to thwart those aims. We should compare the justice of the objectives of both sides, and we should compare the civilian casualties that both sides cause. The distinction between deliberately killing civilians and "unintentionally" but entirely predictably doing so is of very limited moral significance.[31]

In the two wars that Russia has fought to deny the Chechens independence, for instance, Russian forces have killed many thousands of civilians, including children, and have turned more than half the population into refugees. Chechen terrorism has, in contrast, killed hundreds of civilians.[32] In refusing to end its occupation of Palestinian territories and refusing for several years after 2001 to negotiate with the Palestinians to bring about a viable Palestinian state, Israel killed thousands of civilians, while Palestinian terrorists killed hundreds of Israeli civilians. These comparisons are relevant *jus in bello* judgments, judgments about how war is conducted, as are comparisons of the issues involved in *jus ad bellum,* or judgments about the reasons for the war and the goals of both sides. Of course, religious fanatics with unjustifiable aims cannot use violence justifiably, but groups with justifiable objectives may not be more to blame in using violence than are those who wage war against them.

There exist Palestinians who will not be reconciled to the existence of the state of Israel and will continue to support violence to destroy it. There are also Israelis who support expelling the Palestinians from the occupied territories they believe God gave to the Jews. The Palestinian Liberation Organization, however, had long since recognized Israel's right to exist, and elections had affirmed its claim to represent the Palestinian people, yet Israel refused to negotiate with it. Many Israelis believe that Yasir Arafat at Camp David rejected a reasonable offer from Israel for a final agreement; this view is often echoed by U.S. commentators.[33] To many Palestinians, however, Arafat "wouldn't sell out."[34] That reasonable persons among both Israelis and Palestinians could agree to a settlement is shown by the "Geneva Accord," which was reached by unofficial representatives of both sides.[35] This agreement was denounced by Ariel Sharon.

In trying to evaluate *jus in bello* considerations, it is entirely appropriate to compare the numbers of civilian casualties caused by those using terrorism in pursuit of a political goal and by those using military violence in opposing that goal. Of course, higher numbers of civilian casualties are worse than lower numbers, but using actual war or counterterrorism to attempt to eradicate terrorism may be a more unjustifiable means to pursue a political goal than was the violence to which it claims to be a response. Those who have resorted to terrorism often claim to be responding to unbearable oppression and violence rather than initiating aggression.

When states kill civilians, these deaths are often rationalized by the doctrine of double effect and minimized by failures to count or even acknowledge such casualties. Comparing the civilian toll in all uses of violence is appropriate and revealing. The United States in Iraq does not even try to count civilian casualties. Civic, a nonprofit, nongovernmental group that has tried do so, estimates that more than five thousand civilians were killed between the start of the U.S. invasion on March 20, 2003, and May 10 of that year, when major combat was declared at an end. Civic's founder comments that "It says a lot that the military doesn't even keep track of these things."[36] More recent estimates of civilian casualties caused by the war over a longer period are far, far greater. In 2004 a research team at the School of Public Health at Johns Hopkins University put the number of civilian deaths at approximately 100,000; according to a member of the research team this is "a conservative estimate."[37] A report by the same group in 2006 estimated that 655,000 more people died in Iraq since the start of the war than would have died if the invasion had not taken place.[38] Subsequent violence has greatly worsened the death toll of this war.

Violence used to bring about political change and violence used to prevent it are both extremely difficult to justify, and the burden of proof should be against its use on both sides. However, those who have sufficient power to see that political change might be attained in ways other than through violence have an even greater responsibility to avoid bloodshed. Sometimes it is those nonstate groups who could achieve change (e.g., through nonviolent demonstrations, mobilization of outside opinion, and creative use of the media to gain support) who are most at fault for using physical aggression. And sometimes most at fault are the states that have an overwhelming military advantage, use military violence to prevent such other means of achieving change from working, and employ military force and "counterterrorism" measures to preserve an unjustifiable status quo. In such conflicts, terrorism should be thought of as more similar to war than different from it. It can be used for justifiable, as well as unjustifiable, objectives. It is a use of political violence not necessarily more unjustifiable than the means of war.

THE USES OF TERRORISM

A very useful article is Robert Pape's "The Strategic Logic of Suicide Terrorism."[39] In contrast to those who see suicide bombings as a wholly new level of barbaric insanity, he treats even suicide terrorism as best analyzed in strategic terms. Pape shows that, rather than attribute suicide terrorism to religious extremism, it is more convincing to see it as based on rational calculation. Such bombings are nearly always part of campaigns in which violence serves a political objective for those who believe that nothing else will work (or work as well) and that this kind of violence will contribute, based on considerable evidence, to the achievement of their political objectives. Even Al Qaeda is seen as having the stated goal of driving the military of the United States and other Western powers out of "the lands of Islam" and as engaged in strategic thinking of a kind quite compatible with rational calculation rather than religious delusion.

Pape writes: "The vast majority of suicide terrorist attacks are not isolated or random acts by individual fanatics but, rather, occur in clusters as part of a larger campaign by an organized group to achieve a specific political goal....From Lebanon to Israel to Sri Lanka to Kashmir to Chechnya, every suicide terrorist campaign from 1980 to 2001 has been waged by terrorist groups whose main goal has been to establish or maintain self-determination for their community's homeland by compelling an enemy to withdraw."[40]

Pape treats suicide terrorism as "a strategy of coercion, a means to compel a target government to change policy."[41] He also shows that "there have been 188 separate suicide terrorist attacks between 1980 and 2001. Of these, 179, or 95%, were parts of organized, coherent campaigns, while only nine were isolated or random events."[42]

In the case of Hamas and Islamic Jihad, "the terrorist groups came to the conclusion that suicide attack accelerated Israel's withdrawal.... Although the Oslo Accords formally committed [Israel] to withdrawing the IDF [Israel Defense Forces] from Gaza and the West Bank, Israel routinely missed key deadlines, often by many months, and the terrorists came to believe that Israel would not have withdrawn when it did, and perhaps not at all, had it not been for the coercive leverage of suicide attack. Moreover...numerous other observers...came to the same conclusion."[43]

Terrorism, even suicide terrorism, Pape shows, is on a continuum with other uses of violence: "Since 1980, there has not been a suicide terrorist campaign directed...against foreign opponents who did not have military forces in the terrorists' homeland. Although attacks against civilians are often the most salient to Western observers, actually every suicide terrorist campaign in the past two decades has included attacks directly against the foreign military forces in the country, and most have been waged by guerrilla organizations that also use more conventional methods of attack against those forces."[44] Furthermore, "all of the organizations that have resorted to suicide terrorism began their coercive efforts with more conventional guerrilla operations, nonsuicide terrorism, or both. Hezbollah, Hamas, Islamic Jihad, the PKK [Kurdish Workers], the LTTE [Tamil Tigers], and Al Qaeda all used demonstrative and destructive means of violence long before resorting to suicide attack. Indeed...there is a distinct element of experimentation...and distinct movement toward those techniques and strategies that produce the most effect."[45]

James Bennet, reporting for some time on the region for the *New York Times,* writes that "most Palestinians take it as axiomatic that Israelis respond to nothing but force....It is not lost on Palestinians that, during the relatively quiet days under the Oslo peace accords between the two Palestinian uprisings, Israeli settlements in the occupied territories doubled in size."[46]

Bruce Hoffman also emphasizes the calculated aspects of terrorism. "All terrorism," he writes, "involves the quest for power...to effect fundamental political change....Terrorists [are] convinced that only through violence can their cause triumph and their long-term political aims be attained. Terrorists therefore plan their operations in a manner that will shock, impress, and intimidate....Often erroneously seen as indiscriminate or senseless, terrorism is actually a very deliberate and planned application of violence."[47]

One consequence of seeing terrorism as on a continuum with war rather than as wholly different (with war seen as sometimes justifiable but terrorism as absolutely never so) is that it can contribute to reconciliation. After a conflict is settled, both sides can move on. A telling incident was reported of a former member of the African National Congress who had been a "legendary bomb maker" and terrorist in the fight against apartheid. By the time of the report he was a police chief of a large district in eastern Johannesburg. A white police officer serving under him indicated that neither of them held his past against the other: "We fought our war, he fought his war, and we came together."[48] In contrast, those who see terrorists as utterly evil and inhuman can accept nothing less than their total eradication. To them, reconciliation is out of the question, and since terrorism is the weapon of the weak used by many groups, the war against terrorism will presumably be endless.

LEGITIMATE REPRESENTATION

Suppose we agree, then, that to achieve a legitimate political objective, terrorism, like war, can sometimes be a use of violence that is not more unjustifiable than the violence used to resist it. It then raises especially relevant questions about how to decide whether a group using terrorism is actually supported by the people it claims to represent. Established states regularly try to dismiss nonstate groups that use violence as bandits and murderers who do not represent their groups. Terrorists, however, claim to be supported by the groups for whose interests they employ violence. Are there ways to evaluate these claims? Michael Walzer notes "how easy it is to destroy a guerrilla band that has no popular support."[49] One could make a similar point about those who use terrorist violence.

Robert Pape points out that suicide terrorism runs the risk of costing support in the terrorists' own community, so it can be "sustained over time only when there already exists a high degree of commitment among the potential pool of recruits."[50] Bruce Hoffman also notes that the resilience of many groups is "a product of the relative ease with which they are able to draw sustenance and support from an existing constituency," such as the fellow members of their ethnonationalist group.[51] This contributes to the longevity of, for instance the PLO and the IRA. In contrast, various left- and right-wing terrorist organizations that depend on political conviction have often won less support and been more short lived. One estimate claims that "the life expectancy of at least 90 percent of terrorist organizations is less than a year."[52]

Pape argues that "The most important goal that a community can have is the independence of its homeland (population, property, and way of life) from foreign influence and control....In fact, every suicide campaign from 1980 to 2001 has had as a major objective—or as its central objective—coercing a foreign government that has military forces in what they see as their homeland to take those forces out."[53] Hence the risks of losing support involved in suicide terrorism have been thought worth taking. This pattern applies even to Al Qaeda, in Pape's view: A major objective of Al Qaeda has been the expulsion of U.S. troops from the Saudi Peninsula, and "over 95% of Saudi society reportedly agrees with Bin Laden on this matter."[54] Surveys of public opinion in various countries in March 2004 showed that Bin Laden was rated favorably by 65 percent of those surveyed in Pakistan, 55 percent in Jordan, and 45 percent in Morocco.[55] Additionally, "a clear majority of people polled" in these countries said that "the suicide bombings against Americans and other Westerners in Iraq were justified."[56]

Pape concludes the following:

> Suicide terrorists' political aims, if not their methods, are often more mainstream than observers realize; they generally reflect quite common, straightforward nationalist self-determination claims of their community....These groups often have significant support for their policy goals versus the target state, goals that are typically much the same as those of other nationalists within their community. Differences between the terrorists and more "moderate" leaders usually concern the usefulness of a certain level of violence and—sometimes—the legitimacy of attacking additional targets besides foreign

troops in the country....The terrorists are simply the members of their societies who are the most optimistic about the usefulness of violence for achieving goals that many, and often most, support.[57]

They may be more ruthless, but on a continuum they are often matched by the ruthlessness of their opponents.

What would it mean to recognize a terrorist group as legitimately representing a people? What, to begin, is legitimacy? Allen Buchanan recommends that "an entity has political legitimacy if and only if it is morally justified in wielding political power."[58] He distinguishes between political legitimacy and political authority and finds the conditions for any government to have the latter to be so demanding that virtually no government is likely to attain it.[59] However, that does not mean that no government or group can justifiably wield political power. Buchanan concludes that "where democratic authorization of the exercise of political power is possible, only a democratic government can be legitimate."[60] But such democratic authorization is often not possible.

Once a group is recognized, it can engage in constitutional conventions, elections, and the rest of the ways in which leaders may be democratically authorized. However, there is often a prior stage at which those using violence should not be excluded from consideration as legitimately representing a group of people. It is often suggested that groups who employ terrorism must give it up before they can be considered legitimate representatives. This is a demand routinely made of the Palestinians by Israel and the United States. From the point of view of those resisting oppression, however, as usually from an impartial point of view also, this amounts to asking such groups to surrender their leverage in negotiations. Negotiating from a position of weakness, without power to inflict costs on the other side, may be capitulation rather than negotiation.

A group engaged in an armed struggle for a political objective is usually unable to accurately assess popular support. There will be some opposition to its use of violence, which often provokes retaliation. This is illustrated in those Palestinian militants' attacks that result in Israeli destruction of their homes and the buildings from which they operate or in the bulldozing of orchards in which they take cover. Many Palestinians oppose particular actions by militants, although most support the goal of resisting the Israeli occupation.

Despite some opposition, surveys indicate widespread support among Palestinians for the use of violence—including suicide terrorism—because they see it as the only way to hasten the end of the Israeli occupation. According to one 2004 report, "Palestinians have carried out more than 100 suicide attacks...in the past three years. A strong majority of Palestinians have backed them throughout the fighting."[61] When most members of a group think that only violence has any chance of achieving liberation, some groups who use terrorism do seem to represent the popular will.

In her study of the way in which conceptions of political legitimacy were transformed in the West in the late eighteenth century, Mlada Bukovansky examines the interplay between domestic and international factors. Political struggles in Europe and the United States yielded a profound shift from a dynastic monarchical conception of legitimacy to legitimacy as dependent on the popular will; these changes were not only domestic. She shows that "political legitimacy also requires external recognition....Mutual recognition is an essential feature of sovereignty."[62] Today, she asserts, "international political culture...converges on the idea of 'the people' as the ultimate source of political authority," but it does not limit legitimacy to democratic governments.[63] Certainly a revolutionary group may sometimes be thought to better represent a people than does its actual government. "Culture," she argues, "shapes the international system because beliefs about legitimacy are forged through cultural discourse, and without legitimacy power cannot endure."[64] Today, some international discourse seeks to exclude all groups that use terrorism from the possibility of gaining legitimacy. Some such groups, however, may actually meet the basic requirements of legitimacy better than many deemed legitimate by dominant discourses. Legitimacy is one among many contested concepts; questions also about its application will continue to be contested.

Concerning the legitimate authority requirement of just war theory as applied to nonstate entities, Andrew Valls concludes that "if an organization claims to act on behalf of a people and is widely seen by that people as legitimately doing so, then the rest of us should look on that organization as the legitimate authority of the people for the purposes of assessing its entitlement to engage in violence on their behalf."[65]

POLITICAL VIOLENCE AND INTERNATIONAL RECOGNITION

The United Nations has tended to recognize liberation movements as the legitimate representatives of their people. But how should one decide that a liberation movement really is representative, and how should one choose between liberation movements?

Heather Wilson devotes a chapter of her book to the following question: "If it is the case that there is a right of 'peoples' to self-determination and some claim that the use of force to secure this right is justified, then how does a particular liberation movement become a legitimate representative of a people?"[66] Even if there is not such a right and if a liberation movement justifiably uses force to free a group from serious human rights violations, the same question could arise. She writes, "In practice it has been liberation movements and the provisional governments sometimes established by these movements which have often been considered to be the authorities representing a people."[67] Nevertheless, this is not always clear; often more than one resistance movement exists, for instance. Wilson concludes with a sweeping understatement that "recognition of an entity representing a people is still a very primitive and tenuous development for which definitive rules do not appear to exist."[68]

Since 1967 the United Nations has had the general practice of deferring to the Organization of African Unity (OAU), founded in 1963, in deciding which persons or organizations should represent the non-self-governing territories in Africa moving toward ending colonial domination. The PLO, recognized by the League of Arab States, has also been recognized. Although no formally stated criteria for recognition of a liberation movement as the legitimate representative of its people have been announced, there have been implicit standards, discernible in its practices, such as deferring to regional intergovernmental organizations in estimating who should be recognized. The OAU avoids deciding on movements that seek liberation from existing African states, but it has recognized various movements—sometimes more than one in the same territory—fighting against colonial powers.

As Wilson summarizes, a major requirement for OAU recognition has been "that the movement be representative of the people of a territory."[69] Here the OAU emphasizes "control of the loyalty of the population rather than control of land."[70] This is of course difficult to determine and is usually based on conjecture and the ability of members of the movements to persuade neighboring states and the OAU that they indeed have the support of the populations they seek to represent. Another requirement for OAU recognition has been that the movement claims to represent a "people" entitled to statehood, not a particular tribe, religious or ethnic minority, or particular province within a territory. That is, the recognized groups have claimed to represent a whole "self" or people who are seeking self-determination, not just a part of these, though these claims are obviously highly controversial.

If we start with these implicit criteria, how helpful can they be in the context of just war requirements on the use of violence? They suggest that for any group to be a legitimate authority in using terrorist violence, it must have the support of the people on whose behalf the violence is used. This seems to be a reasonable judgment, though (as with political leadership in general) support should be interpreted in terms of not only current polls of popular opinion but also future support of actions taken.[71] Bruce Hoffman notes that all terrorists "exist and function in hopes of reaching" the goals of gaining authority and attaining the ability to govern, though few succeed. "For them, the future rather than the present defines their reality."[72] And so, to some extent at least, should judgments about them, as judgments about the legitimacy of existing governments depend in part on their ability to continue to represent those governed.

It is appropriate to judge terrorist violence, like other violence, in part in terms of its consequences, as well as on more deontological grounds.[73] The requirement that groups that utilize terrorism represent the people they claim to be acting for would allow us to conclude that some terrorism carried out by Palestinians has been undertaken by legitimate authority, as some Israeli terrorism before it may have been. Certainly this does not mean that particular judgments on using violence, even when they meet the requirement of legitimate authority, are correct: For instance, there may well be courses of action open to those involved that make use of less violence and have similar chances of contributing to liberation. However, the possibility exists that a group using terrorism may be a legitimate authority.

The requirement of support would also allow us to be skeptical of some other claims by terrorist groups. For instance, the Baader-Meinhof group in Germany and the Red Brigades in Italy may never have had a great deal of support, and it was unclear whether Kosovars supported the Kosovo Liberation Army when it killed Serbian police and caused Serbs in Kosovo to flee their homes.[74]

Where means other than violence and terrorism are available for achieving a shared and justifiable goal, one certainly hopes that terrorist groups would not have the approval that would contribute to their being the legitimate representatives of people. But then it is often the responsibility of those preventing the achievement of these goals (when they are justifiable) to make available these alternative means (e.g., referenda, international pressure, persuasion) within the obstructing state.

We might do well to avoid giving automatic legitimacy to existing boundaries and political arrangements since the origins of all states in force and fraud make the facts of existing power so morally questionable. At the same time, we can recognize the importance of stability and the degree to which existing states must be acknowledged as effectively existing. Efforts to work out international order and achieve the peace and security for which there is such overwhelming need depend, in general, on accepting existing states as legitimate regardless of their questionable origins. However, there might be a much greater openness than at present to changes in the configurations of states *as long as the change would be brought about peacefully.* This would mean that efforts could be concentrated much more than at present on managing change and less on preventing it. When separation, for instance, is entertained as a possibility instead of repressed as treasonous, political discourse can be directed at the costs of separation: Economic conditions may seriously worsen, for instance. Referenda, where appropriate, can help to indicate popular support or lack of it.

The requirement that a group that claims to represent a "people" represent a "whole" people rather than merely a tribe or subgroup is highly difficult to deal with. Omar Dahbour observes that "what one commentator has remarked about the International Covenants on Rights is generally true of most international documents—that they offer 'no useful guidance as to what counts as a 'people.'"[75] Nonetheless, although it is difficult to be precise about who is included in any group, it is sometimes by no means impossible to specify that a group exists and that it seeks to liberate itself from outside domination. The lines of race in South Africa made the struggle of nonwhites against white domination clearer than in some other cases. Still, many of the other cases discussed by, for instance, Pape and Hoffman make clear the identities of the groups for whose liberation some members have resorted to violence.

To be *legitimate* representatives, must the leaders of a group aiming at statehood agree to abide by the international norms applicable to all states? As long as this requirement is not imposed on powerful, established states (which reserve for themselves the right to decide what is in their national interest regardless of international norms and are still considered legitimate governments), it should not be placed on nonstate groups. It might well, however, be morally justifiable to place the requirement on all states.

I conclude, then, that the requirement of legitimate authority should not be thought impossible for nonstate groups that make use of violence (including terrorism) to meet. Of course, this does not mean that such violence is justified, but neither does it mean that war against them is warranted on the grounds that the violence these groups engage in *cannot* be justified. Groups that employ terrorism are not in a category by themselves. As with war, we need to evaluate the violent acts and consider whether the goals for which they are used are justified.

DEALING WITH TERRORISM

Two broad approaches to terrorism seem to be emerging: first, the Israeli way of massive military response and refusal to consider terrorists' political objectives because that would be rewarding evildoers; second, the European way represented by France, Germany, and more recently Spain, which involves marshalling international support to control violence and to deal with the political problems that fuel terrorism. The United States has opted for the Israeli path: the administration of President George W. Bush and its supporters obviously so, and the public only somewhat less so, at least for some time. A survey in March 2004 showed that 78 percent of U.S. voters believed that Bush is "likely to protect the country from a terrorist attack."[76] This belief in Bush's ability to deal with the threat of terrorism continued high in the United States through his reelection in November 2004, despite harsh attacks from Democrats in the campaign. Commentators on the Right labeled Spain's voters' repudiation of Prime Minister Aznar's support of Bush as "appeasement" and "capitulation to terrorists."[77] Many European officials, meanwhile, argue that relying on military force, especially when it is used unilaterally, is not an effective or justified response to terrorism. Igor Primoratz of Hebrew University, Jerusalem, examines Israel's "use of state terrorism in its rule over the Palestinian territories...and fight against Palestinian resistance."[78] He concludes that this type of counterterrorism "may well prove a dismal failure in political terms, as it has done in the Israeli case." Moreover, it is "utterly indefensible from the moral point of view" since Israel, like other states, has options for dealing with terrorism other than using terrorism itself.[79]

Tomis Kapitan examines the successful efforts of leading Israelis to portray Palestinian resistance in the occupied territories as "terrorism" and thus to shift attention away from Israel's confiscation of land, settlement expansions, and restrictions on Palestinians. Here is his evaluation of Israel's policies: The "principle that the only way to deal with terrorism is with counter-terrorist violence," he writes, "has been the policy of successive Israeli governments since the early 1950s. The result has not reduced but *increased* the amount of terrorism in the Near East."[80] During the ten-year period from 1978 to 1987 Palestinian terrorist attacks killed Israelis at a rate of approximately 8 per year. In the next ten-year period, 1988–1997, that rate had jumped to 42 Israelis killed per year, along with 138 Palestinians per year killed by Israel. By May 2002, after more than a year of Prime Minister Ariel Sharon's refusal to negotiate with Palestinian leaders, intensification of settlement activity, and "iron fist approach to Palestinian resistance,"[81] Israelis were being killed at a rate of 282 per year, and Palestinians at a rate three times as high. "The vast bulk of the fatalities on both sides were civilians."[82]

Here is Matthew Evangelista's evaluation of Russia's efforts in Chechnya over two centuries: "A constant theme has been the counterproductive nature of Russia's military actions. The blunt military instrument most often served to alienate potential allies and turn an indifferent population against the Russian authorities."[83] What he calls Putin's "near-genocidal war" in Chechnya is no exception.[84]

Kapitan writes that "persistent terrorism stemming from a given population is indicative of a serious political disorder. As long as the members of that population are outraged over perceived injustices and decide that terrorism is the *only* viable form of redress, then mere police action, coupled with a repeated failure to address their grievances, will solve nothing, and certainly indiscriminate retaliation will only intensify hatred and resolve."[85]

In a review of a variety of studies by a number of psychologists and political scientists with a view to understanding what we can learn from the social sciences about how to reduce terrorism, Scott Plous and Philip Zimbardo point out that "large-scale military responses to terrorism tend to be ineffective or temporarily to *increase* terrorist activity."[86]

The Bush administration has invaded and occupied Iraq in a preventive war against claimed potential terrorism. This has produced a radicalization of Muslims in the region and a vast increase in recruits available for terrorist attacks against the United States.[87] The United States has virtually ignored the Israeli-Palestinian conflict—the core source of perceived injustice in the Middle East—effectively endorsing Sharon's failed approach and that of his successor Ehud Olmert. It has allowed much of Afghanistan to revert to rule by warlord and sections of the country to be controlled again by the Taliban. If the United States does not change course in its war on terrorism, one can expect an escalation of violence in general and of terrorism in particular. Furthermore, the legitimacy of the United States to act in the world will increasingly be undermined.

If, on the other hand, we try to deal with the political causes of terrorism and are mindful of the moral requirements and empirical realities involved in opposing it, questions of which persons and groups do (and which do not) legitimately represent wider populations will become increasingly urgent.

FOUR

TERRORISM, RIGHTS, AND POLITICAL GOALS

(*With Postscript*)

An examination of usage is particularly unhelpful in deciding what terrorism is and whether it can be justified. Usage characteristically applies the term to violent acts performed by those whose positions and goals the speaker disapproves of and fails to apply it to similar acts by those whose positions and goals the speaker identifies with. In addition, the term is much more frequently applied to those who threaten established conditions and governments than to those using similar kinds of violence to uphold them. There is a tendency to equate terrorism with the *illegal* use of violence, but of course the questions of who decides what is illegal and on what grounds they do so are often precisely those at issue.

Careful analysis can help clarify the issues surrounding terrorism and provide a basis for recommended interpretations. We can recognize that drawing distinctions is difficult and yet agree with Jenny Teichman when she says that "seemingly ambiguous kinds of violence can be distinguished from one another." She suggests that "*revolutions* can be differentiated into the peaceful and the violent.... *Civil protest*, similarly, can be either peaceful or violent. *Guerrilla war* is simply small war. Whether *riots* are crimes or acts of war depends on the intention and the degree of organization of the rioters."[1] Whether or not one shares her ways of drawing these distinctions, one can agree with her conclusion that such distinctions are possible—and important to make. "Terrorism" also, she believes, can be defined, despite being, in her view, "the most ambiguous concept in the list."[2]

Much recent philosophical discussion of the term "terrorism" provides sufficient clarification and demands sufficient consistency to make persuasive the view that terrorism is not committed only by those opposed to governments and their policies. "Terrorism" must be understood in such a way that states and governments, even friendly or democratic ones, can be thought able to engage in acts of terrorism, along with those who challenge the authority and disrupt the order of such states and governments. However, an adequate definition has not yet emerged in the philosophical literature.

In an article called "On Terrorism," R. M. Hare does not even attempt a definition.[3] Carl Wellman offers a wide definition: Terrorism is, he suggests, "the use or attempted use of terror as a means of coercion."[4] But this definition is so wide that, as he admits, it includes nonviolent acts that almost no one else would count as terrorism. Wellman writes: "I often engage in nonviolent terrorism myself, for I often threaten to flunk any student who hands in his paper after the due date. Anyone who doubts that my acts are genuine instances of the coercive use of terror is invited to observe . . . the panic in my classroom when I issue my ultimatum."[5] Although this particular ultimatum may well be an instance of the coercive use of terror, it does not, for most of us, constitute an instance of terrorism, and the very conclusion that, on Wellman's definition it would have to, is enough to suggest to most of us that his definition is unsatisfactory. Violence seems an inherent characteristic of terrorism, so that Wellman's "nonviolent terrorism" seems to be something other than terrorism.

Further, not only does Wellman's definition admit too many acts that are implausibly counted as terroristic, but it also excludes others that should not be ruled out. For Wellman, "coercion, actual or attempted, is of the essence of terrorism."[6] He does not mean only that terrorism is itself coercive, as is violence, for instance, but also that it is a means to further coercion, as when a given group uses terrorism against airline passengers to coerce a government into releasing certain prisoners.

To build the goal of coercion into the definition of terrorism seems mistaken. Among other difficulties, it excludes what can be considered acts of expressive violence, as certain acts can best be deemed. Some terrorism appears to be an expression of frustration more than a means to anything else, or it can have a variety of goals. Terrorism can be intended as punishment or to call attention to a problem even when no ability to coerce anyone further is expected. If we say that punishment is coercive, we can still recognize that, although one may have to coerce people in order to punish them, the two are not identical. Sometimes wrongdoers accept punishment voluntarily, and coercion is often not punitive, so the two terms have different meanings. In the case of terrorism whose purpose is to call attention to a problem, we can again agree that the violence involved is itself coercive but not that its objective is further coercion. If an effort to coerce people to pay attention—to force them against their wills to heed the terrorists' message—counts as an intention to coerce further, we would have to consider a wide range of free speech to be means of coercion, as orators and demonstrators gather and speak in public places in ways that others cannot easily avoid seeing and hearing. If forcing one's message on people would be considered a means of coercion rather than merely itself coercive, then so much of free speech, and especially so much advertising, would be considered coercion that the meaning of this term would lose its reasonable limits. Of course, terrorism is not merely free expression, but whatever else it is is not necessarily a means of further coercion. The violence it involves is coercive, but it can be for the purpose of gaining a hearing for a view rather than, say, extracting a concession from opponents.

One of the most useful recent discussions is that of C. A. J. Coady, even though I disagree with his definition. He defines terrorism as "the tactic or policy of engaging in terrorist acts" and a terrorist act as "a political act, ordinarily committed by an organized group, which involves the intentional killing or other severe harming of non-combatants or the threat of the same."[7] The crucial component of terrorism, in his view, is the intentional targeting of noncombatants. He does not think the intent to spread fear should be part of the definition. Among his reasons for this is that, instead of spreading fear and demoralization, the terrorist act may give rise to defiance and a strengthening of resolve.

In response to this latter point, one can point out that, although of course a terrorist act may fail to have the intended consequence of spreading fear, any act can fail to produce its intended effect. The issue is whether an intention to produce fear as well as damage should be built into the definition of terrorism. Unless we do build it in, we may lack a suitable way to distinguish terrorism from other forms of violence. Coady says that if we refer in the definition to an intention to spread fear, there will be problems in ascertaining the intention behind the act; I do not think such problems will be much more severe in the case of assessing the intention to promote fear than in the case of assessing the intention to harm noncombatants, and this latter intention Coady does incorporate into his definition.

As already discussed, a difficulty with confining terrorism to those acts that involve the intentional harming of noncombatants is that doing so will exclude actions that seem among the leading candidates for inclusion. One such act is the blowing up of the marine barracks in Lebanon in October 1983. In this attack, in which a truck with explosives was driven into a marine compound and exploded, 241 persons, most of them U.S. Marines, were killed.[8] The drivers of the truck were killed as well. The marines were clearly the intended target. According to Coady's definition, this act would not be one of terrorism, and this seems arbitrary.

Additionally, on Coady's definition, such intentional harming of noncombatants by a resistance group as would be caused by, for instance, a long-term campaign of refusing to fill service roles like that of hospital orderly for an oppressing group would count as terrorism, and this seems implausible. Coady cites the work of Brazilian revolutionary Carlos Marighela, whose handbook of urban guerrilla warfare, published in 1969, has been influential with revolutionary groups in Latin America. Marighela confines his discussion of terrorism to only two paragraphs; he means by it "the use of bomb attacks."[9] Though this is certainly insufficient as a definition, it contains a core that should not be dismissed, and that core does not seem consistent with a claim that an intention to harm noncombatants is a necessary component of terrorism.

Another difficulty here is the distinction made between combatant and noncombatant. Coady calls various claims that one cannot distinguish the two "absurd and obscene," but he unfairly loads his own descriptions of the difference.[10] He is surely right that inconsistency often operates here, as those who deny that the distinction can be made among their enemies in wartime fail to accept a comparable argument made by revolutionaries about their enemies. Still, the distinction is considerably more difficult to make—on both sides—than Coady admits, for reasons that I touch on later.

Another useful discussion is Jenny Teichman's, though again I reject the definition it offers. Teichman concludes that terrorism is not a matter of scale, that it is a style or method of government or of warfare, and that it can be carried out by states as well as groups. "Terrorism," she writes, partially agreeing with Coady, "essentially means any method of war which consists in intentionally attacking those who ought not to be attacked."[11] She shows why those who ought not to be attacked may not be equivalent to the category of noncombatant (or that of innocent) as usually understood. Those responsible for the start and the conduct, as well as the carrying out, of violence are not the improper targets the definition rests on. The major difficulty with her definition, in addition to the excessive focus on some version of the combatant/noncombatant distinction, is that it builds a moral judgment into the definition, an approach that I and many others reject for reasons I discuss later.

My own view of what terrorism is remains, then, close to what it was in an article I published some time ago in which I focused on violence rather than on terrorism itself.[12] I there defended the view that violence is "action, usually sudden, predictably and coercively inflicting injury upon or damage harming a person."[13] And I described terrorism as a form of violence to achieve political goals, where creating fear is usually high among the intended effects. For reasons similar to those subsequently argued by others, I limited violence and terrorism to harm to persons rather than to property; sometimes, though not always, one harms persons by damaging their property, but the intention to injure persons must be present.

Judith Lichtenberg speculates on how terrorism induces fear: Violence targeted at ordinary people makes ordinary people everywhere feel uneasy.[14] In the case of the attack on the marine barracks in Lebanon, the target was not ordinary people or noncombatants, but the aim to induce fear can also be present in such cases. The objective can be to induce fear among military personnel: Young U.S. soldiers anywhere, and especially in the Middle East, realize that the most expensive and sophisticated weaponry cannot protect them against the kind of attack that killed so many of their fellows.

We should probably not construe the intention either to spread fear or to kill noncombatants as necessary for an act of political violence to be an act of terrorism. Both are often present, but not always. And there do not seem to be good reasons to make the latter a part of the definition while dismissing the former. Furthermore, other motives can exist as well. As Grant Wardlaw notes in his perceptive book on terrorism, "Whilst the primary effect is to create fear and alarm the objectives may be to gain concessions, obtain maximum publicity for a cause, provoke repression, break down social order, build morale in the movement or enforce obedience to it."[15]

I do not venture to suggest exactly what one or combination of factors may be necessary to turn political violence into terrorism, but perhaps when the intention either to spread fear or to harm noncombatants is primary, this is sufficient.

THE JUSTIFIABILITY OF TERRORISM

A second way in which usage and much popular and some academic discussion has been unhelpful in illuminating the topic of terrorism is that it has frequently built a judgment of immorality or nonjustifiability into the definition of terrorism, making it impossible even to question whether given acts of terrorism might be justified. Thus news reports frequently equate terrorism with evildoing. Politicians often use the term as an automatic term of abuse. British author Paul Wilkinson, in a book on terrorism, characterizes terrorists as persons who "sacrifice *all* moral and humanitarian considerations for the sake of some political end."[16] Benjamin Netanyahu goes even further. He describes the terrorist as representing the kind of prehistoric person who is incapable of morality: "Divested of any moral principle, he has no moral sense, no moral controls, and is therefore capable of committing any crime, like a killing machine, without shame or remorse."[17] Philosopher Burton Leiser says that, by definition, terrorists consider themselves above laws and morality; he equates terrorism with piracy and considers it invariably criminal and immoral.[18] Finally, Michael Walzer begins a discussion of terrorism with the assumption that "every act of terrorism is a wrongful act."[19]

Arguments against building unjustifiability into the definition of terrorism can follow similar arguments against holding that violence is by definition morally wrong. Not only is violence often used in ways usually accepted, as in upholding law, but one can easily cite examples of violence used against governmental authority in which it makes sense to ask whether such incidents were morally wrong. The 1944 bomb plot against Hitler is one obvious candidate. Even if examples of possibly justifiable acts of terrorism, as distinct from other forms of violence, are for many persons harder to acknowledge, we should still be able to consider the justifiability of terrorist acts. We should be able to treat such questions as open, and this requires that we not imagine them to be answerable merely by appealing to a definition.

Many of those who use "terrorist" as a term of denunciation apply it, as noted before, to their opponents and refuse to apply it to the acts of their own government or of governments of which they approve, even when such governmental action is as clearly violent, intended to spread fear, or expectably productive of the killing of noncombatants.[20] But one cannot effectively criticize the terrorism of those Third World revolutionaries who consider various terrorist acts to be admirable[21] unless one also criticizes the terrorist acts of counterterrorism campaigns carried out by one's government and the governments of states one considers "friendly."[22] What to consider "original offense" and what "retaliation" is of course a matter of political judgment. Many of those engaged in acts considered terroristic by existing governments consider themselves to be retaliating against unjustified and violent acts by those governments, such as "reprisal raids," which predictably kill civilians.

In a balanced discussion of forms of violence, philosopher Robert Holmes concludes that terrorism per se is morally no worse than many conventionally accepted forms of violence. Ordinary warfare often uses terror as a tactic, and we should remember that the terror bombings of Dresden, Hiroshima, and Nagasaki undoubtedly killed far more people than have been slain by all of the terrorists, as conventionally labeled, throughout the world in all of the years since.[23]

One can further argue, as does Richard Falk, that one cannot be sincerely or consistently opposed to terrorism unless one is also opposed to the "tactics of potential or actual warfare that rely on indiscriminate violence or that deliberately target civilians."[24] Since those who defend preparing for nuclear war are not willing to reject such tactics, their opposition to terrorism seems more propagandistic than honest. However, the mistake of selective application can be corrected, as we become accustomed to the term "state terrorism" and then reduce the bias so far manifest in usage concerning its application.

Some of those who define terrorism as the intentional harming of noncombatants conclude that therefore, either by definition or not, terrorism is always wrong.[25] Since we can rule out as inadequate the view that terrorism is by definition always wrong, let us consider only those cases in which the judgment is not one of definition but independently arrived at. Then, is intentionally harming noncombatants always wrong and terrorism always wrong because it involves this?

Let us consider some objections to the position that it is never justifiable to harm noncombatants. First let us take up the question of harming noncombatants in wartime and focus on an example. Reports suggest that the Iran-Iraq war of 1980–1988 may have cost some 1 million dead, 1.7 million wounded, and more than 1.5 million refugees.[26] It is also suggested that Iran's decision to accept UN Resolution 598, which called for an end to the fighting, was partly the result of a demoralization within Iran brought about by the Iraqi bombing of Iranian cities.[27] Certainly, from a moral point of view, the war ought not to have been fought, and other means to achieve this outcome should have been found. Iraq was at fault in starting the war and in violation of international law in its use of poison gas.[28] However, once the war was under way, was violence used against noncombatants beyond the possibility of moral justification, even if it did in fact hasten the cessation of violence? Since the Iraqi invasion of Kuwait on August 2, 1990, and subsequently, it became commonplace to demonize the Iraqi leader Saddam Hussein, but it should be possible to evaluate specific actions. An argument can be made that no absolute right of noncombatants to immunity from the violence suffered by combatants should be granted, especially when many of the combatants have been conscripted or misled into joining the armed forces.

Many who serve in armies around the world are children. Iran's conscription age was lowered to thirteen, the contra rebels in Nicaragua recruited boys as young as twelve, and these are not isolated examples. Some two hundred thousand members of the world's armies, according to a UN report, are youngsters. Sometimes they are forcibly rounded up; sometimes they are urged by parents "to enlist in armies to gain food, jobs or payments if the child dies in battle."[29] Such "combatants" are hardly legitimate targets while the "civilians" who support the war in which they fight are exempt.

Now let us apply this objection to terrorism. Is violence that kills young persons whose economic circumstances made military service seem to be almost their only option very much more plausibly justifiable than violence attacking well-off shoppers in a mall, shoppers whose economic comfort is enjoyed at the expense of the young persons who risk their lives in order to eat and thereby carry out the policies of the shoppers? It is hard to see here a deep moral distinction between combatant and noncombatant. If the combatant is a conscript, the distinction between combatant and "ordinary person" is often difficult to draw. Additionally, although one may certainly maintain that any child is innocent, it is still not clear why the children of one group should be granted an absolute right of exemption from the risk of violence when no such right is granted to the children of an opposing group, if the violence is justified on other grounds. When the police use violence to apprehend a suspected criminal and an innocent child is killed in the cross fire, this is normally interpreted as an unfortunate tragedy, not a clear violation of the child's rights. If an act of "unofficial violence" is otherwise justified and an innocent child is killed, it might perhaps be no more clearly a violation of the child's rights. Thus we cannot conclude that terrorism is necessarily always more unjustifiable than other political violence even if harm to noncombatants is always present.

This is not to suggest that we should simply abandon the distinction between combatant and noncombatant. It is certainly harder to justify harming noncombatants than it is to justify harming combatants, other things being equal, and we can try to combine this distinction with usefully drawn notions of "those responsible." But as Coady notes, "If a revolution is unjustified then any killing done in its name is unjustified whether of combatants or non-combatants."[30] The same thing can be said of any repression of opponents of a regime. It is often more important to keep this in mind and to apply the judgments it provides than to rely on a distinction between otherwise legitimate and illegitimate targets.

Many of those who most bitterly denounce terrorism are entirely willing to sacrifice the innocent lives of hostages to uphold the principle that one should never negotiate with hostage takers.[31] They contend that in the long run fewer lives will be lost if one upholds this principle. However, this risks harm to innocent hostages and may rest on justifications quite comparable to those of hostage takers, who are willing to risk harming innocent persons to bring about a political goal on the theory that, in the long run, fewer lives overall will be lost if the goal is achieved than if intolerable oppression continues.

Judith Lichtenberg and the author of the report on terrorism in *QQ* suggest that we should refuse, in retaliating against terrorism, to resort to the tactics of the terrorist by risking the lives of the innocent.[32] Nevertheless—though they do not draw this conclusion—such concern for the lives of the innocent might then indicate that we must be willing rather than unwilling to negotiate with terrorists. The argument is always that negotiating with terrorists now risks more loss of innocent life later, but of course the sincere defender of terrorism makes a parallel claim: that a risk to innocent life now will avoid the further loss of innocent life later, which must be expected as a repressive regime continues its unjust and violent repression.

Much philosophical discussion avoids the mistake of making terrorism wrong by definition. Hare, Wellman, Coady, Holmes, and others agree that, as with violence, we ought to be able to consider whether terrorism can ever be justified. The question should be open, not ruled out by definition. But then, can terrorism be justifiable?

Burleigh Wilkins argues that consequentialism provides weak defenses against terrorism.[33] To a consequentialist, terrorism would have to be justifiable if, on balance, it brings about better consequences than its alternatives. Although consequentialists such as Hare and Kai Nielsen believe that terrorism is hardly ever justified, their arguments depend on empirical estimates that terrorism almost always produces results that are worse on consequentialist grounds than their alternatives. Others find the empirical claims on which such judgments rest to be questionable.

Reading the historical record is notoriously difficult. Some think, along with Walter Laqueur, that terrorist violence has tended to produce "violent repression and a polarization which precluded political progress" rather than the changes the terrorists have sought.[34] The German philosopher Albrecht Wellmer, building on the critical theory of Habermas, concludes that the terrorism of the Red Army Faction in Germany in the 1970s, although it "reflects and brings to a head the pathologies of the system against which it is directed," produced a reactionary net effect: It provided legitimation for political repression and a defamation of the entire Left.[35]

Others think, along with Charles Tilly and Lewis Coser, that violent protests have been an almost normal part of the Western political process and that they have often contributed to progressive developments.[36] Concerning effectiveness, Richard Falk points out that some consider the bombing of the marine barracks in Lebanon to be one of the most successful uses of force "in the history of recent international relations, leading a very strong power to accede to the demands of a very weak opponent."[37] The marines had been deployed in Lebanon as the major expression of a U.S. intent to support the Gemayel government and, as a result of the bombing, were removed from Lebanon by President Reagan.

It may be almost impossible to predict whether an act of terrorism will in fact have its intended effect of hastening some political goal sought by the terrorists or whether it will actually do their cause more harm than good. However, as Wilkins asks, "Is there something special about acts of violence which makes them different from other acts where judgments about their consequences are concerned? We frequently do many things where the outcome is uncertain."[38] If existing conditions are terrible, "they might prompt a prospective terrorist to reason that any chance of altering these states of affairs is worth the risk of failure and the near certainty of harm to property or persons that violence involves."[39]

Furthermore, states use violence and the threat of it to uphold their laws, and some use terrorism. Many theorists still define the state in terms of its monopoly on the use of violence considered legitimate.[40] But if violence can be condemned on consequentialist grounds, it can be condemned in unjustified state behavior, as well as in the behavior of a state's opponents. On the other hand, if violence or terrorism by the state can be justified, its success may be as impossible to predict as that of the violence or terrorism of the state's opponents. Where a legal system violates the human rights of those on whom it imposes its will, the violence or terrorism it uses to do so is surely no more justified than the violence or terrorism used against it, and quite possibly it is less so. When the security forces of an unjust regime kill or brutalize detainees to deter future opposition or shoot at random into groups of demonstrators, they engage in acts of terrorism. Even relatively legitimate legal orders on occasion violate the human rights of some; the violence or terrorism they use to uphold their authority against those they thus mistreat is not more justified than that of their opponents. In both cases, predictions of success may be impossible to make accurately, but in another sense it is impossible to escape making them.

TERRORISM AND RIGHTS

In my view we cannot adequately evaluate social action in consequentialist terms alone.[41] The framework of rights and obligations must also be applied, and in the case of terrorism it is certainly relevant to ask whether rights are being violated, and, if so, whether this can be justified.

In contrast to Hare and others who evaluate terrorism by applying utilitarian calculations, Wellman usefully considers the place of rights in evaluating terrorism. Wellman says that "certain fundamental human rights, the rights to liberty, personal security, life, property, and respect, are typically violated by acts of terrorism."[42] This means not that terrorism can never be justified but that an adequate moral appraisal will have to take violations of rights into account, along with any calculation of benefits and harms produced.[43]

Coady rightfully notes the prevalent inconsistency in many discussions of terrorism. The use of violence directed at noncombatants is judged justifiable on utilitarian grounds if carried out by one's own or a friendly state, as in many evaluations of the justifiability of bombing raids in wartime, in which civilians can be expected to be killed. At the same time, when revolutionaries and rebels use violence that harms noncombatants, such acts are judged on nonutilitarian grounds to be unjustifiable violations of prohibitions on the way in which political goals are to be pursued. As Coady observes, consistency can be achieved by applying either utilitarian or nonutilitarian evaluations to both sides. He favors the latter and concludes that terrorism is "immoral wherever and whenever it is used or proposed."[44] My own suggestion is for a nonutilitarian comparison of rights violations. It could reach a different conclusion.

One of the most difficult problems for political philosophy is that of how to evaluate situations in which human rights are not respected. What are people justified in doing to foster such respect, and how should these actions be judged? Should "bringing about increased respect for human rights" be evaluated in consequentialist terms? But then how should this consequence be weighed against any violations of rights necessitated by the action undertaken to achieve this consequence? If we say that no violations of rights are justified even in this case, this can become a disguised recipe for maintaining the status quo. If we permit violations, we risk undermining the moral worth of the very rights for which we are making efforts to achieve respect.

I propose that we not yield to a merely consequentialist evaluation but that we strive for reasonable comparative judgments. In a well-developed scheme of ensured rights, rights should not be traded off against one another or judged in comparative terms. We do not usefully speak of more (or less) of a right to vote but simply of a right to vote. Moreover, we do not usefully try to determine whether a right to vote is more or less important than a right to nondiscrimination in employment. Where rights conflict, we may order them by priorities or stringency; this, however, is not a matter of maximizing but of seeking consistency. Some rights may be deemed to have priority over others or to be more basic than others, but our aim is not to engage in trade-offs. We seek, rather, to arrive at a consistent scheme in which all of the rights of all persons can be respected and none need be violated.

In a defective society, on the other hand, where rights are not in fact respected, we should be able to make comparative judgments about which and whose rights violations are least justifiable. Was it more important, for instance, for blacks in South Africa to gain assurance of rights to personal safety than it was for white South Africans to continue to enjoy their property rights undisturbed? While some persons' most basic rights are denied respect, it seems worse to continue these violations than to permit some comparable violations of the rights of those who are participating in this denial.

Such an evaluation is not a consequentialist calculation, but it allows us to compare rights violations. It requires us not to ignore the violations involved in maintaining an existing system since, of course, charges of rights violation should not be applied only to those seeking change, while those upholding an existing system are exempt.

I use the expression "effective respect for rights" to mean that an existing legal system recognizes and effectively upholds respect for the rights in question. Of course, this does not mean that violations never occur; no legal system can secure perfect compliance with its norms. It means that violations are on the whole prevented by adequate education, socialization, and police protection and that those who commit such violations are apprehended and dealt with to a sufficient degree to make respect for the rights in question generally high. There is no escaping the fact that effective respect for rights is a matter of degree, but it is quite possible to make an accurate empirical judgment that it is absent when a legal system does not even recognize a particular right as a legal requirement. When using the expression "effective respect for rights," we should specify the type of rights in question, and this we can do.

Let us consider a case in which a certain type of right is recognized as a human right by the major international documents and bodies that establish international norms concerning rights.[45] When a given legal system does not recognize such rights as legal rights for a certain group of people, that legal system will clearly then have no effective respect for those rights of those people. An example would be the right to nondiscrimination on grounds of race recognized as a human right in articles 2 and 7 of the Universal Declaration of Human Rights adopted by the General Assembly of the United Nations on December 10, 1948. Under the system of apartheid in South Africa, especially before the reforms initiated by the government of F. W. de Klerk, this right was not recognized for South Africa's black population. Hence, very clearly there was for blacks in South Africa no effective respect for this right.

Frequently, rights are recognized as legal rights in a given legal system, but respect for them is not effective because either law enforcement agencies are corrupt or prejudiced or the government is inefficient or unfair in its administration, and so forth. The empirical judgment that effective respect for rights is absent may in such cases be difficult to make, and the lack of effective respect for rights can be as serious as in those cases in which the legal system does not even recognize the right. However, an advantage for purposes of moral theory in choosing a case of the latter kind (i.e., where a human right is being violated and is not even acknowledged to be a legal right) is that there can be little dispute at the empirical level that effective respect for rights is absent. So let us consider such a case. Imagine two groups, A and B, and suppose that the failure to recognize the human rights of the members of group B as legal rights in legal system L is advantageous to the members of group A and disadvantageous to the members of group B, insofar as further benefits and burdens accrue to them in exercising or in failing to have the rights in question. However, we will not evaluate the comparative justifiability of rights violations on the basis of these further benefits or burdens.

Now let us ask whether it can be morally justifiable to violate some rights to achieve effective respect for other rights. (First, an aside: If certain legal rights are in conflict with human rights such that we can judge that these legal rights ought not to exist, then what appears to be a violation of them will probably not be morally unjustified. That kind of case will not present the moral difficulties I wish to consider.)

The difficult case occurs when achieving effective respect for the fundamental human rights of the members of one group (which rights ought to be respected) requires the violation of the fundamental human rights of the members of another group (which are also rights that seemingly ought to be respected). If terrorism can ever be justified, it would appear to present this kind of problem. Where there is both a lack of effective respect for the fundamental human rights of the members of one group and a reasonable likelihood that limited terrorism will significantly contribute to achieving such effective respect and where no other effective means are available, can it be justifiable to violate the fundamental human rights of those who will suffer from such terrorism? Their rights to "life, liberty and security of person," as specified in article 3 of the Universal Declaration, are likely to be violated by any act of terrorism. Can this possibly be justified?

Let us specify two situations. In the first, S_1, the members of group A have a human right to X, and they enjoy effective respect for this right in a given legal system, while the members of group B also have a human right to X but suffer a lack of effective respect for this right. In situation S_2, in contrast, the members of both A and B have a human right to X, and they enjoy effective respect for that right. Obviously S_2 is a morally better situation than S_1. It is the process of getting from S_1 to S_2 that is in question.

Here we can make a number of comparative judgments. First, nonviolent methods that do not involve violations of human rights would certainly be morally superior to violent methods, other things being equal. Defenders of nonviolence argue, often convincingly, that nonviolent pressures are actually more successful and lead to the loss of fewer lives than do violent methods in moving societies from situations such as S_1 to those such as S_2. It seems obvious that nonviolence is morally superior, if it can succeed.

I consider myself an advocate of nonviolence, by which I mean that one should recognize strong prima facie principles against the use of violence and always place the burden of proof in a justification on the violent course of action if it is claimed that violence is needed to prevent or to correct serious wrongs or violations of rights. More importantly, one should continually champion what Sara Ruddick calls "a sturdy suspicion of violence."[46] One should strive to invent and promote nonviolent forms of action and try one's best to make nonviolent approaches successful. It is often to this aim that our best efforts can be directed: to create and then sustain institutions that permit, encourage, and are responsive, when appropriate, to nonviolent forms of control or protest, thus deflecting tendencies on any side of a conflict to resort to violence.

To advocate nonviolence is to argue that there are prima facie principles against the use of violence to uphold, as well as to challenge, a legal order. It may well be justifiable to intervene forcefully to prevent, say, violent assault, but force is not the same as violence, and violence usually need not and should not be used. The state has many means besides violence of upholding its legitimate authority and bringing about the effective respect of rights, and such nonviolent means should be developed far more than they have been. Strong prima facie arguments against violence should also apply to groups who seek changes in political and legal arrangements. Nonviolence is not acquiescence; it can be a stubborn refusal to cooperate with injustice and a determination to resist oppression—but to do so nonviolently. Feminists have added greatly to the case for nonviolence. As the author of one collection of essays writes, "Put into the feminist perspective, nonviolence is the merging of our uncompromising rage at the patriarchy's brutal destructiveness with a refusal to adopt its ways."[47]

In important ways, the terrorist often shares the worst macho aspects of his targets by mirroring the fascination with violence and the eroticization of force characteristic of the culture he attacks.[48] However, after this has been said, comparative judgments are still needed. If a judgment is made that in certain circumstances violence to uphold law is justifiable, cannot a judgment as plausibly be made that, in certain other circumstances, violence to bring about respect for rights may be justifiable? And if violence can be justifiable, can terrorism, on occasion, also be? State terrorism to destroy legitimate movements of liberation exists. In contrast, can terrorism as a considered method to overcome oppression with as little loss of life as possible be less unjustifiable than state terrorism?

Gandhi is reported to have said that "it is best of all to resist oppression by nonviolent means" but also that "it is better to resist oppression by violent means than to submit."[49] In his book on Gandhi, William Borman asserts that Gandhi "repeatedly and explicitly makes statements preferring violence to cowardice."[50] Gandhi wrote that "my nonviolence does not admit of running away from danger and leaving dear ones unprotected. Between violence and cowardly flight, I can only prefer violence to cowardice."[51] This leaves us with the task of making comparative judgments concerning the use of violence by all those unwilling or unable to adopt "the summit of bravery," nonviolence, and preferring, on their various sides of any given conflict, violence to flight. It is these comparative judgments with which I am concerned in this chapter.

Let us return to the example of trying to move from S_1 to S_2. If a judgment is made, especially in special circumstances, that nonviolence cannot succeed but that terrorism will be effective in moving a society from S_1 to S_2, can engaging in terrorism be better than refraining from it? Given that it will involve a violation of human rights, can it be better to violate rights through terrorism than to avoid this violation? Table 4.1 outlines the situations and the alternatives. Alternative 1 is to maintain S_1 and to refrain from terrorism; alternative 2 is to employ terrorism and to achieve S_2. Both alternatives involve rights violations. The questions are, can they be compared, and can either be found to be less unjustifiable?

It has often been pointed out, in assessing terrorism, that we can almost never accurately predict than an outcome such as S_2 will be achieved as a result of the terrorism in question. However, I am dealing with the moral issues *given* certain empirical claims. Moreover, *if* the empirical judgment is responsibly made that the transition is likely to achieve S_2 (which situation is clearly morally better than S_1) and that no other means can do so,

TABLE 4.1. Terrorism, Rights, and Political Goals

Alternatives	Assumptions
Alternative 1 S_1 maintained; no terrorism (no T)	Change from S_1 to S_2 requires terrorism; members of both groups have the right not to be victims of terrorism
Alternative 2 terrorism (T); S_2 achieved	Terrorism will violate such rights of members of Group A; it will spare members of Group B

Considerations	
For Group A	For Group B
Alternative 1	Alternative 1
S_1: human right to X; effective respect for this right	S_1: human right to X; no effective respect for this right
No T: no violations of rights versus T	No T: violations of rights to X
Alternative 2	Alternative 2
T: violations of rights versus T	T: no violations of rights versus T
S_2: human right to X; effective respect for this right	S_2: human right to X; effective respect for this right

S_1 is the situation in which members of Group A have a human right to X and enjoy effective respect for this right in the legal system, whereas members of Group B have a human right to X but no effective respect for this right and hence suffer violations of it. S_2 is the situation in which members of both groups have a human right to X and enjoy effective respect for that right.

can alternative 2 be better than alternative 1? Rights will be violated in either case. Are there any grounds on which the violations in alternative 2 are morally less unjustifiable than those in alternative 1?

It is reasonable to conclude that, on grounds of justice, it is better to equalize rights violations in a transition to bring an end to rights violations than it is to subject a given group that has already suffered extensive rights violations to continued such violations, if the degree of severity of the two violations is similar. And this is the major argument of this chapter: If we must have rights violations, a more equitable distribution of such violations is better than a less equitable one.

If the severity of the violations is very dissimilar, then we might decide that the more serious violations are to be avoided in favor of the less serious, regardless of who is suffering them, although this judgment could perhaps be overridden if, for instance, many different (though less serious) violations were suffered by the members of group B, a situation that could outweigh a serious violation for the members of group A. Generally, however, there would be a prima facie judgment against serious violations, such as those of rights to life, to bring about respect for less serious rights, such as those to more equitable distributions of property above what is necessary for the satisfaction of basic needs.

The case on which I focus, however, involves serious violations among both groups. Oppressed groups' rights to personal safety are, for instance, frequently violated. If a transition to a situation such as S_2 involves violations of the oppressing groups' rights to personal safety, why would this violation be less unjustifiable than the other? Fairness recommends a sharing of the burden of rights violation, even if no element of punishment were appealed to. If punishment is considered, it would be more appropriate for those who have benefited from the rights violations of a given group to suffer, in a transition, any necessary rights violations than to allow the further rights violations of those who have already been subjected to them. However, punishment need not be a factor in our assessment. We can conclude that, though nonviolence is always better than violence, other things being equal, terrorism carried out by a group that has reason to believe it can only thus successfully decrease the disregard of rights (where such disregard is prevalent) is less morally unjustifiable than terrorism carried out by a group that maintains such disregard.

That justice itself often requires a concern for how rights violations are distributed seems clear. We can recognize that some distributions are unfair and seek to make them less so. Consider the following: The right to personal security (i.e., freedom from unlawful attack) can be fully recognized as a right in a given legal community, and yet of course some assaults will occur. The community's way of trying to ensure respect for such rights is likely to include the deployment of police forces. But if almost all of the police forces are deployed in high-income white neighborhoods and almost none in low-income black neighborhoods, so that the risk of assault for inhabitants of the latter is many times greater than that for inhabitants of the former, we can judge without great difficulty that the deployment is unfair. Or if we take any given level of effort to protect people from assault and if cuts in protection are then necessary for budgetary reasons and all of the cuts are made in areas already suffering the greatest threats of attack, we can judge that such cuts are unfair.

The basis for such judgments must be a principle of justice with respect to the distribution of rights violations or of risks of such violations.[52] This is the principle to which my argument appeals, and it is clearly a relevant principle that we should not ignore.

What all this demonstrates is that terrorism cannot necessarily be ruled out as unjustifiable on a rights-based analysis any more than it can on a consequentialist one. Depending on the severity and extent of the rights violations in an existing situation, a transition that involves a sharing of rights violations (if this and only this can be expected to lead to a situation in which rights are more adequately respected) may well be less morally unjustifiable than continued acceptance of ongoing rights violations.

POSTSCRIPT

INDIVIDUALS AND GROUPS

In his interesting article "The Morality of Terrorism," Igor Primoratz argues against my view comparing rights violations.[53] Primoratz believes that potential victims of terrorism will maintain that their right to life should not be taken away for the sake of a more just distribution of rights violations; to do so would be to fail to recognize that they are people who are important in their own right, not merely members of a group. Primoratz argues that with respect to rights to life, Robert Nozick's view of rights as "almost absolute side constraints" is correct.[54]

My response is that to fail to achieve a more just distribution of violations of rights (through the use of terrorism if that is the only means available) is to fail to recognize that those whose rights are already not fairly respected are individuals in their own right, not merely members of a group whose interests will be furthered by some goal or whose rights can be ignored. If we can never violate anyone's right to life in the sense that we can never kill anyone, then killing in self-defense when attacked or in the course of law enforcement (e.g., when a convicted murderer tries to escape and is shot) could not be justified. These are not positions to which even Nozick's view would lead, and Primoratz himself makes exceptions for self-defense and punishment. However, if a prohibition on all killing is not what is meant by respecting rights to life as near absolute side constraints, we return to the questions of which rights we have, what they include, and whose rights count—or count more. Presumably everyone's rights should count equally. Respect for rights will never be perfect in practice, but it seems morally less justifiable that those who have already suffered great disrespect of their rights should continue to do so than that the burden of imperfect justice be fairly shared.

Arguments for achieving a just distribution of rights violations need not be arguments, consequentialist or not, that are more than incidentally about groups. They can be arguments about individuals' rights to basic fairness.

FIVE

Group Responsibility
for Ethnic Conflict

When a group such as a nation or a corporation has a relatively clear structure and set of decision procedures, it certainly seems that it is capable of acting and, one can well argue, that it should be considered morally, as well as legally, responsible. Assigning responsibility is a human practice, and there are good moral reasons to adopt the practice of assigning responsibility to such groups.[1] From these judgments, however, little follows about the responsibility of individual members of such groups; much more needs to be ascertained about which officials or executives are responsible for what before we can consider individual members of nations or corporations responsible.

Whether an unorganized group can be morally responsible is much less clear, but useful discussions in recent years have considered the possible responsibility of whites for racism, males for sexism, and the like. This chapter explores arguments for considering ethnic groups or their members morally responsible for ethnic conflict or hatred. Such groups may lack a clear organizational structure, but they are not random assortments of persons. I am especially interested in the grounds for groups and their members to *take* responsibility rather than the more usual and legalistic approach to responsibility of others *holding* them responsible for the purpose of judging or punishing.[2]

Though departing somewhat from her naturalistic view of moral persons, I am thus following the advice of Annette Baier, who has written

that "our philosophical focus *ought* to be as much on collective as on individual responsibility, when we seek to understand ourselves as persons."[3]

GROUP RESPONSIBILITY

Some philosophers hold that only individuals—not groups of people—
can be morally responsible for actions or wrongs that occur. Some deny
that groups can act; hence, they cannot act irresponsibly because, according to this view, only individuals can act.[4] Collective or group responsibility, in the view of these philosophers, is thus impossible.

Such a view is often reached on the basis of metaphysical individualism
or positions taken concerning language.[5] Even in the case of an organized
group with well-defined decision procedures (e.g., a state, a corporation),
many philosophers reject the attribution of responsibility and thus of
praise or blame to them. If these philosophers concede that the law often
holds corporations responsible (e.g., for the harm their products cause),
they maintain that this is merely a legal fiction that says nothing about
moral responsibility. Moreover, if such philosophers acknowledge that
our ordinary discourse is full of claims about what states and corporations
do and what they should be praised or blamed for, they dismiss this talk as
confused, meaningless, or merely metaphorical.

In addition, it is by no means only philosophers who dismiss notions
of group responsibility. In their book, which is highly critical of Western responses to genocide in Bosnia-Herzegovina and of the complicity
of Serbian intellectuals in that genocide, sociologists Thomas Cushman
and Stjepan G. Mestrovic firmly reject what they call "the doctrine of
collective guilt" and chide those who support it because, the authors contend, they should know better.[6]

Like a number of other philosophers engaged for some years in this
debate, I believe that groups can be morally responsible.[7] I believe it
makes good sense to speak about the actions and policies of the United
States, Japan, or Iran and about their moral responsibility for these. It
also makes good sense to speak about the moral responsibilities of corporations for exploitative labor policies or for relocations that have social
consequences. I thus join with philosophers such as David E. Cooper,
Joel Feinberg, Peter French, Larry May, Gregory Mellema, and Burleigh
Wilkins in asserting that the discourse of moral responsibility and thus of
praise and blame can justifiably include claims about the moral responsibility of at least some groups.[8]

This debate, in my view, should not be settled on the basis of positions taken in the philosophy of language or metaphysics. I do not concede their priority. The debate should be conducted on the basis of whether there are good moral reasons to consider groups morally responsible or whether the reasons to refuse to do so outweigh those to do so. Then, if the positions one reaches clash with those in the philosophy of language or metaphysics, one has a reason either to revise the latter or live with the inconsistencies for the time being. To suppose that arguments from the philosophy of language or metaphysics must always trump moral arguments is an indefensible form of ideology that is currently quite fashionable in philosophy—but still wrong. As William Frankena argued in his book *Ethics*, when he considered whether moral responsibility requires contracausal freedom, the question should be discussed in terms of "whether we are morally justified in ascribing responsibility, in blaming, etc., if we take determinism (or indeterminism) to be true."[9] We need to decide on moral grounds whether it is morally better or worse to consider people morally responsible when they act freely in the various senses. And the moral grounds should not be limited to consequentialist ones; among the best reasons to consider persons morally responsible is that it allows them to express their choices in their actions.

Similarly, as Peter French argued for group responsibility, assigning responsibility is a human practice, and we need to consider whether or not to engage in the various aspects of this practice and, if so, under what conditions. In this view, which I share, there are good moral reasons to engage in a practice of assigning moral responsibility to some groups under certain conditions. Doing so enables us to have a much richer and more appropriate understanding of the relevant moral features of human actions, situations, and practices. To refuse to do so impoverishes our moral discourse and weakens moral progress.[10]

Michael Zimmerman makes the ascription of responsibility into a straightforward, moral claim. He says he understands someone "to be morally responsible for an outcome if and only if he deserves to be blamed for it."[11] This may go somewhat too far since we may want to and may have good moral reasons to assign responsibility and to assess blame independently of one another. However, all of these positions recognize that assigning responsibility is not simply an empirical question about causality. It involves at least moral arguments about when we should and should not consider persons responsible and about the kinds of things (e.g., omissions, actions) for which we should consider them responsible.[12]

Others, however, argue on these same moral and appropriate grounds to the opposite conclusion about group responsibility. They contend that collective responsibility is a pernicious notion and that employing it has evil effects. They conclude from this that it should be rejected on moral grounds. Cushman and Mestrovic, for example, demonstrate that Serbian propaganda used "the principle of intergenerational guilt as a legitimation for aggression."[13] They report on how Serbian arguments for ethnic cleansing often relied on claims about the "collective guilt" of Croats and Muslims. They warn of "the dangers—both moral and logical—of the doctrine of collective guilt" and thus reject the notion of group responsibility.[14]

In addition, H. D. Lewis rejects "the barbarous notion of collective or group responsibility" because of what he takes to be the morally pernicious consequences of using this notion, especially the way it encourages individuals, he believes, to escape responsibility as they blame their group but not themselves for its misdeeds.[15]

These are examples of those who oppose using the notion of group or collective responsibility on moral grounds rather than on grounds of philosophy of language or metaphysics. They are thus offering the sorts of arguments that must, in my view, be addressed. They illustrate some of the opposing dangers that using the notion of group responsibility may hold: On the one hand, blame may be unjustifiably extended from a few wrongdoers to a whole group even years after the events, as all contemporary Croats were blamed by some for the crimes of the Ustasha during World War II. On the other hand, the danger exists that individual wrongdoers may unjustifiably escape moral criticism or fail to take responsibility by blaming others and not themselves for wrongs attributed to the whole group of which they are members, as many Serbs seem to have done. In the much-discussed case of Germany, not all Germans, even children, should be blamed for Hitler's crimes; alternatively, if all Germans were guilty of Nazi atrocities, then no particular individuals can be singled out for blame. In the case of the corporation, it would be unreasonable to hold every worker responsible for the pollution a company has produced, but if it is the corporation that is to blame, individual executives may consider themselves not individually responsible for the harms it caused.

Those of us who defend notions of group responsibility are well aware of such dangers in using the notion of group responsibility, but we attribute those outlined to misuses of the concept and believe that the dangers of rejecting notions of group responsibility are greater still.

It is an error to conclude that a group is at fault on the basis of the wrongful actions of some of its members; much more needs to be said about the group and the reasons for considering it responsible. Another frequent error that leads to misuse of the notion of group responsibility is the inference from the responsibility of a group to the responsibility of all of its members. Such an inference should never be made on the basis of logic or empirical fact, and to draw such a conclusion is often highly unjustified. For instance, from finding a corporation responsible for producing a defective product, nothing follows logically about the responsibility of any given employee: We need to know about the corporation's decision procedures, about the relevant participation or nonparticipation of given corporate members in those procedures and their knowledge or ignorance of the relevant events, about the production processes and the activities of individuals in them, and the like. But from the need to know about the activities of individuals and their situations in order to judge their moral responsibility, we should not conclude that judgments about corporate or group responsibility are never justified. Good moral reasons often exist to make just these judgments even though little follows about individual responsibility. For instance, they enable us to reward acceptable corporations with our investments or to shun travel to states that violate international norms. Frequently they are the first steps to further inquiry about the particular responsibilities of individual members of these groups.

Patricia Smith argues that "we need a moral vision of collective responsibility that faces our common problems as *common*."[16] There is rather little we can do as individuals about large-scale social problems such as world hunger or even homelessness and poverty in our own communities. Still, we can recognize affirmative obligations as collective.

Questions about how the responsibility of a group does or does not distribute over its individual members are different from questions about the responsibility of the group itself. As long as we keep these differences in mind and are aware of how they vary according to the issues and the kind of group we are dealing with, we can usefully sort out the various questions involved.

In defending notions of group responsibility we call attention to the dangers of rejecting such notions. Being unable to speak meaningfully about group responsibility hampers our ability to hold both individual persons and social entities of various kinds responsible and to encourage members to take responsibility for the actions of groups. It inhibits many efforts to improve social and political life, for instance, to reduce racism or demand greater corporate accountability. Furthermore, it undermines morally progressive developments in, for instance, international law, where collective entities are called upon to meet standards of international behavior.

The rights of groups are increasingly recognized in political theory and international law.[17] Rights against genocide and ethnic cleansing are among the clearest examples, but there are many others as well. For instance, Article 3 of the European Convention for the Protection of Minorities calls for protection "against any activity capable of threatening [minorities'] existence," and Article 5 asserts "the right [of minorities] to freely preserve, express and develop their cultural identity in all its aspects, free of any attempts at assimilation against their will."[18] S. James Anaya concludes that despite the individualistic bias in international law that has resulted from Western liberal political philosophy, "international legal and political discourse ... has made significant movement toward greater realization of collective or group rights. An important example is in the treatment of indigenous peoples' concerns within the United Nations" and its affiliates.[19] Respecting group rights is often a responsibility of groups.

We thus argue for careful understandings of what groups are and when and how they may be deemed morally responsible.

KINDS OF GROUPS

Not all groups are the same, obviously, and responsibility varies with them. Well-organized groups like states and corporations have explicit procedures for making decisions and are among the best candidates for group responsibility. This is not because they are full-fledged moral persons, as Peter French claims corporations to be.[20] A requirement for being a moral person would seem to be that the entity be able to feel human emotions, as well as to reason and decide. Though a case can be made that a corporation, through its calculations, can have beliefs and can reason and though it certainly can make decisions, almost no one will argue that a corporation has the capacity to have emotions. However, the moral responsibility of an organized group does not require the responsible entity to be a full-fledged moral person; it is enough for the entity in question to have goals, procedures for deciding how to achieve them, and the ability to act accordingly.[21]

Unorganized groups such as people on a beach or pedestrians on a sidewalk at a given time and place may not even be groups; I have in the past called them random collections. They are more questionable candidates for moral responsibility than are organized groups with clear decision-making procedures. Nevertheless, in some circumstances they and/or their members may be morally responsible for not organizing themselves into a group capable of deciding how to take required action.[22] For instance, if, by acting together, the passengers on a subway car could easily alert the train crew and subdue and prevent a child from beating an even smaller child to death, they could be morally responsible for doing nothing and letting the death occur. In these cases, responsibility is more likely to distribute over the members of the group just because it lacks the established decision-making procedures that create differences of authority and responsibility.

The groups most relevant to this chapter may belong to neither of the categories of organized group or random collections. I agree with Juha Raikka that dividing groups into only these categories "does not do justice to ethnic, cultural, and national groups that do not always have clear decision procedures."[23]

In this chapter I do not discuss what constitutes a group or an ethnic group.[24] I bypass important issues such as whether members must identify themselves as belonging to a group or whether they can justifiably be assigned to a group through, for instance, a shared ancestry or history. I assume that a group that comprises only persons who share a certain belief or support a certain policy (e.g., ethnic cleansing) is not the sort of group about which I am speaking.[25] The groups relevant for discussing issues of group responsibility for ethnic conflict must have some identity and continuity over time, have a number of shared characteristics, and be capable of a variety of actions.[26]

Occasionally a single ethnic group may be organized into a single state, but monoethnic states are increasingly rare and increasingly unjustifiable. The more usual kind of ethnic or cultural group and the ones I am largely considering are neither organized groups with recognizable decision procedures nor random collections. Can they be morally responsible, and what are the implications for individual responsibility?

A useful discussion for thinking about these questions is presented in Larry May's book *Sharing Responsibility*. May argues that "people should see themselves as sharing responsibility for various harms perpetrated by, or occurring within, their communities."[27] His grounds for holding this

view are importantly the moral ones I have suggested as central: A practice in which people see themselves as sharing responsibility will decrease
the enormous harms that groups bring about. May writes, "Insofar as
communities enable individuals to do more harm than they could otherwise do, communities also create more responsibility for those whose
lives are woven into the fabric of the community itself."[28]

May considers attitudes to be among the things one can reasonably
expect people to change when such attitudes contribute to the causing of
harm. Among the attitudes he examines are racist ones, and the discussion is highly relevant to a consideration of hatred among ethnic groups
and of the acts engaged in by individuals and purported leaders in contexts of ethnic conflict.

When particularly egregious acts of racism or racist violence occur, a
very common response among members of the communities in which
these incidents occur is that the perpetrators of these actions are at fault
but that other group members such as the speaker are not (even if they
share many of the perpetrators' attitudes) since they themselves did not
directly cause the harm. May argues that this response in unjustified,
"for one's attitudes often are as important to the increased likelihood of
harm in a community as one's overt behavior."[29]

To say that members of a group share responsibility for a harm that
has occurred is not to say that they are all equally responsible—or even
responsible at all. There can well be degrees of responsibility in the
case of the shared responsibility of unorganized groups, as in the case
of the collective responsibility of organized ones. Nevertheless, individuals should not presume that they are guiltless merely because they did
not themselves commit the harmful actions for which fellow members of
their group are more directly responsible.

Interestingly, May's argument raises the responsibility issue from the
inside rather than the outside. He discusses what people themselves should
take responsibility for, as distinct from what outside observers should
judge them responsible for. This shift of perspective may be significant:
We can judge our own attitudes better than others can. Furthermore, the
salutary effect of more people taking responsibility for what their communities bring about can be significant. Recriminations against those who
are judged responsible, as well as those who fail to take responsibility when
they ought to, are often necessary. But the aim of having more people see
themselves as responsible and of more people voluntarily taking responsibility for what their groups bring about holds much greater promise.

If we accept the view, as I believe we should, that ethnic groups can be responsible for ethnic hatred and conflict, we should also recognize that we cannot infer the responsibility of individual members of such groups from judgments about the groups. Juha Raikka examines the grounds on which individuals can escape responsibility for the blameworthy acts of the groups of which they are members. It has been suggested that if individuals disassociate themselves from or actively oppose the morally wrong acts, omissions, policies, or practices of their group, they do not share the group's blame. White Southerners who disassociated themselves from the practices that segregated African Americans into separate schools, waiting rooms, and so on when segregation was the norm in the Southern states of the United States are sometimes cited as examples. Joel Feinberg and Howard McGary have discussed differing views on this issue.[30] Raikka argues that disassociating oneself may help one escape responsibility but may not be enough since one may be participating in the practices one opposes at the same time one is opposing them. He considers the complex example of consumption in a developed country, as in the following hypothetical case:

Every member of a group is at least indirectly using the third-world countries' natural resources in a very blameworthy manner. But only those persons who have not rejected Western living standards altogether are taken seriously in discussions of the problems of poverty in the third world. Thus those who oppose using the resources of the third-world countries have to use them in order for their opposition to be effective.[31]

Thus, a citizen of the United States who disassociates herself from her country's automobile culture and massive overconsumption of the third-world's resources and even works against them but continues to live a more or less "normal" life is still not without responsibility for these blameworthy practices. Furthermore, certainly many whites benefited from the economic and other advantages the system of segregation provided them even if they disassociated themselves from it. In cases of ethnic hatred and conflict, persons who depart too greatly from their group's antipathy to another group may themselves be driven out of their group, be denied its benefits of employment or security, or at least be ignored and without influence. Thus those individuals who retain the advantages of group membership while merely professing to disassociate themselves from the group's policies may fail to escape responsibility for those policies.

However, surely those who oppose the morally blameworthy acts, omissions, policies, or practices of the groups of which they are members have diminished responsibility compared to those who support them. Moral responsibility does have degrees. While we may be required in cases of legal responsibility to conclude that persons are either legally responsible or not, we should resist such rigidity in moral contexts. It is more appropriate to assess degrees of responsibility and degrees of sharing responsibility for the wrongs for which our groups are to blame. Still, unless a group's members acknowledge responsibility for wrongs the group brings about, restraints on the unjustifiable actions of some members are weakened, and, if wrongs occur, it is less likely that reconciliation with the wronged can or should take place.

ETHNIC HATRED

Why are persons with attitudes of ethnic hatred morally blameworthy? Ethnic hatred is animosity toward the members of another ethnic group on the grounds of their group membership. It is an attitude that the members of the hated group are to be at best shunned and avoided and at worst removed or killed. To hate the members of another ethnic group is by and large not illegal. Such hatred may, even when expressed publicly, be protected by norms of free expression, though hate speech is in some countries against the law. However, even if hate speech is or should be legally contained, the law's prohibitions can perhaps do little about the hatred behind it. Yet ethnic hatred may significantly contribute to violent ethnic conflict and to horrible crimes, including genocide, ethnic cleansing, and mass rape. Contributing to a climate of ethnic hatred may considerably increase the risk that harm to people will occur.

Larry May discusses racist attitudes and the reasons they are harmful:

> The members of a group who hold racist attitudes, both those who have directly caused harm and those who could directly cause harm but haven't done so yet, share in responsibility for racially motivated harms in their communities by sharing in the attitude that risks harm to others....Individual racist attitudes considered as an aggregate constitute a climate of attitude and disposition that increases the likelihood of racially motivated harm. The climate of racist attitudes creates an atmosphere in which the members of a community become risk takers concerning racial violence....Insofar as people share in

the production of an attitudinal climate, they participate in something like a joint venture that increases the likelihood of harm.[32]

So even those with racist attitudes who do not themselves directly cause harm by violent acts nonetheless contribute to an increased risk of such acts and are blameworthy.

The arguments are entirely applicable to ethnic hatred and conflict. Those who contribute to a climate of ethnic hatred increase the risk that ethnic violence will occur, and they increase the risk of widespread participation in such violence.

Wole Soyinka has written of the Rwandan carnage that "it was not restricted to a crime of state. True, the massacres were meticulously planned and ruthlessly executed by the state, but the instrumentation was widespread and criminality thus collectivized."[33] Ethnic hatred may play an important role in widening participation in ethnic violence.

Ethnic cleansing can be distinguished from genocide since it may consist of expulsions rather than killings, though ethnic cleansing is often genocidal.[34] Even when ethnic cleansing does not have as its aim, as does genocide, the killing of an unwanted group, it "often uses massacres as a means of getting the group to leave."[35] This process has been gruesomely illustrated in the former Yugoslavia and in Kosovo. A policy of ethnic cleansing, typically involving many acts of violence and terror, is sustained by widespread ethnic hatred.

In the case of mass rape, ethnic hatred may be a strong contributing factor. Although some forms of mass rape (e.g., gang rapes) occur within ethnic groups and can be fueled by misogyny rather than ethnic hatred, mass rape as a component of ethnic cleansing is made more likely by ethnic hatred. Detestation of another ethnic group, combined with everyday misogyny, seems to contribute to turning everyday rape into mass rape. This seems to have been the case in Bosnia. In Claudia Card's account, "although some women have been exploited as sexual slaves and others as sacrificial victims, enslavement and service have not been the apparent primary aims of the rapes of women [by Serbs] in Bosnia-Herzegovina. Rather, the expulsion and dispersion of entire ethnic groups appears to be a primary aim of some perpetrators and failing that, genocide by a combination of murder and forcible impregnation. The idea has not been to bind captive women to captors, but to destroy family and community bonds, humiliate and terrorize, ultimately to drive out and disperse entire peoples."[36]

Rape was not yet considered a violation of women's human rights at the time.[37] The International Criminal Tribunal for the former Yugoslavia is limited to considering the crime of rape as "*ancillary and secondary to the illegitimate pursuit of ethnic cleansing.*"[38] However, the mass rapes that have occurred in the former Yugoslavia are not dismissed as individual breaches of norms; they are seen as a component of ethnic cleansing. They are among the evils to which ethnic hatred contributes.

Even if the greatest emotional contributor to the ethnic strife that has occurred in the former Yugoslavia has been fear, that fear has often been magnified by ethnic hatred as the flames of both fear and hatred have been intentionally fanned by those seeking to use ethnic hostility for their own purposes. Fear is sometimes morally blameworthy but usually not; at least our control over our fear is limited. When fear is based on false information, our own or that of others, persons capable of correcting such false information may well have a moral obligation to do so. Among Serbs and Croats in the former Yugoslavia, these obligations were often flouted as the state-controlled media deliberately distorted the news to increase fear.[39] But we should probably hesitate to blame people for the fear itself that they feel. Ethnic hatred, in contrast, is not morally excusable the way fear may be. It is more an attitude we can adopt or change than an emotion over which we have limited control. Serbs may be excused for fearing the dangers of being in a minority in a non-Serbian state; they should not be excused for turning such fear into ethnic hatred and contributing to a climate that increases the likelihood and the effectiveness of policies of ethnic cleansing and mass rape.

Not all actions that are components of ethnic conflict are unjustified. An ethnic group may respond to hatred and exclusion directed against its members by measures of self-defense. If forced to abandon their own language and cultural practices or denied appropriate representation in governing institutions, an ethnic group may be justified in establishing separate institutions such as schools and "shadow governments" even if they increase ethnic tensions. Even so, neither the ethnic hatred that leads to such responses nor ethnic hatred itself as a response is ever justified.

RESPONSIBILITY FOR ETHNIC HATRED AND CONFLICT

Ethnic hatred can become a shared attitude or feeling among members of a group. When a group can be characterized as having an attitude or a feeling, we rarely mean that every member of the group has this attitude or feeling. However, from our not claiming that every member has this attitude, we should not conclude that we cannot claim that the group has it. For the sorts of reasons I touched on earlier in this chapter, we often have good reasons to make claims about the responsibility of organized groups and also of relatively unorganized ones like ethnic groups.

Can an ethnic group be responsible for so amorphous a shared feeling or attitude as ethnic hatred? I have suggested that an individual can be responsible for an attitude of ethnic hatred even if not for the fear that accompanies it. But can an ethnic group?

We can persuasively argue that an ethnic group can have shared responsibility when it takes responsibility for its members' actions and attitudes. For instance, an unorganized ethnic group in a given community could take responsibility for the negligence that allowed some of its young people to fail to understand the meaning of a swastika and, thinking it an amusing prank, to paint swastikas on the graves of Jews. The members of such a group could then share in taking responsibility for the harm and in making efforts to prevent such negligence in the future, even if the group's members act quite informally and remain a relatively unorganized group. When individuals take responsibility for the actions of groups, they do so not as *individuals* but as *members of the group* and can do so in ways that are open only to group members.[40]

Nevertheless, many groups do not take responsibility for the harms brought about by various of their members. They fail to acknowledge that they share responsibility for such harms. Such a group, even when unorganized, can then be collectively responsible for not taking responsibility or for not sharing in an awareness of its members' responsibility. *The group can be collectively responsible for the failure to take responsibility when it ought to.*

North Americans, for instance, are at present collectively responsible for not taking responsibility for their immoral overconsumption of the world's resources and overproduction of the world's pollution and climate change. North Americans are morally responsible for failing to acknowledge that they share responsibility for these harms and ought to reduce such overconsumption and climate change. Not all North Americans are responsible for these failures; Native Americans, for instance, might be largely exempted from such a judgment. Moreover, the degree of moral responsibility varies greatly among persons and groups within North America. Still, it would make good sense for North Americans collectively to take responsibility for their continued disproportionate contribution to the harms of overconsumption and climate change. For many purposes, such as allocating the costs of reducing pollution, cleaning up the environment, and reducing climate change, such judgments are entirely appropriate.

Applying similar considerations to the former Yugoslavia, we can note that, although atrocities were committed by all sides in the conflict, the worst and by far the most numerous were committed by Serbs (even though in retaking the Krajina region in 1995, from which Serbs had earlier expelled Croats, Croatian soldiers drove out 150,000 Serbs in what has been called "the largest single instance of 'ethnic cleansing' of the Yugoslav war" prior to the massive expulsion of Albanians from Kosovo by the Serbs in 1999).[41] In Kosovo, rough estimates indicate that, in their campaign to drive ethnic Albanians from the region in response to the NATO bombings, 10,000 were killed by Serbian forces, and many hundreds of thousands expelled.[42]

In Bosnia, of the eight reports of atrocities and war crimes in the former Yugoslavia submitted to the United Nations by June 1993 by the U.S. State Department, Philip Cohen writes that "of the 347 incidents contained in the [reports], 304, or 88 percent, were attributable to Serbs, 7 percent to Bosnian Muslims, and 5 percent to Croats.... The victims at the hands of the Serbs numbered in the tens of thousands, while there were approximately 500 victims at the hands of Muslims and approximately 150 victims at the hands of Croats.... 100 percent of the acts of genocide, as defined by the UN Convention on Genocide, have been committed by Serbs alone."[43] On the destruction of cultural monuments and institutions Cohen notes that "Serbs are responsible for the overwhelming instances of destruction of cultural and religious monuments.... In the Serb-occupied area of Banja Luka...Serbian authorities and armed forces destroyed 200 out of 202 mosques...and destroyed or damaged 96 percent of Catholic churches."[44]

Claims of greater Serbian responsibility for war crimes in Bosnia were also made by the report of a United Nations commission of experts, which found that Serbian war crimes and atrocities were systematized and centrally orchestrated and served as an instrument of a state policy of "ethnic purification," in contrast to those of Croats and Bosnians, which were "sporadic and spontaneous."[45] The UN commission of experts concluded that there was no "moral equivalency" between the war crimes of the three groups. This view was also supported by a Helsinki Watch report, which stated that "although all sides have committed serious abuses...the most egregious and overwhelming number of violations of the rules of war have been committed by Serbian forces."[46]

Summarizing the results of a host of reports, Cushman and Mestrovic concluded that "the case against Bosnian Serb leaders as well as their supporters in Belgrade is...overwhelming....Genocide has occurred in Bosnia-Herzegovina and it has been perpetrated exclusively by the Belgrade regime and its proxies....All sides have committed atrocities and war crimes, but only specific parties supported by and controlled by the Belgrade regime are responsible for genocide."[47]

Since the Dayton agreement, which ended the military conflict in Bosnia in 1995, events in Kosovo have greatly complicated but not substantially altered judgments of greater Serb responsibility for the wrongs of the disintegration of Yugoslavia. On May 27, 1999, the International Criminal Tribunal for the former Yugoslavia indicted President Slobodan Milosevic of Yugoslavia and four senior officials of Serbia for crimes against humanity in Kosovo. Many others, very largely also Serbs, had already been indicted for war crimes in Bosnia.

In the case of Kosovo, the Albanians' attempts to achieve independence from Serbia by forming an army of liberation, the KLA, and by killing Serbs, especially police, were no doubt partly responsible for the war that occurred. The Albanians of Kosovo could take responsibility for some of this outcome. The responsibility of NATO members for not preventing the situation that led to the NATO bombing of Serbia and for thus contributing to the death and destruction perpetrated during the Kosovo war can also be persuasively argued. However, the greater responsibility of the Serbian government and its very large number of supporters, as well as of many Serbs in Kosovo, for atrocities against and expulsions of Albanians is relatively clear. And the indictments of Milosevic and other individuals for war crimes do not exculpate many others.

Serbs are in many cases not the kind of unorganized ethnic group to which some of the earlier arguments considered in this chapter applied. Hence there may well be questions about whether responsibility lodges with the Serbian government or the Bosnian Serb leaders rather than with any individual Serbs not in government or even Serbs as a group. We must then raise questions about the extent of the support the Serbian government and various leaders have had, which seems to have been considerable.[48]

Mistakes were surely made before the escalation of violence included large-scale ethnic cleansing and worse.[49] Perhaps the parliament of the Yugoslavian republic of Bosnia-Herzegovina was at fault in declaring the republic independent in October 1991 despite the deep objections of the Serbian third of its population. Perhaps the international community was mistaken in recognizing this new state's independence in April 1992 despite the violent conflict that had by then broken out between its Serbs and the Muslims and Croats who favored independence. Probably the international community was at fault in allowing the conflict to escalate to the extent that it did before involving itself sufficiently to suppress the violence. And so on. But no assortment of previous mistakes excuses the ethnic cleansing and atrocities in Bosnia that resulted in the deaths of hundreds of thousands of people and the forcible displacement of millions. Even if the NATO bombings of Serbia to try to end the brutal conflict in Kosovo greatly provoked the Serbs to take action against the Albanians of Kosovo, this does not excuse the Serbs' very extensive massacres and expulsions of Albanians.

Sometimes atrocities committed against members of a hated ethnic group are performed by individuals acting without the approval of governing structures (sometimes as part of a governmental policy). Such atrocities are usually thought to be even less excusable when they are deliberately carried out as a matter of policy rather than being the result of the uncontrolled and more accidental hatred of individuals since upholding human rights is an explicit responsibility of government. However, that atrocities are carried out by a government may render others not involved in that government less responsible. Nonetheless, when a governing group or person has been elected or has the support of a given ethnic group, the fact that the policy has been decided upon by the group's governing members rather than its membership as a whole only partially diminishes the group members' responsibility. It is not persuasive to maintain that a given leader or leaders are the only ones to be blamed for arousing the nationalistic sentiments that lead to ethnic hatred or atrocities since there must have been a climate of receptivity to such appeals for them to have served those leaders' purposes of using them for political advantage.

CHANGING BORDERS

Arguments that borders should be changed so that an ethnic group can have its own state or that a minority in a neighboring state can be included in an existing one can certainly continue to be made. Some such arguments are persuasive, especially where existing borders are eminently arbitrary, as in many postcolonial situations. Existing state borders should not be accorded automatic moral legitimacy, but there should always be commitments to processes of peaceful change through demonstrations, passive resistance, referenda, and negotiation rather than efforts to achieve such change through violent action. Violence can justifiably be resorted to only for reasons of genuine self-defense, but the commitment to nonviolence should not be required only of those seeking change. When change is aggressively resisted by crackdowns on peaceful expression or when protests, boycotts, and political strikes are forcefully suppressed, then blame for violation of the requirements of nonviolence rests with the government, not with the group seeking change.[50] This may on occasion justify outside intervention. In the breakup of the former Yugoslavia, it has been the Serbs' use of violence, terror, genocide, ethnic cleansing, and mass rape, all magnified by ethnic hatred, that have been most at fault, not the resistance itself of the Bosnian Serbs to the Bosnian independence that rendered them a minority in a new state or the resistance of the Serbs to the desire of the Albanians in Kosovo for independence.

Are Serbs then collectively responsible for the atrocities that have occurred in Bosnia and Kosovo? Available reports are certainly insufficient for concluding this. However, even if we were to answer yes, such a judgment would tell us little about individual responsibility. Many Serbs were not part of the governing structures or armed groups that adopted and carried out policies of ethnic cleansing and did not support them. Many others opposed these policies. Still, Serbs as a group could take responsibility for what was done purportedly in their name. Through mass demonstrations Serbs succeeded in October 2000 in replacing Milosevic when he refused to acknowledge the results of an election he lost. However, reports suggest that the opposition to Milosevic was based more on his government's ill effects on both the Serbian economy and Serbs' own lives than on repudiation of his policies toward Bosnians, Croats, or Albanians.[51] Reports have shown a widespread unwillingness among Serbs to take responsibility for Serbian massacres and expulsions of Albanians in Kosovo.[52] When members of a group fail to take responsibility for what members of their group have done, they may be collectively responsible for this failure and for not accepting responsibility for the consequences brought about by the group's members.

Ethnic hatred is not genocidal ethnic cleansing, though it may further its aims if it occurs. To the extent that Serbs' ethnic hatred of Muslims, Croats, and Albanians provided support for the atrocities committed, are Serbs collectively responsible for this ethnic hatred? Again, some are certainly more responsible than others. Those responsible for the cultural outlook in which Serbs are portrayed as eternal victims and in which victimization is glorified no doubt bear greater responsibility, as do those responsible for the Serbian media's distortions of facts. Many Serbs were led to see themselves as aggrieved victims and to see non-Serbs as fearsome aggressors; those who foster such views are more responsible than those who are misled by them.

Assessing the war in Bosnia, Philip Cohen assigns special responsibility to Serbian intellectuals and claims that a critical mass of them promoted an ideology of expanding Serbia that culminated in the violence. Warren Zimmerman, a former U.S. ambassador to Belgrade, argues along with many others that "the prime agent of Yugoslavia's destruction was Slobodan Milosevic."[53] Some who comment on the events in Bosnia focus more on the failures of other countries to stop the genocide,[54] and some attribute this to the elites who formed public opinion. Cushman and Mestrovic criticize especially the rationalization that all sides in the conflict were equally guilty, a view put forward by Serbian propaganda and accepted by many in the West because it provided a convenient excuse for inaction. They blame those who could have changed the way the West responded to the conflict and claim that "such rationalizations are scripted by political elites, circulated and reproduced by the mass media and by intellectuals, and consumed by the mass public, which is more or less trusting of expert systems of knowledge production and willing to abide by experts' judgments about domestic and international affairs."[55]

Such views seem to overstate the influence of elites, especially in countries where popular opinion as registered in polls makes many political policies virtually impossible. We cannot merely assume that if the public knows more about horrors abroad, it will be willing to make the efforts and sacrifices necessary to address them. However, if elites have less influence than is sometimes thought, then responsibility for the inadequate responses to events in Bosnia must be spread even more widely.

Evaluations of NATO intervention in Kosovo are still being formed.[56] Even if the bombing is deemed to have been justified by the time it occurred to establish limits on a state's ability to disregard the human rights of its members in the name of national sovereignty, it is not hard to judge that more determined action earlier in the disintegration of Yugoslavia might have made it unnecessary. Furthermore, although it may have been the case that only an intervention limited to the use of air power could have gained enough political support to be feasible, the refusal to use ground troops in the intervention made it impossible to prevent many of the atrocities and violations of Albanians' rights, whose prevention would have helped to justify the intervention.

A case can be made that a broad circle of humanity is collectively responsible for the outrages of the 1990s in the former Yugoslavia, but this tells us rather little about the moral responsibility of individual persons. We can conclude, however, that almost everyone involved both could and should take more responsibility than they have for the failures in which they share—failures that led to the calamities and allowed them to happen.

THE MEDIA AND POLITICAL VIOLENCE

In this chapter I review the meanings of "violence," "political violence," and "terrorism." I then consider the responsibilities of the media, especially television, with respect to political violence, including questions such as how violence should be described and whether the media should cover terrorism. I argue that the media should contribute to decreasing political violence through better coverage of arguments for and against political dissidents' and potential terrorists' views and especially through more and better treatment of nonviolent means of influencing political processes. Since commercial pressures routinely conflict with media responsibility, I argue that society should liberate substantial amounts of culture from such pressures.

MEANINGS AND ASSUMPTIONS

As argued elsewhere, I take violence to be the predictable, coercive, and usually sudden infliction of harmful damage or injury upon persons. Such violence is political when it has political aims, such as to change a government's policies or undermine its credibility. I have maintained that the meaning of "violence" should be kept primarily descriptive rather than normative since there can be, most people would agree, justifiable uses of violence, such as in self-defense and in the enforcement of justifiable laws. We should be able to discuss the justifiability of various forms of violence rather than supposing that once we have identified something as violence we have settled the normative questions. I am an advocate of nonviolence, but I interpret this to mean that when nonviolent methods can be effective, they should always be preferred to violent ones and that priority should always be given to trying to bring it about that the conditions that could justify violence do not occur. An early article I published on terrorism[1] has to my dismay been anthologized in a collection on the topic of terrorism, and, whether or not it is justified, in such a way that it appears on the affirmative side.[2] Therefore, I am wary of how views such as mine can be interpreted. Of course, I did not argue for terrorism; I argued that if it is the only effective way to bring about respect for rights such as to personal safety, it may be less unjustifiable than an unchanging continuation of such rights violations. I also argued that it was a basic responsibility of those in positions of power to ensure that the conditions that might justify terrorism are never met. The same applies to political violence. If peaceful protest, for instance, is permitted to have an effect that decreases injustice, violent protest will not be justified. Moreover, it may be useful to remember that, although he argued that resisting oppression by violent means is better than submitting to it, Mohandas Gandhi is known as an advocate of nonviolence.[3]

What is the difference between political violence and terrorism? In both cases, we should not limit them to violence used to attack established authority. Governments and police forces also engage in terrorism and political violence at times.

Terrorism is a specific form of political violence. It usually has the purpose of creating fear or terror among a population. It does not necessarily target innocent people or civilians, but it frequently does so. Political violence may or may not have the purpose of causing fear among a populace: Sometimes it targets a given political figure to remove that individual from power, as in an assassination. Alternatively, it may be a more general insurrection or violent protest on political grounds, or a violent conflict between political groups or states. All of these use violence on political grounds or for political purposes.

Perhaps not all violence used by political authorities need be political. When minimal necessary violence is used to subdue or apprehend those who break justifiable laws, the violence could be legal but not political, in the sense that we can distinguish a legal system from a political system,[4] and such action belongs more properly to the former. When the police force of a governing political authority, however, shoots randomly into a group of demonstrating opponents to warn dissidents and strike fear into potential demonstrators, that is political violence or terrorism. Even when routine police work uses brutality (since states as presently constituted represent dominant political power), the violence employed is usually best understood as political violence.

Much of the violence against the enforcement arms of established political authority is not political in nature, as when those engaged in crime for personal gain become violent in resisting arrest by the police. It is possible to interpret a certain amount of crime, rioting, and looting in the United States in recent years as a kind of political protest against the economic conditions of depressed urban areas and populations. However, such cases are often ambiguous; much better examples would be organized efforts openly declared to be violence for the political purpose of changing those conditions.

In his essay "Approaches to the Study of Political Violence," Peter H. Merkl adopts what he calls a "nominalistic route toward definition." He relies on the "direct identification of all politically violent phenomena by the observer rather than on first defining a quasi-Platonic 'essence,' or concept of political violence."[5] Then, however, imposing a preselected criterion on the observer, he proceeds to deliberately leave out all examples of government-ordered political violence, thus illustrating how his supposed complete nominalism is as unsatisfactory as would be a pure a priori definition for understanding the phenomenon of political violence. My proposed conception has been developed through a process of trying out a variety of definitions and revising them in the light of judgments of reasonable persons concerning actual cases of political violence.

Since this chapter discusses the media's responsibilities, I dwell no further on these definitional questions. Nonetheless, it may be useful to have in mind certain recent cases that can be classified as political violence and then to see what the arguments I develop imply for cases such as these. Examples of political violence that I have in mind include the Los Angeles riots in April 1992, which occurred in response to the perceived injustice of the acquittal of police officers engaged in the beating of Rodney King; the World Trade Center bombing in New York City on February 26, 1993; the bombing of the Federal Building in Oklahoma City in April 1995; the assassination of Israeli prime minister Yitzhak Rabin on November 4, 1995; and the vicious beating of suspected illegal aliens carried out by law enforcement officials in Riverside County, California, in early April 1996. I make certain assumptions about these cases without claiming very substantial factual accuracy about the empirical aspects involved. My concern is with the normative issues, given certain presumed facts. The conclusions seem applicable to the more recent and even more salient examples of terrorism discussed in earlier chapters of this book.

In all of these cases we may say that the agents carrying out these acts of political violence were greatly influenced by their beliefs about what is politically right and wrong and that their beliefs about these matters were formed in contexts of cultural influences. In at least two of the cases, religious teachings and beliefs were heavily involved.

It is sometimes argued that the causes of such actions are primarily psychological rather than political or intellectual and that certain psychological profiles "explain" the acts of terrorists and others who commit violent acts better than does attention to their beliefs. What is more, in the case of rioting or the beating of suspects, it may be that uncontrolled rage rather than any belief about the injustice of the criminal justice system or beliefs that illegal aliens and the perpetrators of crime ought to be punished immediately and "made to pay" is the primary cause of the brutality. However, we are still left with the need to understand how some persons with given psychological tendencies toward violence are led to commit actual acts of political violence whereas others are not, and we still need to understand the component of the action that was affected by such beliefs and by the social and cultural contexts in which these beliefs were formed and acted on. It is thus entirely reasonable to suppose that, in cases such as those mentioned, words said and unsaid, as well as images and ideas present or absent, need to be considered as possibly strong influences on the commission of political attacks.

Studies of men who engage in domestic violence are revealing on these issues. The men routinely deny their wrongdoing and uphold for themselves the view that they have done nothing wrong. They do this by means of a belief system that supports male dominance, depersonalizes women, and claims that women invite violence by their behavior, that women enjoy being raped, and that children deserve to be beaten. These convictions seem clearly to contribute to these men's use of violence.[6]

On the plausible view, then, that beliefs affect the occurrence of political violence and that culture affects the formation of beliefs, what responsibilities do those who shape culture have for political violence? In addition, which contexts of culture are relevant here? The cultural context that probably had much to do with the beliefs of those who carried out the 1993 World Trade Center bombing is far removed from the media culture that dominates in the United States. The persons who likely influenced those accused in the Oklahoma City bombing are also far removed from this media culture, but in different ways. The same issues can be raised for the other cases of political violence I have mentioned, as for all the other political violence of which these are examples. However, in this chapter I focus on the responsibilities, if any, of the media, and I confine my discussion to the media in the United States.

The media consist of television, at the center, along with radio, film, music, and the print media. Included also are all of the ways in which images and sound are distributed, from movie theaters to recordings, as well as video games and the programs, networks, and hardware of the computer culture.

It is unpersuasive to suggest that the media have no responsibility for political violence. Each of the narrower cultural contexts that may more directly and closely shape the beliefs of those who engage in political violence is embedded in a wider cultural context, of which the media are not only an important but also an increasingly overwhelming part. Moreover, political violence is clearly a kind of violence. If the media promote a "culture of violence," this may well promote political violence, along with other, less focused kinds.

Many studies offer substantiated charges that the media in the United States indeed promote a culture of violence[7] and that this is a significant contributing cause to the high levels of violent acts that take place in the United States.[8] Other studies dispute these allegations. I find the claims of a connection between media violence and violent acts far more persuasive than the claims of no connection, though I agree that many attempts to "blame the media" are misplaced efforts to deflect attention from and responsibility for even clearer connections between, for instance, poverty, social injustice, and crime or the easy availability of guns and violence. To many of those unwilling to address the social problems of the central cities and the deep economic injustices of U.S. society, the media are an easy target. Nonetheless, this does not change the valid judgment that the media are in part responsible for the high levels of violence and injustice in the United States.

Although leading media voices refuse to take responsibility for the effects (whether of increased violence or anything else) of their activities, I want to focus on the more particular questions of what, if anything, the media contribute to political violence and what can be done about it. The kinds of question I address here thus include the following: What ought the media to do with respect to political violence? And what ought society to do with respect to the media?

First, however, just how serious a problem is political violence? Perhaps people perceive it to be a very serious problem in part because of the amount of media coverage devoted to it. Thomas Schelling speculated on "why international political terrorism is such an infinitesimal activity on the world scene when measured not in audience appeal but in damage actually accomplished or even attempted."[9] Still, dismissing terrorism as unimportant seems highly questionable; the potential is alarming. For some time we have been urged to consider the dangers of terrorist attacks being nuclear and reminded that obtaining nuclear material is not impossibly difficult.[10] So let us consider what the media ought to do about political violence, whether it originates in the United States or comes from elsewhere.

THE RESPONSIBILITIES OF THE MEDIA

One of the major responsibilities of the news media in covering political violence is deciding what descriptions to use of the act itself. A difficult issue for the media is "when is one accurate in labeling an act of violence, an individual, or group terrorist, and when should the more sympathetic label freedom fighter(s) be conferred on an actor or group of actors"?[11] It is apparent that governments apply such labels to suit their foreign policy and other interests, as when the Reagan administration called the contras in Nicaragua "freedom fighters" while accepting the Israeli government's descriptions of comparable Palestinian efforts as "terrorist."

A related problem is whether to describe a particular action as a terrorist act or as retaliation. Many acts of political violence are described by those supporting them as retaliation for earlier acts of political violence, though described by their detractors as "new," "fresh," or "renewed" acts of terrorism. For the media to decide where to begin the cycle such that one act is called an "act of terrorism" but another "retaliation" is often fraught with arbitrariness or bias. Nonetheless, the responsibility cannot be evaded, and it has enormous influence on how an audience views political violence.[12]

The media have sometimes been asked not to give coverage to terrorists since attention gives them what they seek. In addition, the media have been asked to avoid making heroes of those who use violence.

Some worry that media coverage of terrorist activity has a "contagion effect." They advise the media to resist covering acts of political violence to avoid setting off imitators.[13] Grant Wardlaw doubts that media coverage significantly affects the occurrence of terrorism,[14] and Robert Picard shares such doubts.[15] Although there may not yet be adequate studies to establish a causal link between television coverage of political violence and the incidence of it, it may well be, Picard admits, that television contributes to the diffusion of information and ideas that, together with personal contacts, encourages this form of action. However, with the sharing of images and ideas on the Internet, this diffusion takes place regardless.

In any case, political violence is newsworthy and should not be ignored, though it should be covered truthfully rather than as a drama to exploit for increased ratings, as some producers advocate.[16] What the media should not ignore are the issues and the background of the political disaffection that fuels violence, and what they should cover far more than at present are more appropriate and successful ways in which the disaffected can engage in political processes. One effect of the request to avoid making terrorists seem attractive to others who share their views was for a time a ubiquitous tendency of every official involved to link the word "cowardly" with every act of political violence. Without further discussion of why it is more courageous to organize and persist in political struggles than to make a bomb in secret, however, the sound bite that came through in every reference to terrorism as "cowardly" seemed fake or silly. Instead of such sound bites, media coverage of efforts to organize and achieve change nonviolently, as well as media dramatizations of nonviolent struggles to achieve political liberation, economic justice, and the like, should be offered frequently.

What else should the media do to decrease political violence? Since those who engage in political violence seem to be influenced by their beliefs about what is politically right and wrong, can the media have any influence on such beliefs? The answer is undoubtedly yes. To have a beneficial influence on such beliefs, the media need to engage in meaningful discussion of what positions are politically better or worse and make strong cases for justifiable positions. This means they would have to consider questions such as whether it may be justifiable to break laws against political violence and why it usually is not. They would also have to raise questions of the priority of morality over law and deal with them in substantial and adequate ways. The law itself cannot recognize a priority for morality, but where freedom of expression is protected, the media are entirely able to engage in moral discourse over the justifiability of civil disobedience, illegal dissent, political violence, and the like. The media could make clear that, for breaking the law on moral grounds to be justifiable, the moral positions appealed to must be sound and tenable.[17] Even though civil disobedience, for instance, may well be justified on grounds of achieving racial justice, this does not mean the same disobedience can be defensible on grounds of racial supremacy. So the media would need to engage in moral discussion that would further understanding of the best available positions on moral issues of political significance, as well as furthering moral understanding of the justifiability or unjustifiability of various methods of furthering those positions. In addition, they would need to discuss and critique foreign policies and corporate activities.

In addition to moral discourse, the media could easily provide relevant images and ideas that would promote understanding of the best moral positions available and the most effective ways to promote them. The media could, for instance, have appealing and exciting films and programs on the greater effectiveness and justifiability of nonviolent efforts compared to violent ones to advance political aims. These could demonstrate the greater courage required and the enhanced admirability of character demonstrated in nonviolent resistance. Alternatively, they could show the futility, stupidity, and moral unattractiveness of violence, in particular, of political violence.

The media would need to present such discussions and images in ways that are likely to reach potential recruits for political violence, as well as those who influence them in more proximate ways, such as their mentors and friends. One way to do this would be to give a hearing to members of disaffected groups who oppose violence and are able to answer the arguments made by those within groups who advocate violence. Though members of disaffected groups may pay little attention to mainstream, establishment views, they may well attend to arguments among members of their own groups. The media could seek out members of various groups that might give rise to political violence and give arguments against violence by members of such groups a wider hearing than they might otherwise receive. In the wake of the Rabin assassination, many observers believed that the failure of opponents of Rabin's policies to speak out against violence contributed to the beliefs and conditions that made possible the violence that occurred. The strident political attacks on illegal aliens and the blame heaped on them for the economic insecurities of many citizens quite possibly contributed to the beliefs that permitted law enforcement officials in California to engage in the violent beatings of suspects. These are the kinds of positions that the media could and should counter.

A major reason the media, in news reports, attend to acts of violence and ignore the reasons for them is that coverage of such acts is relatively inexpensive, and the media, including their news divisions, are driven by commercial interests.[18] Local news in particular, where much more understanding of disaffected groups and the evaluation of their possible methods of pursuing their goals would be possible and suitable, is at present composed of the cheapest possible footage from the police and the fire stations, together with lengthy fillers on the weather and sports.[19] All of television programming is essentially a means to bring an audience to a station's commercials, but the local news is a particularly egregious example of how television fails to meet its responsibilities. Democracy undoubtedly requires an informed citizenry, and it is the responsibility of the press, including those who produce the news on television and radio, as well as in newspapers, to provide the information citizens need. The only news many citizens encounter is the local television news, yet it leaves them dangerously and irresponsibly misinformed.

What the news media do cover may well contribute to the problem of political violence rather than to its decrease. As James Fallows writes, "the message of today's news coverage is often that the world cannot be understood, shaped, or controlled, but merely endured or held at arms length....All countries fall into two categories: those that are so messed up we shouldn't waste time thinking about them, and those that are messed up in a way that threatens our security...so we should invade them" and quickly withdraw. "One inch beneath its surface," he continues, "most domestic news carries a similar despairing message....We have a system of news media that tells people constantly that the world is out of control, that they will always be governed by crooks, that their fellow citizens are about to kill them."[20]

Those inclined toward distrust and imagining that only violence can attract attention to their political views are encouraged in such tendencies by the standard fare of media news. Studies show that even when crime is decreasing, people believe it is increasing because that is what the media cover.[21] Moreover, studies show that people are greatly influenced, in evaluating the seriousness of problems, by which ones are covered by the media in comparison with others that are not so treated. The journalists who gather news from around the world, risking their lives and health, deserve respect and appreciation. But when the journalistic enterprise becomes more and more driven by ratings and economic considerations, such journalists are unable to do the work they should. As Thomas Friedman has noted, "with today's cacophony of magazine shows...and talking-head news commentaries, many people have lost sight of what real journalists do. Journalists do not appear on the McLaughlin show and scream at each other....Journalists don't have their own shock-jock radio shows."[22] Yet this is the kind of journalism that is increasingly offered to the public and that crowds out the responsible kind of reporting and commentary.

THE RESPONSIBILITIES OF SOCIETY

Let us consider next what society should do about the media. It is in many ways the major question because the idea that the media will themselves take responsibility for the political violence they fail to help prevent is preposterous in the context of the U.S. media. Despite decades of criticism of the levels of violence on television, such violence has continued to rise, and the industry has for years opposed any limitations on it. The V-chip, which the industry opposed, was required by the telecommunications law enacted early in 1996 to be installed in future television sets. In response, the industry was induced to change its stand and agree to a ratings system of its own devising to activate the chip. This would enable parents to block certain violent programs their children might otherwise watch. It would give many children and young adults a signal as to what to choose to see. According to Frank Rich, the industry "finally agreed to a ratings system when it realized that it can be as broad (and hard to enforce) as the movie ratings system it will mimic," under which movies have continued to become ever more violent.[23]

The failure of commercial television to take responsibility for the effects of its activities is well illustrated in its positions concerning children's programming. The industry has turned children's programs into vehicles for the commercial manipulation of children by making "programs" that are effectively program-length commercials for toys and related products. It has consistently resisted all efforts to increase the educational offerings for children. In April of 1996 a political effort was made to urge the Federal Communications Commission (FCC) to require broadcasters seeking license renewals to provide at least three hours a week of educational programming for children; the industry lobbied hard against such an utterly modest requirement. Although in 1951, twenty-seven hours of relatively high-quality children's programming was offered each week,[24] by the mid-1990s few commercial stations came close to offering three hours of educational programming.[25]

Recent decades have seen the media become ever more blatantly commercial and any alternatives to the commercial media, such as public broadcasting, ever more beleaguered. Republican presidents and congresses have very nearly killed public broadcasting altogether. Even though they have not quite succeeded, public broadcasting is a shoestring operation that must constantly scrounge for minimal funds to stay afloat. A comparison between spending on public broadcasting in the United States and several other countries shows how marginalized everything but the commercial media is in the United States.[26] In the late 1980s Japan was spending $14 per person per year on public broadcasting, Canada $23.60, and Great Britain $24.52, while the United States was spending only 77 cents.[27]

The near total commercialization of the media is in no way confined to television. Newspapers' practices and coverage have become more and more driven by commercial considerations, as have the publishing industry's decisions. To take just one example, the Book-of-the-Month Club, which once based its choices of which books to promote on at least some level of merit, has come to consider only potential profit.[28]

One can conclude that, unless it would be commercially advantageous to address issues of political violence, there is no reason to suppose that the media will do so. Furthermore, there is no reason to suppose that doing so would be commercially advantageous. If society, then, wishes to deal more effectively with violence and political violence and wishes the media to contribute to this task, it will have to consider measures other than merely suggesting suitable measures for the media to adopt.

One avenue that will no doubt be explored is more social control over runaway media. Talk of such control becomes more politically feasible from time to time, as politicians find that it is politically popular to attack the media as irresponsible. The introduction of the V-chip opened up some possibilities for more social control of violence in the media than in the past, but a television ratings system is unlikely by itself to contribute seriously to a decrease of whatever violent programming on television does to promote political violence. More stringent controls may be suggested. However, it is hard to imagine governmental censorship of violent programs surviving First Amendment challenges in the United States. What it is possible to imagine is that the Federal Communications Commission, whose legal requirements specify that licenses be granted on the basis of serving "the public interest," would take its responsibilities more seriously.[29] Under public and political pressure, the FCC could become more demanding in its licensing requirements and require an overall decrease in the quantity of violent programming. This might be a small, though significant, improvement.

Controls on anything in the culture other than broadcasting, however, are harder to envisage. The influence of certain books on those who commit acts of violence and of political violence appears to be considerable in a number of cases. Peder Lund's Paladin Press of Boulder, Colorado, publishes what critics describe as murder manuals; one is titled *Hit Man: A Technical Manual for Independent Contractors,* and another, *How To Kill* (six volumes).[30] Some reflect the concerns of militia groups, with titles such as *Modern Weapons Caching: A Down-to-Earth Approach to Beating the Government Gun Grab.* However, although Canada has banned the sale of two Paladin books, various civil liberties experts doubt that U.S. courts would agree to curb them or that those who might sue the publisher when a murderer seems to have followed the directions of one of Lund's books could win their case.

In recent years much discussion has centered on restricting hate speech. Germany and France have very serious restrictions on such speech, but legal curbs in the United States face fairly impervious constitutional barriers. The arguments developed in favor of restrictions of hate speech have centered on environments such as a university, and even here it is questionable whether such restraints can be effectively defended, though Diana Meyers's proposal for the university's compensation to the victims may seem promising.[31]

Feminists have had little success in gaining acceptance of the link between pornography and violence against women and thus in establishing the harm that could provide a basis for legal restrictions on pornography. The conclusion should probably be drawn that attempts in the United States to restrict speech, images, and ideas are not likely to be successful. The ideology of a near total opposition to censorship is too deeply embedded in law and culture. Nevertheless, the position that misguided speech and images should be vigorously opposed through better and more persuasively good arguments and ideas is ripe for development, expansion, and institutional implementation.[32] Additionally, the position that the media have a responsibility to counter speech and images that lead to violence with those that promote nonviolence could become a popular position.

The idea could also begin to take hold that, just as culture should be free from governmental censorship or control, so should it be free from commercial censorship or control. Since commercial interests and control have led the media to provide less and less educational programming for children and more and more violent programming for everyone, we should consider how the media could be freed from these pressures. There are many available suggestions, such as fees on television sets to fund noncommercial broadcasting at very substantial levels or taxes on advertising to support noncommercial cultural production. We are accustomed to considerable public support of education, together with standards of academic freedom from governmental and corporate interference; a comparable combination of significant public support of noncommercial culture, together with standards of cultural independence from both governmental and corporate control, should also be developed. Most of those who work in commercial cultural enterprises long for greater independence from commercial pressures; their professional standards should demand it more vigorously.

If our commercialized culture is failing to perform the functions that society needs culture to perform, as it clearly is, we should create a noncommercial culture to do so. Among these functions are to inform the public as the press in a democracy has the responsibility to do.[33] Another is to offer critiques and evaluations of existing structures of power, not mere reinforcements of the dominant interests of the major economic structures and corporate power. Yet another is to deal with the deep ills and traumas of the society and the world, such as their violence, political wounds, and grievances.

Part of the difficulty we face in developing a noncommercial media culture is the failure of progressives to have built an adequate media politics. Progressive efforts have not been able to match religious broadcasting, with its network of radio outlets around the country or to counter the right-wing talk radio that so often poisons the political atmosphere.[34] Instead, there are what may well be exaggerated hopes that the Internet offers vast new possibilities for progressive organizing, though it can be used for any objective.[35] At the same time, there are unhelpful dismissals of media critics as elitist or as failing to understand the interests of ordinary working-class people.[36] Some leftists hold that their proposals are inevitably dull, and they merely accept that what they offer is boring. Of course, it should not be conceded that progressive views must be boring. The stories of labor struggles, civil rights activities, and feminist organizing can be highly dramatic and exciting, and current treatments of the possibilities for political actions of various kinds can be extremely engaging. Nonetheless, the possibilities and their expression in the terms of a media culture need badly to be developed.

In the United States, society has developed a media culture, one that is dominated by the media, and this media culture is overwhelmingly commercial. Other components of the overall culture have become marginalized or are being absorbed into the media as soon as they develop a following. "High art" is increasingly indistinguishable from popular culture, and every day we see new examples of corporate sponsorship of and influence over museum and other exhibitions.[37] The "news" is harder and harder to distinguish from media entertainment, and those religious groups that are growing adopt the marketing techniques and the stylistic forms of the media. When songs or musical styles that begin as expressions of protest become popular, they are turned into the background music of television advertisements. In addition, styles of dress originally developed to oppose the fashion industry's commercial hold on people are taken over by the designers and manufacturers of the "looks" promoted through endless advertisements in magazines, whose pages of editorial material are increasingly impossible to differentiate from their advertising pages.

So commercial has the culture become that vast numbers of people eagerly turn their very persons into advertisements by promoting brands of beer, soda, or sports equipment on their clothes and accessories. The commercial media culture shapes consciousness so thoroughly that most people find it hard to imagine a culture not dominated by commercial interests.

Douglas Kellner writes that "a media culture has emerged in which images, sounds, and spectacles help produce the fabric of everyday life, dominating leisure time, shaping political views and social behavior, and providing the materials out of which people forge their very identities....Media culture helps shape the prevalent view of the world and deepest values: it defines what is considered good or bad, positive or negative, moral or evil."[38]

THE POTENTIAL OF MEDIA CULTURE

The potential of a media culture is extraordinary. Traditionally, societies have arrived at decisions and resolved disputes within and between them through the use of force, economic coercion, majorities' imposing their wills on minorities, or negotiation, with force in the background influencing the outcome. In contrast, in a society in which an independent media culture was the dominant influence in the society, social decisions could be reached and disputes could be resolved through discourse rather than coercion. Potentially this could be possible between, as well as within, societies. It would represent remarkable progress in human development. Moreover, the discourse could be based on the honest reporting of events and conditions and on participants' imaginatively and empathetically entering into the narratives of others' histories and situations. The discourse could be characterized by rational discussion and consideration of alternative courses of action and the reasons in their favor. It could also promote the kind of trust on which social stability and peace between groups depend. It could invite those who disagree with existing arrangements to enter the discourse and encourage the hope that those with the best arguments would win over others, and it could lead to the widespread belief that this would be so.

Among other extraordinary achievements in moral progress that such a culture would provide, it would undermine the beliefs that encourage political violence among potential opponents of political authority both at home and abroad. It would no longer be possible for the disaffected to maintain that their views cannot gain a hearing without the use of violence or that power rather than good arguments will overwhelm their positions or that the violence of established authorities must be met with that of the disaffected because no other means of effecting change is possible.

The picture I have painted, however, of the potential of media culture is of course *only* about its possibilities. The reality of the media culture we have in the United States bears almost no resemblance to it. All of the directions in which society and the media are headed in the United States are away from this potential and toward ever greater subservience of the media to commercial interests, ever increased concentration, homogenization, and control by a few media giants whose primary interest is financial gain, ever fewer honest interpretations of reality, ever fewer presentations of non-U.S. perspectives, and ever less free and useful moral discourse.

In such a climate, the chances that political opposition at home and abroad will take violent forms are also likely to increase. As the media increasingly set the agendas of political and social attention and increasingly affect the outcomes of elections and of what few genuine public debates of issues occur, the belief that the views of the disaffected can gain a hearing on their merits cannot be maintained. Violent expressions of political emotion are thereby promoted.

Yet however unlikely, given current trends, may be the development of a responsible media culture, we should not lose sight of the potential of a culture not dominated by commercial interests and in which moral and political discourse would shape society's decisions and policies. Such a media culture could provide the standard against which any measures to deal with the media are considered. It would require a vast freeing of the media from the commercial control under which they now labor. Such a culture not commodified and not commercialized is almost never mentioned in the media. Nevertheless, we could develop a social movement to educate students and citizens about the realities of the media and the more promising alternatives. We could develop a social movement to liberate culture. On every ground that I can think of, I believe we ought to do so.

SEVEN

THE MORAL ASSESSMENT
OF VIOLENCE AND
TERRORISM

That is why all armed prophets have conquered, and unarmed prophets have come to grief.

—Machiavelli, *The Prince*

Suffering injury in one's own person is ... of the essence of nonviolence and is the chosen substitute for violence to others. ... It results in the long run in the least loss of life.

—M. K. Gandhi, *Nonviolence in Peace and War*

The moral problems of violence or terrorism arise in actual contexts. Addressing them may be thought to be a task for applied ethics. However, only if we had adequate normative theories suitable for the diverse contexts of human experience would we be in a position to make valid applications of ethical theory. Along with many others, I doubt that the theories we now have are adequate, but I believe that the moral views and judgments we can come to in exploring actual problems can help us to improve our moral theories and to test them in experience.

What shall we say about those acts of moral agents in which violence or terror is used to achieve moral objectives? Can they ever be justified? And what, if anything, can our deliberations in this domain indicate about the methods by which we ought to conduct moral inquiry?

In developing the arguments of this chapter I concentrate on the question of the justifiability of violence. I then briefly consider whether the arguments apply also to terrorism, and, if not, why not. Finally I consider the implications for moral inquiry that the discussion may suggest.[1]

VIOLENCE

It is sometimes suggested that violence is by definition wrong, but to maintain this is not a satisfactory position, as I have argued earlier in this book. It is easy enough to think of examples of acts of violence of which it is meaningful to ask whether they were wrong. To answer questions about the justifiability of acts of violence requires that we not construe the issues as ones that we can settle merely by appealing to a definition.

Violence can be defined as action, usually sudden, that predictably and coercively inflicts injury upon or damage that harms a person.[2] The threat of such action is a violent one. Property damage is sometimes called "violence" by those who deplore it but should be included only insofar as it risks injury or harm to people.[3]

Some maintain that failures to act can also be instances of violence, as when people are harmed by being deprived of food.[4] It might, however, be more accurate to see the violence involved as the injury inflicted when those who are deprived attempt to change their position. Moreover, failures to act can certainly be morally outrageous without being violent. To starve a person slowly may be as blameworthy as killing the person quickly (or sometimes even more so), but it is not more violent.

Harm can be inflicted through psychological as well as physical pressure, and the injuries caused by violence may be both psychological and physical.

A dissident who blows up a car, intentionally killing its occupants, is violent. The police who capture him with guns threaten violence to do so. If he is wounded or killed in the capture, violence has been used against him. A competent doctor operating on a patient is not inflicting harm. An honest tennis player injuring another does not do so predictably. Automobile driving unavoidably risks injury, but to the extent that it is voluntarily engaged in, it does not do so coercively.

Violence is distinct from force and coercion since force may be used to coerce without violence, and coercion is not always violent, though violence is always coercive.[5] Force is power to cause people to do something against their will. Coercion is the activity of causing people to do something against their will, whether that will is actual or is what they would will if they knew what was going to happen to them or to others and still had what could be described as a capacity to will.[6]

The use of force to coerce may often be justified, whereas the use of violence for the same purpose would not be. For instance, a parent may coerce a child to surrender a dangerous object by gently forcing the child's fingers open, whereas to retrieve the object by a violent blow would not be justified.

If we agree with Plato that it can never be right to injure or harm anyone, we will be back with the view that we rejected at the outset—that violence is by definition unjustifiable. However, we can retain a meaning of "inflicting injury," which is descriptive and morally indeterminate and does not allow us to call every form of causing pain a kind of violence. To injure someone in self-defense or in the upholding of a just law may be not only a legally allowed but also a morally justifiable case of injuring.

The rules of almost any legal system permit the use of violence to preserve and enforce the laws, regardless of whether these laws are just, but forbid most other uses of violence. Where laws are morally unjustified, the use of violence to uphold them will be morally unjustified even if legally permitted. Moreover, legal rules sometimes permit the use of violence to uphold highly corrupt and harmful political power. Violence is also often used in the enforcement of law in excess of what might be needed for this purpose and in excess of what the law allows.

In an improving political system, violence not allowed by law will seldom be found legal by new judicial decisions, so we can rarely speak of illegal violence as coming to be legally justified, at least not without first becoming politically acceptable. However, it is not unusual for illegal violence to become politically justified in the sense that within the political system it will come to be considered justified. Let us examine these issues.

If we have made a higher-level moral judgment that a given political system is worthy of existence or that it is satisfactory enough for us to consider ourselves to be members of it and that it ought to be changed rather than destroyed but that it cannot be adequately changed within its existing legal forms and legally allowed political processes, we may consider engaging in acts of violence that are illegal but will come to be seen as justifiable on political grounds. And if we deem a given political system so thoroughly corrupt and productive of harm that it cannot be repaired, we may consider whether we would be morally justified in engaging in violence to rid human beings of the violence it inflicts or to express our outrage.

POLITICAL VIOLENCE

To consider whether violence can be politically justified we need to distinguish political violence from other forms of violence. We may say that political violence is violent action against individuals or groups for political or social reasons. Usually we can consider any attacks upon public officials to be instances of political violence unless they are for obviously personal, nonpolitical reasons. Furthermore, when government agents employ violence beyond what is needed for the enforcement of justifiable law, this is also political violence.

For an act of violence to be justifiable within a political system, it must at least be an act of political violence. However, can any of these acts be justified *within* a political system? Or can they be justified only by appeal to moral considerations in opposition to what the political system will approve?

The legal rules of almost any political system are likely to prohibit the use of violence as a means of interpersonal and intergroup conflict in favor of other forms of interaction: voting, political and economic pressure, lobbying, judicial decision, executive decree, and so on, all of which involve power, and some of which involve force but none of which need involve violence. From a legal point of view, it would be hard to maintain that acts of violence on grounds other than self-defense narrowly conceived and law enforcement are ever justifiable within a political system. However, such a view assumes that the legal system is above political control and is more inclusive than the political system and that both may be changed only in ways the legal system permits. The legal system may still be subject to moral criticism, but if it is subject only to moral criticism, it may, as a system, be changed only internally, according to its own rules, or as a result of moral influence, which may be inordinately weak.

In a world in which moral persuasion exercised considerably more power than it does at present, this might be the appropriate hierarchy:

the political system subsumed under the legal, and the legal under the moral. However, it is hard to suppose that this is always the appropriate hierarchy for the world as we know it since many legal systems represent as finite a stage of moral understanding as the political systems to which they are attached, and they sometimes represent attitudes frozen into law that are unsuited to a new situation. In one sense, the law records and embodies political decisions already made,[7] and, although we should not assume that whatever is later in time is morally superior, we need not assume, especially in realms as much in need of change as most legal and political ones, that it is never so.

If we do not, then, give priority to legal judgments over political ones, although we may give priority to moral judgments over both, can we consider some acts of political violence justifiable within a political system?

Historically, such acts have played a significant role in the political systems that have emerged in recent centuries. But it is quite possible that the violence that has taken place has been a manifestation of changes within the political system rather than a cause. As power configurations shift, they may be reflected in acts of violence, as those fearful of losing power (quite accurately, in many cases) attempt to hang on to their positions, and those angry at having suffered years of injustice (quite justifiably angry, in many cases) lash out when they dare. If violence has merely accompanied a change rather than contributed to it in a causal sense, this would not supply grounds upon which the violence might be found justifiable in terms of its political consequences. The historical record, however, can be read in various ways. Charles Tilly presents political violence as a fairly normal and central factor in Western political life as both a cause and an effect. "Men seeking to seize, hold or realign the levers of power," he writes, "have continually engaged in collective violence as part of their struggles....Violent protests seem to grow most directly from the struggle for established places in the structure of power....Instead of constituting a sharp break from 'normal' political life, violent protests tend to accompany, complement, *and extend* organized, peaceful attempts by the same people to accomplish their objectives."[8] Tilly concludes that in the disturbances of the more recent past, "men contend over the control and organization of the State and the economy"[9] and that, as before, "collective violence is part and parcel of the Western political process."[10]

Lewis Coser asserts even more clearly that violence can be a causal factor having results that are approved. Surveying the efforts of the working class to gain some political power in England in the nineteenth century, he writes:

> Far from being but an epiphenomenal manifestation of temporary maladjustment, Chartism had a direct impact by leading to a series of reform measures alleviating the conditions against which it had reacted. Violence and riots were not merely protests: they were claims to be considered.... It is not to be doubted that legislative remedies, from factory legislation to the successive widening of the franchise and the attendant granting of other citizenship rights to members of the lower classes, came, at least in part, in response to the widespread disorders and violent outbreaks that marked the British social scene for over half a century.[11]

Assuming that acts of political violence sometimes cause political changes that are significant improvements, politically and morally, can they then be justifiable within the political system? The difficulty of saying yes or no is effectively portrayed by Sorel:

> Certain acts of violence have rendered such great services to democracy that the latter has often consecrated as great men those who, at the peril of their lives, have tried to rid it of its enemies.... Each time an outrage occurs, the doctors of the ethico-social sciences, who swarm in journalism, indulge in reflections on the question, Can the criminal act be excused, or sometimes even justified, from the point of view of the highest justice? Then there is an irruption into the democratic press of that casuistry for which the Jesuits have so many times been reproached.[12]

There may always be the danger, empirically well established, that violence is hard to control, no matter how rational the original intentions of those who decide to employ it. As Hannah Arendt suggested, "the danger of the practice of violence, even if it moves within a non-extremist framework of short-term goals, will always be that the means overwhelm the end.... The practice of violence, like all action, changes the world, but the most probable change is a more violent world."[13] And Sorel, despite his commitment to total, unyielding class warfare, advocated nothing more truly violent than a general strike, for fear of losing control and inviting repression. "It is easy enough," he wrote, "to arouse popular anger, but it is not easy to stifle it. As long as there are no very rich and strongly centralized trade unions whose leaders are in continuous relationship with political men,[14] so long will it be impossible to say exactly to what lengths violence will go."[15]

Furthermore, the historical record on the uses of violence is thoroughly mixed. Contemporary defenders of aggressive tactics often assume that some violence was necessary to achieve the gains of organized labor in its early struggles, but one can dispute this claim. In their study spanning the period from the 1870s to the 1960s in the United States, Philip Taft and Philip Ross conclude the following:

> The effect of labor violence was almost always harmful to the union. There is little evidence that violence succeeded in gaining advantages for strikers. Not only does the roll call of lost strikes confirm such a view, but the use of employer agents, disguised as union members or union officials for advocating violence within the union, testifies to the advantage such practices gave the employer.... A community might be sympathetic to the demands of strikers, but as soon as violent confrontations took place, the possibility was high that interest would shift from concern for the acceptance of union demands to the stopping of violence.... The evidence against the effectiveness of violence as a means of gaining concessions by labor in the United States is too overwhelming to be a matter of dispute.[16]

The danger that violent action will produce consequences that are worse than the situation under attack is often severe. The successful use of violence almost certainly requires a tight discipline and capacity for secrecy in direct conflict with the open, participatory decision processes its advocates sometimes espouse. Still, an outbreak of violence may provide a signal that the political system, in its own interest, should heed. It may increase the likelihood that those who would rather ignore the issues raised by the discontented will pay attention to more moderate leaders. This may well have been the situation in which progress in civil rights was achieved in the United States in the 1960s.[17] Since those with political power are often insensitive to the distress of others and since those who are sensitive often lack political power, it may be that violence can provide a shock that will lead to improvement in an area of distress in a political system.

THE JUSTIFICATION OF VIOLENCE

Let us suppose, then, that an intentional act of political violence, V_p, does not lead to additional, more extensive, unintended violence and produces what can be considered good results. What can be meant by holding the judgment "V_p was justifiable" valid within political system P?

We may well argue that one of the primary functions of a political system is the validation of political positions as justifiable or nonjustifiable, just as one of the primary functions of a legal system is the validation of legal claims as justifiable or nonjustifiable. The grounds upon which a judgment may be valid may be different in the two systems, but both provide a method of deciding between conflicting claims.

If an act not permitted by existing laws but concerning which there are strongly felt conflicting positions turns out to have results that are generally considered to contribute to the well-being of the political system, the act will be considered justifiable within this system. Moreover, if we decide at a moral level that the continued well-being of that political system is at least better than its destruction, then the act, even if it is an act of violence, may not only be *considered* justifiable within a political system but may also be politically justifiable.

Let us examine the case of England adapting to the industrial revolution. If Lewis Coser is correct, violent outbreaks can be said to have caused changes that the political system later found justifiable within that system:

> The often violent forms of rebellion of the laboring poor, the destructiveness of the city mobs, and other forms of popular disturbances which mark English social history from the 1760s to the middle of the nineteenth century helped to educate the governing elite of England, Whig and Tory alike, to the recognition that they could ignore the plight of the poor only at their own peril. These social movements constituted among other things an effective signaling device which sensitized the upper classes to the need for social reconstruction in defense of a social edifice over which they wished to continue to have over-all command.[18]

Hannah Arendt considered all justification to depend upon future consequences: "Legitimacy, when challenged, is claimed by an appeal to the past, while justification relates to an end which lies in the future. Violence can be justifiable, but it never will be legitimate."[19] I do not share the view that justification is possible only in terms of future outcome; political justification is more often arrived at this way because of the nature of political systems, but legal justification is and should be more often arrived at by appealing to the past and to deontological principles because of the nature of legal systems.[20] Because an acceptable set of legal rules should rule out violence on grounds other than self-defense and law enforcement, most advanced legal systems do not in fact find such violence justifiable or legitimate. However, this is not a requirement for every legal system, as some have allowed private individuals to carry out violent revenge, and others have permitted excessive violence to be used in enforcing their rules. In addition, within certain political systems, violence might be justified by reference to a prior political rule that recommends it in certain circumstances. It is not only pure Machiavellians who might agree, however reluctantly, to a political rule that a promising political system struggling for survival may occasionally be justified in taking violent measures against corrupt opponents. So we cannot say that only the future can justify violence, though political violence should normally be judged by its results.

Political justification presupposes the existence of a political system with methods of deciding between conflicting claims, just as legal justification presupposes the existence of a legal system. Within various established political systems now in existence, some acts of violence seem to be capable of being found justifiable if they have the following characteristics:

1. They do not lead to additional, more extensive violence.
2. They directly and promptly bring about political consequences that are more decisively approved within the political system than the actions were disapproved.
3. No effective alternative means of bringing about these consequences were possible.

Perhaps acts of violence can be justifiable on other grounds as well; I am suggesting characteristics such that, if an act has them, it is justifiable. I intentionally evade the language of necessary and sufficient conditions.

A few words about the first characteristic: It is not meant to require that other acts of violence not occur since the same kinds of reasons or causes that lead to one act of violence may lead to another, but it suggests that each act needs to be justified independently and that a given act of political violence has this characteristic only if *it* does not produce further, more extensive violence.

Since violence is the inflicting of injury and damage rather than the creation of any political good, we may say that the only consequences it is in fact capable of producing (relevant to the second characteristic) are negative ones: the harm to or the destruction or removal of some person, power, or obstacle. But sometimes this is a result that will be widely approved and will make possible further good consequences. Furthermore, although political systems ought to develop in ways such that the third characteristic is in fact *never* present, until they do, violence can sometimes be politically justifiable.

Whenever the conditions are present that would give what Joan Bondurant calls "the process of creative conflict" a chance of successes, it should be favored.[21] The Gandhian method of winning over one's opponents through nonviolent pressure may well be more effective than violence in undermining people's attachment to mistaken views. However, one should not ask people willingly to accept genocide even if one believes—and it would be a position for which little evidence could be marshaled—that the world would be so shocked that it would be the last case of genocide. In addition, one should not assume that nonviolent protest is always worth the risk. Walter Laqueur believes that "civil disobedience would not have had the slightest effect in Nazi Germany; Gandhi was quite mistaken when he recommended it."[22] He may be mistaken. Joan Bondurant points out that "had the Jews offered satyagraha against the Nazi regime their losses could scarcely have been greater....Had the Jews of Germany been schooled in the art of satyagraha, an organized effort of satyagraha might have got underway. The chances for success are certainly as great as are the chances for violent revolution under the modern police-state system."[23] Still, if the empirical judgment is made that those preventing the alternative means in the third characteristic from being available are totally unlikely to change, then refraining from violence might be harder to justify than resorting to it.

There are those, such as Sorel and Fanon, who stress the positive value of violence in molding group solidarity; Sartre goes even further. But the justification of this aspect of violence is that it will contribute to the group's destructive potential, a potential that the group then may or may not be justified in exercising, or else to action *not* within the political system.[24] We will consider the latter issue later.

Before contemporary advocates of violence to achieve progressive change take heart from the kind of analysis here presented, they should observe that on this analysis of political justification, the violent actions justified within a political system may be those taken in behalf of the system against a dissident individual or group, as well as those taken against established power by those who would reform it. For violence to be politically justifiable, it must be justifiable in some sense within a political system even though the system may change dramatically. The judgment will be made by the system itself.

CAN VIOLENCE BE MORALLY JUSTIFIABLE?

Future judicial decisions about constitutionality will find some acts of civil disobedience legally justifiable. Others will never be found legally justifiable within a given legal system—but are still morally justifiable. Similarly, some violence aimed at changing a political system will be found acceptable within that system, while other violence aimed at changing a system may be morally justifiable even though that system will never find it politically justifiable. An example might be a violent political protest against the jailing of political opponents in a state that will never reform itself in such a way as to find the protest justifiable.

If individuals have no sincere expectation that their act of political violence may be found justifiable within the political system in which they carry it out, dependent as that system must be for its very existence on certain configurations of prevailing power, they may consider whether the action can be morally justifiable. An act of political violence may be morally justifiable, in my view, if it has the following characteristics:

1. It does not lead to additional, more extensive violence; and either
2. It directly and promptly brings about consequences that are, in terms of a justifiable moral system, of sufficiently greater moral good than evil to outweigh the violence itself, and no effective alternative means of bringing about these consequences are possible; or,
3. It is prescribed by a moral rule or principle that is valid and applicable to a situation facing an agent, and no alternative way of fulfilling this rule is possible.

In the foregoing statements I have included reference to a deontologically based rule among the grounds for moral justification and excluded reference to any such rule from the grounds for political justification. This reflects the view that political justification presupposes the existence of a political system with the power to make its decisions effective for the members of that system and that political justification depends upon an examination of consequences more significantly than it depends upon reference to deontologically grounded rules. Legal justification presupposes the existence of a legal system capable of effectively enforcing its decisions but depends upon reference to deontologically grounded rules more than upon estimations of consequences.[25]

Moral justification, in contrast, depends upon both deontologically based rules and an examination of consequences and proceeds by an activity loosely analogous to the scientific activity of first constructing and then testing hypotheses. Moral justification presupposes the existence of a moral system in some sense but not in that of being able to impose and enforce its decisions. A moral system should be authoritative because it is able to win the voluntary assent of free moral agents in a way comparable to that by which a scientific system gains authority by winning the acceptance of free and impartial inquirers. Conflicts between moral systems, obviously rife at present, should be settled by argument and persuasion on the basis of sincere and impartial deliberation and extensive moral experience. However, some states refuse to allow this process to occur. Though it can proceed to some extent even under repressive conditions, it ought to be enabled to develop freely.

If the effectiveness of a moral system should depend upon its power to win voluntary agreement, one may wonder whether any moral rule can ever prescribe a violent act or any good consequences justify such an act.

Kant argued that "everyone may use violent means to compel another to enter into a juridical state of society."[26] Nonetheless, we might agree that a state, with legal provisions that allow violence in self-defense but forbid it generally would be better and stronger if founded on agreement rather than on forcible imposition. Those who agree might use violence to defend themselves *against* those who do not, but this would be collective self-defense, not the imposing of a legal system on those who do not accept it.

The most plausible view, then, might be that we are not justified in using violence to force others to cooperate with us but that we may defend ourselves against those who prevent us from entering into cooperative, morally justifiable relations. And we may use violence to defend our moral rights to express our views on the reasons others ought to join in arrangements for the resolution of conflict through argument and political decision rather than through violence.

When there is no viable alternative way to defend our moral rights to free expression or to be given a hearing, violence may be morally justifiable. This view reflects the primacy that is often felt for the moral rights of freedom of thought, of expression, and of conscience.

VIOLENCE AND THE SELF

The argument is made, particularly by Sartre and Fanon, that violence can contribute significantly to the psychological health of oppressed peoples. They argue that, through the commission of a violent act, subjugated persons can come to recognize their human freedom. Sartre writes, "We only become what we are by the radical and deep-seated refusal of that which others have made of us." Of the Algerians' struggle for independence, he says:

> First, the only violence is the settler's; but soon [the rebels] will make it their own; that is to say, the same violence is thrown back upon us. . . . By this mad fury, by this bitterness and spleen, by their ever-present desire to kill us . . . they have become men: men *because of* the settler, who wants to make beasts of burden of them—because of him, and against him. . . . This irrepressible violence is neither sound and fury, nor the resurrection of savage instincts, nor even the effect of resentment: it is man recreating himself.[27]

One may respond that the capacity to say "no" to the command of one's oppressor may indeed be an essential part of the process of becoming aware of one's freedom but that the form of the refusal need not therefore be violent. One may even assert that the awareness of freedom is greater when people recognize that they possess a capacity both for carrying out violent action and for refraining from it. They may become conscious of a higher degree of freedom by defying those who taunt them to prove themselves through violence, as well as by defying those who oppress them.

If, however, an existing political system refuses to allow the expression of moral arguments designed to transform it and if an act of political violence can constitute such an expression, it may be morally justifiable. There will be grave danger that any violent political act will cause unforeseeable consequences and even graver danger that a violent action intended to change a political system will instead be seen as one intended to destroy that system and thus unleash the responses that such an act would precipitate. Then the consequence may be to entrench repression rather than to shake it. If any such acts are to have any chance of achieving their purposes it will be necessary to evolve tacit rules to keep them within bounds and make their intentions clear. As in the case of civil disobedience, there will have to be an understanding of the possible moral sincerity of both the actor and those members of the political system faced with responding to such action, both of whom may be acting in accordance with what they conscientiously consider to be their moral obligations. In the case of civil disobedience, the sincerity of the actors can sometimes be demonstrated by their willingness to limit themselves to nonviolent actions. Sometimes, but not always, a willingness to accept the penalty that the legal system imposes or to perform the action in public can contribute to a demonstration of sincerity.[28] Comparable evidence of sincerity is much more difficult to offer in the case of violent action that is not justifiable within the political system, but it is not impossible. The provision of fair warning to minimize unnecessary injury and the offering of unmistakable evidence of restraint that the violence can be ended in as disciplined a way as it is undertaken may both contribute.

When those to whom a political system fails to give a voice constitute a large number of that system's members, the argument may be persuasive that an act of violence that warns that system of possible danger to itself may have to be justifiable within that political system or it will not be justifiable at all. However, when those to whom a political system denies a voice are too small in number or too powerless to represent a significant threat to the existence or even the health of that system, the requirement that for an act of violence to be morally justifiable it must also be politically justifiable may be mistaken. Political systems have been known to be long lived, though highly immoral.

Quite clearly, the world should be such that violent but illegal actions are *never* morally justifiable. Persuasion and argument should always be the forms through which moral judgments succeed in being authoritative for political actions. Political systems should be such as to provide the forums within which moral argument can take place and to transform the clash of forces behind the arguments into an interaction of minds, wills, and political power rather than into violent actions.

Polemarchus's observation to Socrates on the road from Piraeus is, however, still with us: You cannot persuade those who will not listen.[29]

Although it is almost never the case, if an act of violence is the only way to open the possibilities for persuasion and argument through nonviolent forms, to channel intractable conflicts into intellectual, political, and legal processes of resolution, or to express nonacceptance of the despicable acts of evil regimes, it may be morally justifiable. War to end war has been a miserable failure; violence to end violence is no less likely to fail. Nonetheless, the requirements for an act of violence to be morally justifiable may not be impossible to meet either logically or empirically.

DESTRUCTION OF THE STATE

If we decide, finally, at the moral level that efforts to transform an existing state through legal means, civil disobedience, political strikes, or the kind of violence that may be politically or morally justifiable to gain a hearing or express opposition to torturers and tyrants are all futile or impossible, a moral decision may be made that the very existence of a given state is unacceptable.[30] Can violence to destroy a state and defend a new one being brought into existence then be morally justifiable? One will need to take account of the possibilities of uncontrolled violence and vicious repression as the system defends its existence and its attackers increase their stake in success. After every breakdown of nonviolent measures to bring about the changes sought, one should continually assess the chances for new nonviolent measures to succeed. The inability of destruction to provide, of itself, any better alternative system should never be forgotten. Nevertheless, in some circumstances, violent action may result in less violence than otherwise and may be justified.

If one believes that it may be morally justifiable to punish criminals, the same sorts of arguments would provide moral justification of the "punishment" on moral grounds of tyrants and torturers where existing law and political power allow them otherwise to go unpunished. Even though there may be, in a given situation, no realistic expectation of vindication within a given political system, the victims or intended victims or defenders of victims of torture or political violence carried out by tyrants may be morally justified in trying to ensure that those who commit evil deeds cannot do so without cost to themselves. Violence to punish torturers and tyrants may be more justifiable than violence to uphold unjust regimes. And where no other way exists to punish the violent and immoral use of power, violence to do so may be justified if punishment ever is (though one may well doubt that punishment can ever be justified).

Of course, the danger exists that those judging whether a given case of torture or tyranny deserves punishment are making a mistaken judgment, but we must allow for the possibility that such judgments are correct. We should not make the faulty assumption that those with political power are always more nearly right than those without it.

Additionally, although these should never be the only choices, where the inescapable choice is between supporting either violently evil regimes or those who use violence against them, we will be responsible either way for excusing violence. Whether we choose the less wrongful use of it will be a necessary aspect of determining whether the act of violence we excuse is morally justifiable. Narrow descriptions of the acts themselves, stripped of their contexts, the intentions with which they are performed, and their place in the progression or diversion of social movements, cannot provide a basis for adequate moral judgment. Whether the violence is used to maintain repression and exploitation or to bring about a respect for human rights will make a difference.

What is apparent from the history of revolution and violent action outside the political system is that the levels of the violence, suffering, destruction, and tyranny that occur as a delayed consequence of the acts in question have seldom been adequately anticipated. Moreover, arguments are usually hard to sustain that alternative, more peaceful means of effecting the approved changes were not available. There are many means of exerting pressure, forcing changes, and coercing even highly tyrannical regimes into transforming themselves without ending a state's existence.

Sartre's assertion that "no gentleness can efface the marks of violence; only violence itself can destroy them" ignores the fact that the process is never the neatly discontinuous one in which A commits violence upon B, and B "effaces" it by returning the violence upon A.[31] What actually happens is more nearly that A commits violence upon B, B commits violence upon C (the heir, representative, symbol, etc., of A), D commits violence upon E (the heir, representative, symbol, etc., of B), and so on in a progressively widening spiral. As existing governments increase their knowledge of the degrees of repression that may contain opposition without provoking full-scale rebellion and as the weapons of violence increase in destructiveness and the forms of violence become ever more sophisticated and insidious, resorting to violence becomes increasingly dangerous. Occasionally morality may recommend the destruction of a state. But we can reject any number of aspects of the states we are in— and no morally responsible person can fail to do so under most present conditions—without acting to destroy the state itself.

CAN TERRORISM BE JUSTIFIED?

Do the arguments I have considered concerning violence apply also to terrorism? As we have seen in this book, terrorism is sometimes defined as "the systematic use of murder, injury, and destruction" to create terror and despair through "indiscriminate" attacks in which "no distinction" is made that might exempt the innocent from being targets of such attacks.[32] Terrorists are sometimes said to "sacrifice all moral and humanitarian considerations for the sake of some political end."[33] As we have also seen here, if terrorism is defined this way, we may be unable even to raise the question of whether it could be justifiable. As with violence, however, the question should be open, not shut by definition, as several of the discussions in this book illustrate. Any adequate definition of terrorism must be able to include terrorism carried out by a government, as well as by its opponents. If, as some report, terrorist acts "are often viewed in many Third World countries as noble acts of 'freedom fighters,'" we should be able to examine the reasons without having precluded them by definitional fiat.[34]

Robert Young, in an article on terrorism, agrees with most definitions that terrorism is "intimidatory in intent" but does not agree that terrorist attacks need be "indiscriminate."[35] The targets of terrorism may be the armed forces, the police, and those with political power responsible for repression. Although surprise is "central to the potency of terrorism," this is not inconsistent with warnings to minimize harm to the innocent.[36] In Young's view, terrorism should be a tactic of last resort only where other means of political action are unavailable. However, as part of an ideological "program of revolutionary struggle," it may be justified, he believes, as certain wars can be. Its casualties and violence are very limited compared to war. A program that includes terrorist acts may in his view be the only realistic means to counter state-inspired terrorism, and, if its cause is just and success likely, terrorism may thus be justified. In one of the most comprehensive discussions, Grant Wardlaw defines political terrorism as "the systematic threat of violence to secure political goals."[37] The purposes may be very varied: The primary effect may be to create fear, but the objectives may be to gain concessions, achieve publicity for a cause, provoke repression that will increase sympathy for the cause, build morale in a movement, or increase obedience to it. A single incident may aim at or achieve several such objectives simultaneously.[38]

Amar Ouzegane, a leader of the Algerian FLN movement that struggled to achieve Algerian independence against the French, wrote of the functions of terrorism that "urban terrorism, our liberating terrorism, functioned as a safety valve. It permitted patriots ulcerated by the unequal struggle, revolted by French injustice...to liberate themselves from an unconscious psychological complex, to keep cool heads, to respect revolutionary discipline."[39]

Interestingly, those who defend terrorism often employ arguments familiar from "just war" discussions. John Dugard writes that "the Third World argument is based largely on a Western philosophical tradition: that of the 'just war.'"[40] He points out that many states, "including the major Western powers, have on occasion engaged in acts of terror against civilian populations which completely overshadow the acts of terror committed by national liberation movements."[41] While prohibitions against state terrorism remain unenforced, "it is asking too much," he states, "of Third World countries to collaborate in the suppression of the most effective means to counter terror available to national liberation movements."[42]

We might conclude that if the massive violence of war can be justified, which is dubious, terrorist acts can also be, if they have certain characteristics. However, if terrorism includes, not by definition but in fact, the unnecessary killing of the innocent, it is at least not more justified than war in doing so, though the scale may be smaller. In addition, if comparable good results can be accomplished with far less killing, an alternative to war that would achieve these results through acts intrinsically no worse than those that occur in war would be more justifiable.

It is almost always possible to show that, as limited terrorism is better than war, less violent alternatives to terrorism are better than terrorism, and nonviolent pressures are better than violent ones. We might agree that the causing of war, whether through aggression, violent repression, the extermination or expulsion of unwanted populations, or the deprivation of the means to maintain life is the ultimate crime of violence. If war to prevent the success of those who cause war can be justified, lesser uses of terror and violence can also sometimes be justified. However, the more tyrants and torturers depend on the support of those around them, the better may be the chances of eroding that support through nonviolent pressure. The opponents of violence should not have to sacrifice their lives, but those who use violence must also be prepared to risk theirs.[43] To jeopardize one's life in nonviolent opposition—if the risk is no greater and the chance of success and the rightness of the cause are only no less—is surely more justifiable.

EIGHT

MORAL INQUIRY, ACTION, AND CARE

What can discussions such as those in this book indicate about the ways in which we ought to conduct moral inquiry? If we decide that the issues should be handled in accord with the moral requirements of political and legal relations among persons, we can turn to the moral theories developed for such relations. Discussions of violence show, I believe, that an adequate treatment of the relevant problems requires consideration of both their deontological and consequentialist aspects and more.

We must be able to assess the rightness or wrongness of an act that is an instance of a moral rule such as "resist violent oppression," even if it has no further good or bad consequences. We should be able to consider whether such an act is justifiable when its effects are unknowable. However, we must also be able to evaluate many acts of violence on the basis of the good or bad consequences they bring about. And here the very great importance of reliable empirical estimates and findings is clear. We need to know far more than we seem to about the actual results of violence and its alternatives and to be able to realistically compare the expectable outcomes of nonviolent versus violent efforts. Such empirical information is certainly insufficient for even our consequentialist moral judgments since we also need to have adequate views on why we should judge various consequences to be good or bad and on how good or bad to consider them. Moreover, it is certainly of no help in determining the deontological justifiability of acts of violence. However, we might more easily agree on the overall conclusions of our deliberations if we could agree on the empirical components.

On the other hand, discussions such as these may suggest that we can make considerable progress in understanding what we think we ought to believe concerning violence and terrorism without being able to settle the disputes between the standard ethical or metaethical theories available, such as Kantian morality or utilitarianism, though we might be able to reject emotivism as unable to account for the ways in which the discussions make sense.[1] We should recognize how attention to such actual problems might inform and improve our moral theories and our views of how to conduct moral inquiry.

I have in previous work spelled out arguments for a division of moral labor. They assert that different moral theories may be more suitable than their alternatives for different moral contexts.[2] Also, the ways the conflicting claims of individual interest and collective good should be resolved should be different in different domains; for instance, the moral considerations suitable for an economic context may be unsuitable for a family one. I argue that teleological or consequentialist forms of justification are particularly appropriate for political decisions and for actions designed to uphold or change political institutions. The discussion of political violence in this book reflects that position, but consequentialist considerations certainly do not exhaust the moral considerations relevant for evaluating political violence. Deontological forms of justification are particularly appropriate for some violent actions, such as those that are or should be matters of law, as violence usually is.

More recently I have argued for the ethics of care as suitable for the widest web of relations connecting all human beings and potentially bringing them together, as care is suitable for the most intense and intimate relations connecting human beings in small groups such as families or groups of friends.[3] Considerations of care should always be taken into account in situating the political and legal in a wider context, as I discuss in the last section of this chapter. Our deepest considerations should be ones that ask what appropriate caring for all human beings requires.

Experience and Moral Inquiry

In previous work I have developed a method of experimental moral inquiry.[4] It ought to enable us to make progress in deciding what types of moral theory to appeal to in various contexts and progressively to improve our moral theories. For the foreseeable future we can expect to make more progress in specialized moral explorations than in what can remain a distant objective: the development of one true, unified field theory for everything anyone should do in any domain. We should try to work out and achieve coherence and confirmation for the very general moral assumptions, the intermediate-level principles and generalizations, and the multiplicity of particular moral judgments relevant to given and often special domains.

While moral inquiry is not a form of empirical inquiry (since a distinction between description and prescription should be preserved, and ethics is above all prescriptive), it can nevertheless proceed by a process analogous to scientific inquiry. We can develop moral theories or hypotheses and subject them to the "tests" of moral experience. Moral experience allows us to arrive at moral judgments about particular actions and attitudes and, under certain circumstances, to view these judgments as tests of our moral theories. The process can be analogous to that by which particular observations refute or support scientific theories. Philosophical analysis and discussion are needed for the achievement of greater coherence and the clarification of the claims one makes. But moral theories, like scientific theories, ought to be accepted or rejected on the basis of experience. Coherence alone is inadequate. In science, the relevant experience is that of observation; in ethics it is that of action, decision, and active approval or disapproval. However, action is as much a part of experience as perception.

A context in which persons subjected to centuries of oppression finally act to resist that oppression is a fertile one in which to consider the plausibility of this argument. People who have been taught (and who have come to accept) that they ought to obey existing political authority are at a given time committed to a set of moral prescriptions about how they ought not to defy that authority. If they then decide that they ought to engage in a given violent challenge of that authority, they may decide this in terms of a moral judgment about a particular case, arrived at independently of the moral principles to which they previously believed they were committed. If, after engaging in or observing the violent challenge, they continue to believe that the challenge was morally justifiable, this will require them to revise the moral theories they may previously have accepted, according to which it was not justifiable.

Quite possibly the judgment "this act of defiance was justifiable" could be reached only when embedded in a developed alternative moral view rather than in pure isolation. However, this claim would not present more difficulty for moral inquiry than does the claim about scientific inquiry that we can recognize the truth of particular observation statements that conflict with a given theory only when these statements make sense in terms of a rival theory.

We should not conclude from this latter claim that scientific inquiry is a purely rational enterprise in which experience is superfluous. Comparably, we should recognize that moral inquiry requires the component of moral experience. It cannot be adequately developed as a purely rational investigation. Moral theories should be thought of as analogous not to mathematics but to empirically interpreted scientific theories. Moral theories, like scientific theories, should enable us to confront actual, not merely imagined or hypothetical, experience.

What is moral experience? It is, in my view, the experience of voluntarily accepting or rejecting the various moral recommendations we encounter, the experience of willingly approving or disapproving the actions of others and the social arrangements in which we live, and above all the experience of acting and living with these actions and their outcomes and of discussing the relevant moral aspects with others. Such experience is the most fruitful source of independently determined moral judgments with which to test our moral theories.[5]

A wide range or a certain depth of such experience is more promising as a test of our theories than is further theorizing. We should listen to those engaged in and affected by various acts to hear what they intend and feel and think. We should enlarge our experience beyond the academic settings of moral theory and professional discussion. What we do not experience ourselves, we should try more often to experience indirectly through literary accounts, reportage, and especially the statements of participants.

The context in which persons engage in, refrain from, or respond to acts of violence can indicate how the process I have discussed can take place. In a context in which violent repression or protest seems morally acceptable to many persons, a commitment to nonviolence requires the development of an alternative position in a way comparable to how one might develop a position of defiance of accepted authority. In all such cases, people can bring to their experience the moral theories available to them, but they may on occasion have grounds to accept them or their parts on the basis of the independent judgments they may reach in their particular circumstances.

Since applied ethics deals with the actual contexts in which one must make specific moral decisions, it can offer much helpful support to the process of moral inquiry. But in doing so it is not then applied ethics but an integral part of the process of moral inquiry. Once an adequate theory for a given domain has been developed and satisfactorily tested in that domain, it might be suitable to apply it to further problems. In most of the special regions of moral concern that have received the attention of the public and of philosophers in recent years, the special moral theories needed for the adequate treatment of the moral problems in them are still highly underdeveloped. It is thus still premature to think we are applying an adequate moral theory to particular problems in them. Nonetheless, philosophers and others can make greater progress toward the development of such adequate theories by paying attention to the particular problems and circumstances in, say, medical practice, business decisions, political protest and terrorism than we can by retreating to the antiseptic atmosphere of pure rationality or pure moral theory.

In the progress of scientific inquiry there is no substitute for observation. In some comparable way, there is in the conduct and possible progress of moral inquiry no substitute for the experience of making moral choices and acting on them as human beings sincerely trying to be morally conscientious and responsible. Attention to many actual moral problems and to the ways in which conscientious persons try to deal with them can illustrate this conclusion.

THE MORAL IMPORT OF ACTION

Let us consider further how to interpret and evaluate actions. What is the import of intentional action for our moral views and morality? One type of moral import has to do with justifiability as judged not only by the agent but also by the community of moral inquirers or the relevant group engaged in a process of evaluation. This may include the agents themselves—typically at a later time—looking at their action from a point of view external to themselves as agents. Here the action may be evaluated on whatever moral grounds the moral inquirers and participants in discussion bring to their inquiry, whether these are deontological principles, consequentialist calculations, considerations of care, and so forth. Evaluating the moral import of actions, as I have argued elsewhere, should not be limited to just those actions done for the sake of purposes their agents regard as good.[6] Actions done for no reason or because an agent failed to decide to change a course of action already undertaken or done for purposes that the agent did not value may merit moral condemnation or praise. Additionally, actions done inadvertently may have this kind of moral import. All of this can be thought of as the external moral import of actions.

Here I am concerned with what one might think of as the internal moral import of action, that is, its moral import to the agents as both agents and sincere moral inquirers. I argue that certain actions can constitute our way of testing whether we judge our moral theories to be justifiable. In testing our moral theories through action, we would arrive at various principles that resemble those of familiar moral theories, but these would not be arrived at entirely through rational deduction and empirical reasoning, as they would, for instance, for Alan Gewirth.[7] The process would involve whatever attitudes arise through lived experience and discourse with others, acted on and reflected on, and the principles would be interpreted for actual historical situations and in actual moral experience and would be thus tested through these. The results of our moral inquiry would thus be far stronger and more persuasive than those of purely rational deliberation supplemented by general empirical knowledge.

To Alan Gewirth, rationality requires us to accord to everyone the rights to freedom and well-being needed to be an agent, rights that in the process of acting we inherently claim for ourselves. Gewirth's argument is about the *generic* features of action, reasoned about, and it yields his supreme moral principle, "act in accord with the generic rights of your recipients as well as of yourself."[8] His arguments about any particular action we should or should not take will then be derived from the moral principle, together with the appropriate reasoning and empirical knowledge. My approach to moral inquiry relies less on reason and more on what can be called *moral experience*. It requires us to evaluate our *particular* actions through their normative import for us as we act and not just to reason about their generic features. Moreover, it requires us to subject any moral principles and rules based on them to the tests of further moral experience.

The judgments we arrive at concerning particular actions that test our theories need not be based primarily on reason. They may appropriately be based on feelings of empathy or sympathy, as well as reason;

we can be Humeans, as well as Kantians, or advocates of the ethics of care. Alternatively such particular judgments may be based on anger at what we feel to be unfair, which positions, like all others, we should seek to have consistent with our moral principles and other judgments. This may require revisions of particular judgments, moral principles, or the guidelines in between.

Let me outline how we are to test our moral theories. Moral theories include general moral principles, more specific or intermediate-level moral recommendations, an indication of how they are to be applied in particular cases, and a vast and indefinite array of particular moral recommendations and judgments consistent with the principles and general recommendations.

We can begin with any set we take to be plausible; perhaps they have been taught to us by parents, teachers, or public figures we have admired or suggested to us by books we have read. If they are moral theories they should offer justifiable guidelines for everyone, including ourselves, to act on. Moral principles will always need interpretations of their meaning and how they are to be applied to particular circumstances, which are often very different depending on historical developments. No moral theory could be complete, but it should offer a general idea of what it would recommend in a wide variety of cases.

For instance, our theory would probably include the moral principle to be truthful. We would interpret this as a recommendation to be honest rather than deceptive and to avoid lying except in cases in which some other general moral principle such as that we ought to avoid contributing to the death of innocent persons might be given priority. Then, if we are asked by an investigating committee that we deem to be legitimate whether we witnessed a certain event, we should normally tell the truth even at some inconvenience to ourselves. Of course, further details could make this a hard case rather than an easy one; here I am outlining an easy case of our moral theories recommending action in a way we take to be justifiable. Then, let us suppose we act as our theory recommends, and despite the inconvenience we continue to believe, on reflection and with discussion with others, that we did what we ought to have done. We might conclude that, in this case, the principle that recommends truthfulness could meet the requirements of discourse ethics[9] or of reflective equilibrium.[10] We might think it entirely consistent with the moral reasoning recommended by Alan Gewirth. If we actually act on it, however, deliberately choosing this act over its alternatives and expressing through and with our action the moral stance of judging the action to be right, the principle would have the added strength of having stood up to the test of being acted on by us in actual circumstances and of having the action taken in accord with it judged on reflection by us as being the right action if we continue to judge that we acted rightly. Thus the moral principle interpreted for this kind of case would have been put to the test of experience and found satisfactory.

What I am suggesting is that the *practice* of moral inquiry is different— and better—when it includes action, as well as discourse and reasoning, than when it does not. Furthermore, action should be part of the inquiry, not just evaluated by the results of a process of inquiry composed only of reasoning or discourse.

Here one might object that the element of action I have added to the discourse or reasoning that might occur concerning the action does not really add anything since the action would be judged justifiable by us just because it accorded with the principle to which reasoning had led us; if it did not do so, we would not judge it justifiable.[11] Hence, no test would have occurred. But it is at the heart of my argument that this objection is mistaken. It rests on an assumption that the only way we can judge our actions to be justifiable or unjustifiable is by referring them to the moral principles we either held prior to the action we took or hold independently of our actions, and this misrepresents our actual experience of trying conscientiously to figure out how we ought to act.

Our actual experience shows that we can sometimes act in a way not in accord with what we thought our moral principles recommended, expressing in such an action a moral position in favor of that action. We can then come on reflection and on the basis of discussion with others to continue to judge that what we did was justifiable rather than unjustifiable. Of course, this will require a revision of the moral theory we thought we held—adherence either to a moral principle or interpretation of it different from before or to a different ordering of the principles. But this is just how moral inquiry ought to proceed.

We should not suppose that whenever we do not act in accord with our moral principles we suffer from weakness of will. And we should not suppose that every judgment (after the fact that the action we took was justifiable even though contrary to our previously held positions) is the result of self-serving rationalization rather than of appropriate moral reevaluation. Sometimes we revise and improve our moral theories by acting in ways that conflict with what our previously held theory recommended (thereby making the particular moral judgment incorporated in the action) and then concluding on reflection that what we did was indeed right. When this process is deliberately engaged in with the intention of putting our moral theories to the test of experience, we can be engaged in moral inquiry that leads to finding moral theories valid. Additionally, when the action we take is undertaken as part of such a process, it has the clear normative import of either supporting or challenging any given moral position. When we tell the truth in accordance with a moral theory that recommends we do so in cases like the one we are in, we attach value to that action and to the principle recommending it. And when we consciously, voluntarily, and deliberately act in a way contrary to what a moral principle recommends, we attach value to a particular judgment that challenges that principle. We can then seek to incorporate this judgment into a different theory in which an opposing moral principle, interpretation, or ordering of the moral considerations recommends that we do what accords with our judgment. Here the internal normative import of action is clear.

Another objection that might be made is that the process I am outlining is merely an account of the way that our thinking actually proceeds and that I have offered only an empirical description of it rather than dealing with what moral theory genuinely is justifiable and how we ought to seek it.[12] However, this objection misrepresents my argument, which is not that my account is of how we conduct moral inquiry for ourselves or how we in fact come to our moral beliefs, however mistaken they may be. I am offering an account of how human beings *ought* to conduct moral inquiry. I certainly aim to offer normative recommendations for conducting moral inquiry, the way Gewirth recommends how we ought to reason to our moral principles and then to their implications. The arguments for any process of moral inquiry can be that it better reflects what human beings seek in looking for guidance in their efforts to decide what to do and that it produces better moral theory than its alternatives. I believe the method of moral inquiry I recommend can do this, and it has the significant advantage of according with the implications of a wealth of feminist criticism of traditional approaches to moral theory.[13]

I have long argued that the kind of moral theory we should seek is theory that can guide us in the actual, imperfect world in which we must act, not theory fit only for an ideal world of perfect justice or goodness. I believe that for the time being we should work with different likely theories for different contexts rather than seeking one fully unified theory that will serve for all contexts, though the latter should remain a distant goal while we develop more pluralistic approaches.

We live and act and make moral evaluations in given historical contexts, as well as in different contexts such as those of law, war, the family, and so on. The way we become aware of many of the issues we need moral theory to address depends on our historical and other situations. For example, equality, the equal worth of persons, and equality of opportunity all can be and have been discussed in the abstract, but until gender equality became a matter of public debate, almost no philosophers or others even raised the question of whether gender was a legitimate basis on which to exclude people from a wide range of occupations, as was the practice. Again, until the environmental movement of the 1970s brought concerns for the environment to the attention of many people, it did not occur to most philosophers that our moral theories should include guidance on our responsibilities with respect to pollution, global warming, or endangered species. What is more, contemporary genetic, medical, and computer technology are raising many new issues of great moral significance. Whether any previous moral theory is adequate for them is unclear.

A moral theory developed without regard to historical or other contexts can be a useful beginning by providing something like the basic concepts and principles to be tried out. However, we will not have a moral theory able to do what we look to it to do—guide our actions—until it is interpreted for historical and other contexts and tested in actual action.

Moreover, I have long argued that we should think in terms of validity rather than truth when dealing with moral claims. Moral theories should not be thought to be composed of judgments that describe or correspond to some reality "out there," whether in nature or some realm of Platonic forms. We make moral theories valid in a way somewhat—but only somewhat—analogous to the way we make the laws of a legal system valid. Unlike legal validity, moral validity is not bound to any given culture, social structure, or institution. The "we" who can make moral theories valid are all human beings sincerely engaged in moral inquiry, and the validity is what we can eventually agree on if we engage long and appropriately enough in moral inquiry. Moral theories can be valid when chosen for good enough reasons and on the basis of sufficient moral experience.[14]

How much objectivity can this kind of moral validity offer? At the end of her article on acting and choosing, Hilary Bok considers the issue of objectivity in ethics: "We are not primarily trying to describe and explain our experience, but to determine what we should do. One cannot show that moral claims are not objective by showing that they do not meet the criteria of objectivity appropriate to scientific claims....As ethicists, we try to understand what we should do, and why we should do it. If moral objectivity requires more than this, it requires more than we need."[15] I share this view.

Moral experience is not the empirical experience of sense perception to which so many philosophers have reduced "experience." Moral experience is the human experience of conscientiously trying to act as we think we ought or of being aware that we fail to do so. Moral experience is the experience of trying to live what we think are good lives and trying to evaluate our own and others' choices of how to act and to live. Moral experience includes acting, as well as observing and evaluating.

Most of us have had the experience that our choices on occasion have diverged from what we thought we would decide about a moral issue, and the divergence has been not because we failed to do what we thought we should but because, in the actual context in which we had to decide, we came to see the moral issues differently or to think or feel differently about what we ought to do. It cannot plausibly be said, then, that we can never decide what we ought to do independently of the theories we think ourselves committed to since many of us have had just this experience of doing so and of then having to revise our moral views accordingly. Experiences such as these, conscientiously engaged in, reflected on, and discussed with others, can test our moral theories, as can the cases in which we find the recommendations of our theories satisfactory when we act on them.

An action performed in the context of putting our moral theories to the test contains within itself a choice either in favor of or challenging the moral imperative that recommends that action or in favor of or challenging the moral judgment that the action we perform is the right one. The choice may be based on deontological grounds or consequentialist ones, or it may express our sense of the kind of person we choose to be or of our commitment to a human relation we value. Or we may be unclear on how best to justify it, but we judge it in itself in a way that is independent of what we think our moral theory would recommend—to be the action we ought to do. Perhaps we only later discover the grounds on which we can best consider it what we ought to have done. We should then seek as coherent a theory as possible consistent with our judgments about particular actions, our own and those of others, and about persons and their characters and relationships. Thus do we engage in moral inquiry and improve our moral theories.

An Illustration

Let me illustrate my argument with an examination of a controversial moral problem: the case of doctor-assisted suicide. It is a moral issue that involves what the law should permit or forbid and what people should consent to or resist.

Suppose someone has come to agree with Gewirth, whether or not on the basis of his reasoning, that everyone has rights to freedom and well-being. When trying to interpret this principle in the case of doctor-assisted suicide, that person may think that respecting the freedom of terminally ill patients entails respecting their own decisions on whether suicide would be more in accordance with their values than the continued pain and what they take to be the indignities of a slower death and that it requires that such patients have a legal right to assistance from a willing doctor, under appropriate safeguards, in carrying out this decision. However, those who agree with Gewirth might think instead that respecting people's rights to well-being entails restrictions on doctors that do not permit them in such cases to assist in causing death but only to alleviate pain.

A purely rational moral theory such as Gewirth's will provide resources for debate about these various interpretations. Writings such as "Assisted Suicide: The Philosopher's Brief,"[16] which concerns the Supreme Court's decisions in *State of Washington et al. v. Glucksberg et al.* and *Vacca et al. v. Quill et al.*, and the decisions themselves can help clarify what respecting persons' rights to freedom and well-being implies for this kind of case. Empirical data on the actual conditions of dying patients, the capacities and limitations of drugs in reducing pain, the effects of permitting doctor-assisted suicide, the history of abuses of power on the part of the medical profession, and so forth can be brought into the argument and their relevance considered. However, the moral theory will be untested as long as it remains in the domain only of rational debate.

If, however, those who are sincerely engaged in moral inquiry act deliberately in this context of doctor-assisted suicide, reflect on their actions, and decide on the evaluations to accord their actions, whether seeing them as justifiable or as actions they regret, the theory consistent with these judgments can attain a standing as tested in practice that it cannot have when it is a merely rational deliberation. Those who do not have direct experience of doctor-assisted suicide (e.g., because they are not doctors or have not had dying family members who requested help in dying, and so forth) can come close to the direct experience of others through conversation, through reading their accounts, and especially through literary and other treatments that enable them to have vicarious experience of it. What is important is to be an agent or to identify with an agent in the context for which the moral inquiry is conducted.

Philosophers may tend to think that human beings judge an action justifiable only in light of the theory or beliefs they hold prior to acting or when deciding to act, but this misrepresents the actual experience that many of us have.[17] It can often be the action itself that contains the internal normative import we are giving it in acting. To this extent, Gewirth's account of the inherent normativity of action is very valuable and illuminating. I believe this normativity should not be extended to all action, and much action with normative import in my sense is not a test of moral theory but merely routinely in accord with what our moral theories permit or require. Nonetheless, some actions can be the tests I describe, and their internal moral import is crucial for moral inquiry.

We can and do at least sometimes choose a particular action, in all its particularity and complexity, not as an instance of a type or an instantiation of a principle or general judgment but as what we in the immediate context think we ought to do, perhaps without quite being able to articulate the reason. The action may clash with, rather than conform to, the moral positions we thought we held. And if we do not then interpret this as a failure on our part to live up to our principles and beliefs and if we on the contrary think on reflection that the action was justifiable, then we will need to adjust our moral positions and our moral theory accordingly, perhaps by reversing our positions completely or subscribing to a quite different moral theory, or perhaps by making a minor adjustment or reinterpretation but keeping the basic principles and framework intact.

A person may thus think she is opposed to doctor-assisted suicide on the grounds, among others, that it is always wrong for doctors intentionally to cause death. However, if her dying parent asks for assistance in dying, if she is convinced that the parent's decision is a stable one and has been arrived at freely, and if the parent's doctor is willing to provide such assistance only if the daughter agrees, she may rethink her opposition. Still relatively undecided, she may nevertheless give her consent, and in the act of doing so she takes a position in favor of permitting doctor-assisted suicide. If on further reflection she does not regret her action, she will have to modify her earlier opposition rather than merely imagine she should make an exception of this case unless there are strong reasons that this case is different from others she knows about; then those reasons would apply to cases like her own if they arise. In working out a view on the permissibility of doctor-assisted suicide under safeguarding conditions, she will develop a view that has met at least this one test of being put into practice, of being acted on, and her view will be an improvement over one based merely on reasoning and the empirical facts that might influence some of the reasoning.

Because many persons who are sincerely engaged in moral inquiry not only reason, argue, and reflect but also subject moral theories to the tests of action, the normative import of action makes possible the progressive improvement of our moral theories. Not all action has this potential; however, actions that we deliberately take as tests of our moral theories (though we may do this after the fact rather than beforehand) or those that we happen to perform even almost inadvertently but later interpret as tests can give us moral theories that are more than merely coherent and rational. They are theories with the greatly added strength of being supported by moral experience.

If we try to bring the moral evaluation of terrorism into this picture of theorizing and testing through experience, there are problems, of course. Most of us will not and should not be directly involved in terrorism either as victims or as perpetrators. But we are all involved in current efforts to counter the feared violence (e.g., in supporting or opposing the "war on terror" and components of it such as military intervention). In addition, we should make far greater efforts than are usual to experience acts of violence and their precursor conditions vicariously through responsible reportage, writings on others' experiences, and literary, dramatic, and artistic depictions.[18] Such experience should be that of not only victims but also participants in violence. We should try to understand what those who support and carry out terrorist acts think and feel, as well as what it is like to be harmed by violence. We need to understand the violence of those who enforce their rule as well as of those seeking political change.

After 9/11 it was easy for Americans to identify with the victims and imagine what it must have felt like to be trapped in a burning office tower or to have lost a person one loved in that horrible event. It was easy to feel outrage and hatred for those who caused this terror. A balance, however, needs to be sought in exploring the experience that contributes to moral assessments of terrorism. We need to imagine how people around the world experience U.S. and European imperialism and privilege and how their grievances can mount and eventually lead to eagerness to promote what they see as necessary though violent resistance. We ought to make the effort to experience vicariously the ways in which people are sometimes drawn to violence, including suicide attacks. We need to understand the hatred and desire for revenge that affects those who believe they are the victims of our own routine behavior, as well as of our more dramatic actions. Louise Richardson explains that, to contain the threat of terrorism effectively, one needs to understand disaffected individuals, enabling communities, and legitimizing ideologies.[19] To evaluate violence, one needs understanding from multiple points of view.

When the United States seeks through military intervention and political coercion to bring freedom and democracy to people deprived of them and to further its own interests, it may well create more opponents than it can eliminate, as experience makes apparent. When its policies and corporations cause economic pain and dislocation on a massive scale, as they often do, it may create the conditions that foster violent resistance, and this resistance may not be vulnerable to the military destruction the United States is prepared to deliver. Quite the contrary, as we should have learned.

As we engage in moral inquiry and subject our moral theories to the trials of experience, we can improve them. And as we consider which theories to employ in these inquiries, we should, I propose, expand the possibilities beyond the traditional and dominant ones to the more recently developed ethics of care, even in a context such as that of political violence.

THE ETHICS OF CARE

The ethics of care is only a few decades old. Of course, it has precursors (e.g., in the work of Aristotle and Hume), but its sources and outlines are very different from more established theories. It is by now a distinct moral theory or normative approach. Although the personal relations of family and friendship can most clearly exemplify the values and practices of care, the ethics of care is highly relevant to global and political issues as well. That the ethics of care is a promising alternative to more familiar moral theories becomes evident when one considers its central ideas, characteristics, and their potential importance.

The ethics of care has developed out of feminist thinking and can be a morality with universal appeal. It rests not on divisive religious traditions but on the experience every person has had of being cared for and on the experience many persons have had and are having of caring for others. No child would survive without extensive care, and most persons need additional care for some periods of their lives. The ethics of care examines the values implicit even in existing care, unjustly structured as it usually is, and provides guidelines for improving care and extending its values. It focuses on the cluster of values involved in fostering caring relations, values such as trust, empathy, mutual consideration, and solidarity. It appreciates the importance of the emotions in understanding what morality requires and the importance of cultivating caring emotions, not only of carrying out what reason dictates. Where other moral theories such as Kantian morality and utilitarianism demand impartiality above all, the ethics of care understands the moral import of our ties to our families and groups. It evaluates these ties, thereby differing from virtue ethics in focusing on caring relations rather than on the virtues of individuals. How more traditionally established values such as justice, equality, and individual rights should be meshed with the values of caring relations is being worked out.

The idea that care is only for children or those who are ill or have a disability and is thus not relevant to political and social life reveals the extent of the libertarian myth that pervades so much of Anglo-American thought and theory: the myth of self-sufficiency. Those who imagine themselves self-sufficient have already benefited from enormous amounts of unacknowledged care when they were still dependent in ways that even they must recognize. They are still dependent on webs of social relations that enable them to earn their income, invest their money, and hold on to their property. Without these webs, their property would be looted, their money worthless, and their jobs nonexistent. Everyone needs the care and concern for others that foster their willingness to participate in such webs and respect others' rights. They benefit from the valuing of care that supports public concern for health care and education and would support concern for child care for all if attended to. The values of care can guide the improving of governmental policies, as well as actual respect for rights.

As a moral theory or new approach toward morality, the ethics of care differs markedly from other moral theories. It is not merely a concern that can be added on to or included within the most influential moral theories, as some of their advocates suggest. As a fully normative theory it has developed far beyond its earliest formulations in the work of Sara Ruddick, Carol Gilligan, and Nel Noddings. It rests on feminists' distinctive appreciation of the importance of care and caring labor, and it sees its values as worthy of extension far beyond the personal.

The ethics of care recognizes that much of the caring labor that actually takes place does so in oppressive conditions, where it exploits women and ill-paid minority workers. It includes concern for transforming the social and political structures within which practices of care take place so that such oppression can be overcome. It develops recommendations on how the values of care should be reflected in political institutions and relations between cultures. In this it has the advantage of being based on truly universal experience, the experience every person has had and could not have survived without, the experience of having been cared for as a child.

When we examine what exactly we mean by "care," we can see that for the ethics of care, "care" is both various practices that take place and various values by which to evaluate these practices and envision improvements in them. As human beings we have developed both practices of justice and theories of justice with which to evaluate the practices. Comparably, we need ethics of care to evaluate caring practices.

Practices of care, whether care of children or those who are dependent or have unusual needs, as well as practices of care in a global context, involve work. Such work should be undertaken with appropriate motives and meet suitable standards. Practices thus incorporate values but also need to be evaluated and improved.

In the ethics of care, although it is virtuous to be caring, caring persons should do more than have the right motive or disposition. They should adeptly engage in activities of care and in the cultivation of caring relations. Caring relations are characterized by responsiveness to need, sensitivity, empathy, and trust. To the ethics of care, persons are relational as well as capable of autonomy.

The ethics of care includes examination of how to avoid being paternalistic (or maternalistic) in providing care. Good care is neither domineering nor more coercive than necessary to safeguard or educate the recipient. It promotes the appropriate relational autonomy of the recipient. Caring practices are often best evaluated from the point of view of those cared for. Analogies between care as perceived by those cared for in family contexts on the one hand and the insights of weak states receiving aid and the self-delusions of imperialistic powers on the other hand are often illuminating.

A contrast has often been drawn between care and justice. In comparison to men's activities in public life, historically care, women, and the household have been devalued and believed irrelevant to morality. There are significant differences between Kantian moral theory and utilitarianism, but both are theories of justice thought suitable for public life because they emphasize impartiality, rationality, universal principles, equality, and rights. Neither one is adequate as a moral theory for the contexts of family and friendship. Feminist philosophers developing the ethics of care have explored questions of how care and justice might be interwoven into a satisfactory, comprehensive, moral theory.

As I have suggested, one way of doing this is to conceptualize caring between fellow human beings as the wider network of relations within which we can agree to treat persons as if they were liberal individuals for the limited purposes of legal and political interactions guided by justice. The ethics of care does not imply that the discourse of justice and rights is dispensable, but it does suggest arguments for limiting the reach of law and legalistic thinking. The feminist roots of the ethics of care make the demand for equality fundamental, but the ethics of care reinterprets such equality. It suggests that the model of morality based on impartial justice and liberal individualism is persuasive only for limited legal and political contexts, not for the whole of morality, as has been supposed.

Traditional liberal theory is designed for contractual agreements between "strangers" and is thought to have the advantage that it does not require that persons care about one another. Yet the assumed strangers are not so distant after all since the bounds of the group within which contractual agreement is sought are already assumed. In the world as it is, however, issues about who is included are often the most contentious and, in relations between states, can often lead to conflict.

How should we conceptualize what is meant when we say that "within" caring relations we can agree to relate to one another in ways that are other than caring, such as making contractual agreements with relative strangers? An analogy that may be helpful is that of friends playing a competitive sport. Their relationship of friendship or care must be based on more than self-interest, but in the narrower context of the game they each seek to win and agree to abide by the rules. The rules presume that both persons seek their own advantage. If this perspective were expanded to characterize the whole of their relationship, they would no longer be genuine friends, but it does not preclude areas of competition. Morality is no game, but between persons with weak ties of caring, normative rules can be adopted to deal with political, legal or other types of interactions. Yet without the initial moral stance of caring, the motivation to seek such agreement and to respect each other's interests (as opposed to imposing a solution that promotes their own advantage) would be lacking, as states and groups have routinely done to weaker states and groups when they could.

The ethics of care has deep implications for political and social issues. Consider the question of whether corporate and market ways of conducting a range of activities should be expanded through privatization and commercialization or limited through restrictions on markets. The ethics of care is more promising than the dominant moral theories for dealing with the questions involved since it makes clear how values other than market ones should have priority in areas such as child care, health care, education, and cultural activities. The ethics of care can provide strong arguments for limiting markets and for cultural expression freed from commercial domination. These issues are especially relevant in the context of economic globalization.

One can also connect the ethics of care with the rising interest in civil society and in the limits to what law and rights are thought able to accomplish. Actually respecting the rights we recognize as important presupposes that persons are sufficiently interconnected through caring relations to be concerned about whether others' rights are respected. The ethics of care has the resources to understand community and shared identity and can suggest what a caring society might be like. It also has the resources for dealing with power and violence. It should not be thought to be built on idealized images of family peace and harmony, but it does consider caring ways to deal with violence.

Sara Ruddick has explored what those working to enhance the chances for peace can learn from practices of care such as mothering. Discussing the lessons of maternal practice, she suggests we attend to how "to keep the peace, a peacemaking mother, as best she can, creates ways for children and adults to live together that both appear to be and are fair.... In reinforcing the fragile affections that survive rivalry and inevitable inequality, mothers who are guided by ideals of nonviolence work for the days that their children will come to prefer justice to the temporary pleasures of tyranny and exploitation."[20] This illustrates the argument I make in chapter 2 that the ethics of care would advocate respect for international law based on fairness and justice even though it would go on to envision ways to deal with many issues within and among societies that are better than legalistic ones.

The ethics of care should lead to the transformation of the particular domains within society as, for instance, we ask that legal or health care institutions be more caring. It should also (and especially) bring about the transformation of the interrelation of these domains. For instance, in a caring society, it would not be the case that child care and much health care would be marginalized activities whose participants are left to fend for themselves, while the ever-expanding powers of the state and the economy are marshaled for military prowess and economic dominance of the region or the globe. In a caring society, multiple forms of care, education, and noncommercial cultural expression would move to the center of attention. We could show that markets should not be continually expanding, thereby turning human relations into market relations, and that law and legalistic approaches to handling problems should be limited to an appropriate domain. We could show not only that international law and diplomacy are better routes to peace than domination by military force but also that the development of more caring approaches to building global connectedness should be greatly expanded.

The ethics of care has been developed to understand and guide the closest of human relations, those of family and friendship, and it has been found to have profound implications for the world beyond. I have argued that it is an ethical outlook suitable for the weakest and most distant of human ties, as well as for the strongest relations.

Between the two extremes of very weak and very strong relatedness lie domains of intermediate ties such as those of political interactions, legal orderings, and economic pursuits; for these, more familiar moral theories may better address the relevant issues. However, it is not only for the closest human relations but also for the most distant that the ethics of care has important insights to offer. When violence is not contained by the legal and political bounds that seek to mitigate its multiple damages, we may want to turn to the ethics of care for illumination. Sara Ruddick shows how maternal practice gives rise to ideals of nonviolence and how these ideals could contribute to the politics of peace. Of course, actual mothers are sometimes violent, and some are often violent, but an ideal of nonviolence "governs the practice" of maternal care. Care work—"sheltering, nursing, feeding, kin work, teaching of the very young, tending the frail elderly—is threatened by violence.... Mothering begins in birth and promises life; military thinking justifies organized, deliberate deaths."[21] Peace between peoples, she argues, should not be thought of as aiming "to be left alone in safety," but as achieving "peace as active connectedness."[22] Understanding connectedness and guiding its progress are the focus of the ethics of care.

Of course, the suggestion is not that one can deal with the politically violent in the same ways that one deals with a violent child, as critics who mock the approach of care imply while promoting what they imagine to be their own tough, realistic, hard-line policies. One can, however, be guided by many similar moral considerations: to deter and restrain rather than obliterate and destroy; to restrain with the least amount of necessary force so that reconciliation remains open; and, in preventing violence, to cause no more damage and pain to all concerned than are needed.

It is indeed the case that violence leads to more violence. Rather than trying to "wipe out once and for all the enemies that threaten us," which is impossible, the more successful, as well as more justifiable, approach to violence is to lessen its appeal. Those who answer violence with greater violence engender hatred among those who share the grievances that drive some to turn to political violence and who share the spreading casualties caused by war against them. Those on the sidelines damaged by the greater violence aimed at destroying those they consider evil will increasingly identify with the victims of that increased violence. The objective of the strong should be to oppose violence in ways such that sympathy for those using violence will decrease rather than grow. One might think this would be obvious, but to the macho, the martinet, and the fake tough guys of families and governments, it often is not.

As war and other violence kills children, mutilates young bodies, and causes terror, horror, and extraordinary pain, any morally responsible person should aim to understand how best to reduce it in morally acceptable ways.

NOTES

INTRODUCTION

1. For extended discussion of the ethics of care see Virginia Held, *The Ethics of Care.*

2. See ibid., especially chapters 7–10.

3. See, for example, ibid., chapter 10; John Keane, *Global Civil Society?;* Fiona Robinson, *Globalizing Care: Ethics, Feminist Theory, and International Affairs;* and Anne-Marie Slaughter, *A New World Order.*

4. Sara Ruddick, *Maternal Thinking: Toward a Politics of Peace.*

5. Ibid., xviii–xix.

6. On just war theory see especially Michael Walzer, *Just and Unjust Wars,* and Steven Lee, ed., *Intervention, Terrorism, and Torture: Challenges to Just War Theory in the 21st Century.*

7. See Virginia Held, "Gender Identity and the Ethics of Care in Globalized Society."

8. See, for example, Helena Cobban, *Amnesty after Atrocity: Healing Nations after Genocide and War;* and Margaret Urban Walker, *Moral Repair: Reconstructing Moral Relations after Wrongdoing.*

CHAPTER I

1. Alison Mitchell, "Israel Winning Broad Support from U.S. Right," A1, 13.

2. Kofi Annan, "Kofi Annan's Blunt Words Criticizing Israeli Tactics." Text of Letter, A12.

3. James Bennet, "Israelis Storm a Gaza Camp; 11 Palestinians Are Killed," A10.

4. Sam Dillon, "Reflections on War, Peace, and How to Live Vitally and Act Globally," A28. Benjamin R. Barber offers a response to this way of thinking: "Do we think we can bomb into submission the millions who resent, fear and sometimes detest what they think America means?" "Beyond Jihad vs. McWorld," 12.

5. Nicholas D. Kristof, "A Toast to Moral Clarity."

6. Ted Honderich, *After the Terror.*

7. Noam Chomsky, *Power and Terror,* 49.

8. See Paul W. Kahn, "The Paradox of Riskless Warfare."

9. See chapter 4, this volume.

10. U.S. Department of State, "Patterns of Global Terrorism 1997," vi.

11. "Under international law, terrorism cannot be committed by states qua states. State sponsored terrorism, however, is another matter." John Alan Cohan, "Formulation of a State's Response to Terrorism and State-sponsored Terrorism," 88–89.

12. Neve Gordon and George A. López, "Terrorism in the Arab-Israeli Conflict," 110.

13. Ibid.

14. Michael Walzer, "Five Questions about Terrorism."

15. C. A. J. Coady, "Terrorism and Innocence," 37–58.

16. Igor Primoratz, "What Is Terrorism?"

17. Tony Coady has suggested in discussion that what makes the attack on the Pentagon an attack on civilians and thus terrorism is that a plane with civilians on board was hijacked and civilians were killed in attacking the Pentagon. But if we pursue this line of argument, we would need to separate the two events of hijacking the plane and then crashing it into the Pentagon rather than some other target, and it is the latter that causes a problem for the definition in question.

18. Robert Fullinwider, "Terrorism, Innocence, and War," 22.

19. David Rodin, "Terrorism without Intention." See also Lionel McPherson, "Is Terrorism Distinctively Wrong?"

20. Chris Hedges, *What Every Person Should Know about War.*

21. For a report see Jeffrey Gettleman, "The Perfect Weapon for the Meanest Wars."

22. Serge Schmemann, "Not Quite an Arab-Israeli War, but a Long Descent into Hatred."

23. James Bennet, "Israeli Voters Hand Sharon Strong Victory."

24. This point was made by Sigal Ben-Porath at a conference called "Moral and Political Aspects of Terrorism" at the University of Arizona, Tucson, March 8, 2003.

25. Angelia Means, "The Idea of the Enemy."

26. Amy Waldman, "Masters of Suicide Bombing: Tamil Guerrillas of Sri Lanka."

27. Ibid.

28. Kamel B. Nasr, *Arab and Israeli Terrorism,* 57.

29. Benjamin R. Barber, "The War of All against All," 77, 88.

30. Lloyd J. Dumas, "Is Development an Effective Way to Fight Terrorism?" 73.

31. Ibid.

32. Ibid.

33. Andrew Valls, "Can Terrorism Be Justified?" 66.

34. Fullinwider, "Terrorism, Innocence, and War," 24.

35. Benjamin Netanyahu, ed., *Terrorism: How the West Can Win*, 29–30.

36. Michael Wines, "Mourners at Israeli Boys' Funeral Lament a Conflict with No Bounds."

37. Bruce Hoffman, *Inside Terrorism*, preface.

38. See, for example, Robin Morgan, *The Demon Lover: The Roots of Terrorism;* and Virginia Held, *Feminist Morality: Transforming Culture, Society, and Politics*, chapter 7.

39. Laura Blumenfeld, *Revenge: A Story of Hope.*

40. "Q & A; Punishing a Terrorist By Showing Him His Victim's Humanity," *New York Times* (Apr. 6, 2002), B9.

41. See, for example, Richard A. Falk, "Ending the Death Dance."

42. Barber, "War of All against All," 78.

43. Ibid., 79–80.

44. *The Philosopher's Index* for the entire period from 1940 to 2002 lists only six articles or reviews that deal substantially with humiliation and none for which it is the major topic.

45. Avishai Margalit, *The Decent Society,* 9.

46. Ibid., 1.

47. Avishai Margalit, *The Ethics of Memory,* 118.

48. Of course, a few suicide bombers have been women, as a few rulers of states have been women, but the numbers are comparatively small.

CHAPTER 2

1. Virginia Held, Sidney Morgenbesser, and Thomas Nagel, eds., *Philosophy, Morality, and International Affairs.*

2. George Packer, "Comment: Unrealistic"; and James Traub, "Old World Order," *New York Times Book Review.*

3. Anatol Lieven and John Hulsman, *Ethical Realism: A Vision for America's Role in the World.* The book actually contains many sensible suggestions for being more realistic about various foreign policy issues, but it has been interpreted to show that morality has no place in international affairs.

4. See Thomas M. Franck, "The Power of Legitimacy and the Legitimacy of Power: International Law in an Age of Power Disequilibrium."

5. For an analysis of the George W. Bush administration's "aggressive unilateralism" see John L. Hammond, "The Bush Doctrine, Preventive War, and International Law."

6. It is worth recalling the views of Anthony Lake, who was soon to be President Clinton's national security advisor, in early 1993: "The new foreign policy debate, Mr. Lake has argued, is between those who see the world through a classic balance of power prism and those who, like President Clinton and himself, take a more 'neo-Wilsonian' view in which the United States uses its monopoly on power to intervene in other countries to promote democracy" (Steven Holmes, "Choice for National Security Advisor Has a Long-Awaited Chance to Lead").

7. Maureen Dowd, "Who's Hormonal? Hillary or Dick?"

8. Thomas L. Friedman, "No More Mr. Tough Guy."

9. See Held, *Ethics of Care,* especially chapter 10.

10. William H. Taft IV, "A View from the Top: American Perspectives on International Law after the Cold War," 502.

11. For a report on and critique of this view see Harold Hongju Koh, "Commentary: Is International Law Really State Law?"

12. *Roper v. Simmons,* 125 S. Ct. 1183, 1228 (2005) (Scalia, J., dissenting).

13. Judith Resnik, "Law's Migration: American Exceptionalism, Silent Dialogues, and Federalism's Multiple Ports of Entry."

14. Franck, "Power of Legitimacy," 89.

15. Taft, "View from the Top," 510.

16. Ibid., 511.

17. Ibid.

18. Brian Urquhart, "The Outlaw World," 25.

19. Franck, "Power of Legitimacy," 90.

20. Ibid., 97.

21. Louise Richardson, *What Terrorists Want: Understanding the Enemy, Containing the Threat,* 176.

22. Adam Liptak, "Suspected Leader of Attacks on 9/11 Is Said to Confess."

23. Richardson, *What Terrorists Want,* 177.

24. Ibid., 180.

25. Robert A. Pape, *Dying to Win: The Strategic Logic of Suicide Terrorism.*

26. See Hoffman, *Inside Terrorism;* and Pape, *Dying to Win.*

27. Richardson, *What Terrorists Want,* xvii.

28. Ibid., xv.

29. Ibid., xix.

30. See, for example, Martha Crenshaw, "The Debate over 'New' vs. 'Old' Terrorism."

31. I am grateful to John Kleinig for clarification of this issue at the Conference on Terrorism held at John Jay College of Criminal Justice of the City University of New York, Nov. 10–11, 2006.

32. Robert E. Goodin, *What's Wrong with Terrorism?*

33. John Mueller, *Overblown: How Politicians and the Terrorism Industry Inflate National Security Threats and Why We Believe Them.*

34. William Langewiesche, *The Atomic Bazaar.*

35. Tom J. Farer, "The Prospect for International Law and Order in the Wake of Iraq."

36. Benjamin R. Barber, *Fear's Empire: War, Terrorism, and Democracy.*

37. See, for example, Laura W. Reed and Carl Kaysen, eds., *Emerging Norms of Justified Intervention: A Collection of Essays from a Project of the American Academy of Arts and Sciences;* Stanley Hoffmann, *The Ethics and Politics of Humanitarian Intervention;* Simon

Chesterman, *Just War or Just Peace? Humanitarian Intervention and International Law;* International Commission on Intervention and State Sovereignty, *The Responsibility to Protect;* J. L. Holzgrefe and Robert O. Keohane, eds., *Humanitarian Intervention: Ethical, Legal, and Political Dilemmas;* Deen K. Chatterjee and Don E. Scheid, *Ethics and Foreign Intervention.*

38. Franck, "Power of Legitimacy," 99.

39. Tom J. Farer, "Humanitarian Intervention before and after 9/11: Legality and Legitimacy."

40. Ibid.; also Jane Stromseth, "Rethinking Humanitarian Intervention: Gradations in Sovereignty."

41. Franck, "Power of Legitimacy," 104.

42. Iris Marion Young, "Violence against Power: Critical Thoughts on Military Intervention."

43. Independent International Commission on Kosovo, *The Kosovo Report: Conflict, International Response, Lessons Learned,* 89.

44. Chris Brown, "Selective Humanitarianism: In Defense of Inconsistency."

45. Richard W. Miller, "Respectable Oppressors, Hypocritical Liberators: Morality, Intervention, and Reality"; see also Michael Blake, "Reciprocity, Stability, and Intervention: The Ethics of Disequilibrium."

46. But see Rex Martin, "Just Wars and Humanitarian Interventions."

47. See Virginia Held, *Rights and Goods: Justifying Social Action.*

48. John Rawls, *The Law of Peoples.*

49. John Rawls, *A Theory of Justice.*

50. Rawls, *Law of Peoples,* 93.

51. Ibid., 81.

52. Ibid., 93.

53. See chapter 5.

54. Thomas M. Franck, "Interpretation and Change in the Law of Humanitarian Intervention."

55. Richard A. Falk, "What Future for the UN Charter System of War Prevention?" 591.

56. W. Michael Reisman, "Why Regime Change Is (Almost Always) a Bad Idea," 516.

57. Kofi A. Annan, "Two Concepts of Sovereignty," 49.

58. See Anne F. Bayefsky, ed., *Self-determination in International Law: Quebec and Lessons Learned;* and chapter 3, this volume.

59. Alain Pellet, "Legal Opinion on Certain Questions of International Law Raised by the Reference," 118.

60. Reisman, "Why Regime Change," 517; see also Lori Damrosch, "Commentary."

61. Stromseth, "Rethinking Humanitarian Intervention."

62. Franck, "Interpretation and Change"; Carsten Stahn, "Enforcement of the Collective Will after Iraq." For a nuanced and different interpretation of

retroactive justification see Michael Byers and Simon Chesterman, "Changing the Rules about Rules?"

63. Farer, "Prospect for International Law," 626.

64. Ibid.

65. Thomas M. Franck, "What Happens Now? The United Nations after Iraq," 608.

66. Falk, "What Future for the UN Charter System?"; Franck, "Power of Legitimacy"; and Stahn, "Enforcement of the Collective Will."

67. Franck, "Power of Legitimacy," 97n35.

68. Stahn, "Enforcement of the Collective Will," 822.

69. See especially Held, *Rights and Goods,* chapters 4 and 15; also see chapters 7 and 8 of this volume.

70. For discussion of how international law can be changed see Allen Buchanan, "Reforming the International Law of Humanitarian Intervention"; Franck, "Interpretation and Change"; and Stromseth, "Rethinking Humanitarian Intervention." However, see also Neta C. Crawford, "Decolonization as an International Norm: The Evolution of Practices, Arguments, and Beliefs."

71. Stromseth, "Rethinking Humanitarian Intervention."

72. Rosalyn Higgins, "Intervention and International Law," 42.

73. Hedley Bull, ed., *Intervention in World Politics,* 183.

74. Ibid., 181, 186.

75. Ibid., 189.

76. See Held, *Ethics of Care.*

77. Joan C. Tronto, "Is Peace Keeping Care Work?" On a right to be rescued from extreme violence see Morton E. Winston, "The Right of Rescue."

78. Damrosch, "Changing Conceptions of Intervention in International Law," 106.

79. Stanley Hoffmann, "Commentary on 'Beware the Slippery Slope,'" 89.

80. See Richard A. Falk, *The Declining World Order;* and Jonathan Schell, "Too Late for Empire."

81. See, for example, Keane, *Global Civil Society?;* and Slaughter, *New World Order.*

82. Falk, *Declining World Order.*

CHAPTER 3

1. Doubts that terrorists can have adequate authority to undertake political violence are raised by McPherson in "Is Terrorism Distinctively Wrong?"

2. Graham Boynton, *Last Days in Cloud Cuckooland: Dispatches from White South Africa.*

3. Noam Chomsky, "Terror and Just Response," 70.

4. Hoffman, *Inside Terrorism,* 184.

5. Heather A. Wilson, *International Law and the Use of Force by National Liberation Movements.*

6. Ibid., 14.

7. Ibid., 15. Wilson relies on James Turner Johnson, *Just War Tradition and the Restraint of War.*

8. Wilson, 15.

9. Ibid., 55; see also Omar Dahbour, *Illusion of the Peoples: A Critique of National Self-determination.*

10. Robert Young, "Political Terrorism as a Weapon of the Politically Powerless," 59–60.

11. Wilson, 127.

12. Wilson, 135.

13. See chapters 1 and 4.

14. The definition adopted by the U.S. government is "Terrorism is premeditated, politically motivated violence perpetrated against noncombatant targets by subnational groups or clandestine agents, usually intended to influence an audience." U.S. Department of State, "Patterns of Global Terrorism, 1983–2001."

15. Walzer, *Just and Unjust Wars,* chapter 12, and Walzer, "Five Questions about Terrorism," 5–10.

16. Coady, "Terrorism and Innocence," 37–58.

17. Primoratz, "What Is Terrorism?"

18. Valls, "Can Terrorism Be Justified?"

19. Robert Young, "Political Terrorism."

20. Walter Laqueur, *No End to War: Terrorism in the Twenty-first Century,* 233.

21. For further argument see chapter 1.

22. Shannon E. French, "Murderers, Not Warriors: The Moral Distinction between Terrorists and Legitimate Fighters in Asymmetric Conflicts."

23. Walzer, *Just and Unjust Wars,* 199.

24. Ibid., 198.

25. Ibid.

26. James Sterba, "Introduction," 11.

27. Ibid.

28. Alison M. Jaggar, "What Is Terrorism, Why Is It Wrong, and Could It Ever Be Morally Permissible?" 204.

29. Fullinwider, "Terrorism, Innocence, and War," 10.

30. French, "Murderers, Not Warriors," 44.

31. Of course, there is a large philosophical literature that examines this distinction; I do not cite it here but merely state my conclusion in the context of terrorist violence.

32. Matthew Evangelista, *The Chechen Wars: Will Russia Go the Way of the Soviet Union?* 1, 192; Laqueur, *No End to War,* esp. 185–189.

33. For example, Thomas L. Friedman, "Footprints in the Sand."

34. Steven Erlanger, "Palestinian Politicians Try to Head Off a Power Struggle."

35. Elaine Sciolino, "Self-appointed Israeli and Palestinian Negotiators Offer a Plan for Middle East Peace." See also the Web site of Americans for Peace Now at http://www.peacenow.org.

36. Jeffrey Gettleman, "For Some Iraqis in Harm's Way, $5,000 from U.S. and 'I'm Sorry.'"

37. Elisabeth Rosenthal, "Study Puts Iraqi Deaths of Civilians at 100,000."

38. David Brown, "Study Claims Iraq's 'Excess' Death Toll Has Reached 655,000."

39. Robert A. Pape, "The Strategic Logic of Suicide Terrorism."

40. Ibid., 344.

41. Ibid., 346.

42. Ibid., 347.

43. Ibid., 353.

44. Ibid., 349.

45. Ibid., 350–351.

46. James Bennet, "On the West Bank, a Hint of Resistance without Blood."

47. Hoffman, *Inside Terrorism,* 183.

48. Sharon LaFraniere, "A South African Journey: Bomb Maker to Police Chief."

49. Walzer, *Just and Unjust Wars,* 195.

50. Pape, "Strategic Logic of Suicide Terrorism," 348.

51. Hoffman, *Inside Terrorism,* 171.

52. Ibid., 170.

53. Pape, "Strategic Logic of Suicide Terrorism," 348.

54. Ibid., 349, citing Elaine Sciolino, "Saudi Warns Bush."

55. Susan Sachs, "Poll Finds Hostility Hardening toward U.S. Policies."

56. Ibid.

57. Pape, "Strategic Logic of Suicide Terrorism," 349.

58. Allen Buchanan, "Political Legitimacy and Democracy," 689.

59. Ibid., 696.

60. Ibid., 689.

61. Greg Myre, "A Palestinian Asks, Who Made My Son a Suicide Bomber?"

62. Mlada Bukovansky, *Legitimacy and Power Politics: The American and French Revolutions in International Political Culture,* 3, 8.

63. Ibid., 8.

64. Ibid., 211.

65. Andrew Valls, *Ethics in International Affairs,* 71.

66. Wilson, *International Law and the Use of Force,* 137, chapter 6.

67. Ibid.

68. Ibid., 138.

69. Ibid., 145.

70. Ibid., 144–145.

71. Valls is very cautious here since he wants to rule out "vanguard" organizations that "claim representative status despite lack of support among the people themselves"; *Ethics in International Affairs,* 71. The point I am making is in agreement with his further argument that "the standard should not be higher [for nonstate entities] than that used for states" (ibid.).

72. Hoffman, *Inside Terrorism,* 184.

73. I deal with these issues in the next chapter.

74. Independent International Commission on Kosovo, *Kosovo Report.*

75. Dahbour, *Illusion of the Peoples,* 65.

76. *New York Times*/CBS News poll, *New York Times* (Mar. 16, 2004), A24.

77. David Brooks, "Al Qaeda's Wish List"; Edward N. Luttwak, "Rewarding Terror in Spain."

78. Igor Primoratz, "State Terrorism and Counter-terrorism," 123.

79. Ibid.

80. Tomis Kapitan, "The Terrorism of 'Terrorism,'" 57.

81. Ibid., 58.

82. Ibid., 57.

83. Evangelista, *Chechen Wars,* 12.

84. Ibid., 196.

85. Kapitan, "Terrorism of 'Terrorism,'" 60.

86. Scott L. Plous and Philip G. Zimbardo, "How Social Science Can Reduce Terrorism," *Chronicle of Higher Education* (Sept. 10, 2004), B9.

87. See, for example, Craig S. Smith and Don Van Natta Jr., "Officials Fear Iraq's Lure for Muslims in Europe"; and Daniel Benjamin and Gabriel Weimann, "What the Terrorists Have in Mind."

CHAPTER 4

1. Jenny Teichman, *Pacifism and the Just War: A Study in Applied Philosophy,* 89–90.

2. Ibid., 90.

3. R. M. Hare, "On Terrorism."

4. Carl Wellman, "On Terrorism Itself," 250.

5. Ibid., 252.

6. Ibid.

7. C. A. J. Coady, "The Morality of Terrorism," 52.

8. U.S. Department of State, "Patterns of Global Terrorism: 1984." The State Department classifies this attack as an act of terrorism.

9. Carlos Marighela, *Handbook of Urban Guerrilla Warfare,* 89.

10. Coady, "Morality of Terrorism," 59.

11. Teichman, *Pacificism and the Just War,* 96.

12. Virginia Held, "Violence, Terrorism, and Moral Inquiry."

13. Ibid., 606.

14. See *QQ: Report from the Institute for Philosophy and Public Policy*, 2.

15. Grant Wardlaw, *Political Terrorism* (1982), 41. See also Aziz Al-Azmeh, "The Middle East and Islam: A Ventriloqual Terrorism."

16. Paul Wilkinson, *Political Terrorism*, 17 (emphasis added). In a more recent book, Wilkinson does not build the moral judgment quite so directly into the definition. He defines political terrorism as "coercive intimidation. It is the systematic use of murder and destruction, and the threat of murder and destruction in order to terrorize individuals, groups, communities or governments into conceding to the terrorists' political demands" (51). Then, on the basis of a useful though not unbiased survey of terrorist activity, he concludes that terrorism is "a moral crime, a crime against humanity" (66).

17. Netanyahu, ed., *Terrorism*, 29–30.

18. Burton Leiser, *Liberty, Justice, and Morality*, chapter 13. Leiser considers the Palestinians to have provided the foremost examples of terrorist acts. Israeli "reprisals" and the children and noncombatants killed in them are not mentioned.

19. Michael Walzer, "Terrorism: A Critique of Excuses," 238. His position is effectively criticized by Robert K. Fullinwider in "Understanding Terrorism."

20. The essays collected in Netanyahu, ed., *Terrorism*, provide many examples.

21. See John Dugard, "International Terrorism and the Just War."

22. On this point see especially Richard A. Falk, *Revolutionaries and Functionaries: The Dual Face of Terrorism.*

23. Robert L. Holmes, "Terrorism and Other Forms of Violence: A Moral Perspective."

24. Falk, *Revolutionaries and Functionaries*, 37.

25. See, for example, Coady, "Morality of Terrorism"; Leiser, *Liberty, Justice, and Morality;* and Jan Schreiber, *The Ultimate Weapon: Terrorists and World Order.*

26. Fox Butterfield, "8-Year Gulf War: Victims but No Victors."

27. Bernard Trainor, "Turning Point: Failed Attack on Basra."

28. Ibid.

29. New York Times (AP), "200,000 Youths Said to Be in World's Armies."

30. Coady, "Morality of Terrorism," 63.

31. See, for example, Leiser, *Liberty, Justice, and Morality*, 395.

32. *QQ: Report.*

33. Burleigh Wilkins, "Terrorism and Consequentialism."

34. Walter Laqueur, *The Age of Terrorism.*

35. Albrecht Wellmer, "Terrorism and the Critique of Society," 300.

36. See Charles Tilly, "Collective Violence in European Perspective"; and Lewis A. Coser, "Some Social Functions of Violence."

37. Falk, *Revolutionaries and Functionaries*, 34–35.

38. Wilkins, "Terrorism and Consequentialism," 150.

39. Ibid.

40. The classic statement is Max Weber's: "The state is considered the sole source of the 'right' to use violence....The state is a relation of men dominating men, a relation supported by means of legitimate (i.e. considered to be legitimate) violence" (*From Max Weber: Essays in Sociology,* 78).

41. See Held, *Rights and Goods.*

42. Wellman, "On Terrorism Itself," 258.

43. Ibid.

44. Coady, "Morality of Terrorism," 58.

45. See, for example, Committee on Foreign Affairs, comp., *Human Rights Documents.* For discussion see, for instance, James W. Nickel, *Making Sense of Human Rights.*

46. Ruddick, *Maternal Thinking,* 138. See also Adrienne Harris and Ynestra King, eds., *Rocking the Ship of State.*

47. Pam McAllister, Introduction, iii.

48. See, for example, Robin Morgan, *Demon Lover.*

49. Quoted in McAllister, Introduction, vi.

50. William Borman, *Gandhi and Non-violence,* xiv.

51. Quoted in ibid., 252–253.

52. This argument is in response to a comment by Rogers Albritton.

53. Igor Primoratz, "The Morality of Terrorism," 221–233.

54. Ibid., 231.

CHAPTER 5

1. For one such argument see Virginia Held, "Corporations, Persons, and Responsibility."

2. For a related discussion, see Iris Marion Young, "Responsibility and Global Justice: A Social Connection Model."

3. Virginia Held, "Moral Subjects: The Natural and the Normative"; and Annette Baier, "A Naturalist View of Persons," 6.

4. See, for instance, the chapters by H. D. Lewis, R. S. Downie, and Manuel Velásquez in Larry May and Stacey Hoffman, eds., *Collective Responsibility.*

5. See Anthony Quinton, "Social Objects." See also Margaret Gilbert's discussion of ontological and analytic individualism in *On Social Facts,* 427–436. John Ladd, in "Morality and the Ideal of Rationality in Formal Organizations," argues that the organizational language game is such that social and corporate decisions are not and cannot be governed by moral principles and that to think they should be is to make a category mistake.

6. Thomas Cushman and Stjepan G. Mestrovic, eds., *This Time We Knew: Western Responses to Genocide in Bosnia,* 18.

7. See Virginia Held, "Can a Random Collection of Individuals Be Morally Responsible?"; Held, "Corporations, Persons, and Responsibility."

8. See David E. Cooper, "Collective Responsibility," 167; Joel Feinberg, *Doing and Deserving: Essays in the Theory of Responsibility*; Peter A. French, *Collective and Corporate Responsibility*; Larry May, *The Morality of Groups: Collective Responsibility, Group-based Harm, and Corporate Rights* and *Sharing Responsibility*; Gregory Mellema, *Individuals, Groups, and Shared Moral Responsibility*; and Burleigh Wilkins, *Terrorism and Collective Responsibility*.

9. William K. Frankena, *Ethics*, 73.

10. Philip Pettit has suggested in correspondence that we distinguish between cases in which people really are responsible and those in which we just hold them responsible because it may increase their good behavior; he mentions bringing up children as a source of such examples and worries that a view such as mine might undermine our ability to make this distinction. I believe we can still make it, as we do with strict liability. In most cases we have good moral reasons for considering people or groups responsible only for what they causally and intentionally bring about, but in some cases we have good moral reasons to hold them responsible even if not all of the usual conditions are met, such as when a manufacturer is strictly liable for the safety of a product even if some consequence of using it was not foreseen because this is likely to increase the care with which products are put on the market. What we are doing here is distinguishing one set of moral reasons from another, which we can also do in bringing up children, though the reasons will often be different.

11. Michael J. Zimmerman, "Sharing Responsibility."

12. See especially Patricia Smith, *Liberalism and Affirmative Obligation*.

13. Cushman and Mestrovic, *This Time We Knew*, 25.

14. Ibid., 18.

15. H. D. Lewis, "Collective Responsibility," in May and Hoffman, *Collective Responsibility*, 17.

16. Smith, *Liberalism and Affirmative Obligation*, 222.

17. See William F. Felice, "The Case for Collective Human Rights: The Reality of Group Suffering"; Will Kymlicka, ed., *The Rights of Minority Cultures*.

18. Felice, "Case for Collective Human Rights," 51–52.

19. S. James Anaya, "The Capacity of International Law to Advance Ethnic or Nationality Rights Claims," 326.

20. French, *Collective and Corporate Responsibility*. For arguments that the necessary conditions for corporate responsibility may not be the same as those for individual responsibility see Held, "Corporations, Persons, and Responsibility." Angelo Corlett argues that the necessary conditions for collective and individual responsibility are the same but that collectives rarely if ever in fact satisfy them. See J. Angelo Corlett, "Collective Moral Responsibility."

21. Held, "Corporations, Persons, and Responsibility."

22. Held, "Can a Random Collection of Individuals Be Morally Responsible?"

23. Juha Raika, "On Disassociating Oneself from Collective Responsibility," 106n6.

24. Thomas Pogge writes: "To constitute an ethnic group, a set of persons must satisfy three conditions: commonality of descent, commonality of continuous culture, and closure. The members of the set must understand themselves as descendants of members of an historical society (in a broad sense, including tribes, principalities and the like, as well as systems of interacting tribes or principalities). They must share a common culture, or partial culture, which they take to be connected, through a continuous history, with the culture of their ancestors (however different from the latter it may have become in the process). And the group must contain all, or nearly all, of the persons who, within the relevant state, are taken to share the descent and culture definitive of the group." Thomas W. Pogge, "Group Rights and Ethnicity," 194.

25. I am grateful to Paul Grieco for raising this question.

26. For very useful discussions of some of these issues see Ross Poole, *Nation and Identity;* and Karen Kovach, "Who We Are and What We Do: Ethnicity and Moral Agency."

27. May, *Sharing Responsibility,* 1.

28. Ibid., 4.

29. Ibid., 37.

30. See Feinberg, *Doing and Deserving;* and Howard McGary, "Morality and Collective Liability."

31. Raika, "On Disassociating Oneself," 103.

32. May, *Sharing Responsibility,* 47.

33. Wole Soyinka, "Hearts of Darkness."

34. James W. Nickel, "What's Wrong with Ethnic Cleansing?"

35. Ibid., 6.

36. Claudia Card, "Rape as a Weapon of War," 9.

37. Liz Philipose, "The Laws of War and Women's Human Rights."

38. Ibid., 56.

39. See Aleksandar Pavković, *The Fragmentation of Yugoslavia,* 143–146; and Warren Zimmerman, *Origins of a Catastrophe,* chapter 5.

40. For an illuminating discussion of how it is open only to group members to align themselves with a group and to see a group as an extension of their own agency, see Karen Kovach, "Ethnic Groups and Moral Agency."

41. Mark Danner, "Operation Storm."

42. John Kifner, "Inquiry Estimates Serb Drive Killed 10,000 in Kosovo."

43. Philip J. Cohen, "The Complicity of Serbian Intellectuals in Genocide in the 1990s," 46.

44. Ibid., 47.

45. Ibid., 52–53.

46. Helsinki Watch, *War Crimes in Bosnia-Hercegovina,* 6.

47. Cushman and Mestrovic, *This Time We Knew,* 15–16.

48. See Cohen, "Complicity of Serbian Intellectuals," and Stacy Sullivan, "Milosevic Is One Problem; National Denial Is the Other."

49. See Pavković, *Fragmentation of Yugoslavia,* and Susan L. Woodward, *Balkan Tragedy: Chaos and Dissolution after the Cold War.*

50. For discussion see Held, *Rights and Goods,* and chapter 4 of this volume. David Copp argues that with respect to secession, what is needed is regulation, and he shows how a moral right to secession might be implemented in international law. See David Copp, "International Law and Morality in the Theory of Secession."

51. See, for example, Steven Erlanger, "Did U.S. Bombs Help or Hinder?" 16; and Roger Cohen, "Who Really Brought Down Milosevic?"

52. See Blaine Harden, "The Milosevic Generation"; and Sullivan, "Milosevic Is One Problem."

53. Warren Zimmerman, *Origins of a Catastrophe,* viii.

54. David Rieff, *Slaughterhouse: Bosnia and the Failure of the West.*

55. Cushman and Mestrovic, *This Time We Knew,* 21.

56. See, for example, the Independent International Commission on Kosovo, *Kosovo Report,* and chapter 2 of this volume.

CHAPTER 6

1. Virginia Held, "Terrorism, Rights, and Political Goals."

2. S. Satris ed., *Taking Sides: Clashing Views on Controversial Moral Issues.*

3. Pam McAllister, ed., *Reweaving the Web of Life: Feminism and Nonviolence;* Borman, *Gandhi and Non-violence,* xiv.

4. Held, *Rights and Goods.*

5. H. Merkl, ed., *Political Violence and Terror,* 54.

6. Stanley G. French, *Interpersonal Violence, Health, and Gender Politics.*

7. Bill Carter, "A New Report Becomes a Weapon in Debate on Censoring TV Violence."

8. E. Donnerstein, R. Slaby, and L. Eron, "The Mass Media and Youth Aggression"; W. Grimes, "Does Life Imitate Violent Films?"

9. Thomas C. Schelling, "What Purposes Can 'International Terrorism' Serve?" 19.

10. J. Stern, "Preventing Portable Nukes."

11. A. O. Alali and K. K. Eke, eds., *Media Coverage of Terrorism: Methods of Diffusion,* 6.

12. Schlesinger, G. Murdock, and P. Elliott, *Televising "Terrorism": Political Violence and Popular Culture.*

13. Brian Jenkins, "Research in Terrorism: Areas of Consensus, Areas of Ignorance."

14. Grant Wardlaw, *Political Terrorism: Theory, Tactics, and Counter-measures.*

15. Robert G. Picard, "News Coverage as the Contagion of Terrorism."

16. See Schlesinger, Murdock, and Elliott, *Televising "Terrorism."*

17. See Held, *Rights and Goods.*

18. Douglas Kellner, *Television and the Crisis of Democracy.*

19. Max Frankel, "The Murder Broadcasting System."

20. James Fallows, *Breaking the News: How the Media Undermine American Democracy*, 142.

21. N. Seppa, "News Shows Exaggerate Prevalence of Violence," 9.

22. Thomas L. Friedman, "At God's Elbow."

23. Frank Rich, "The V-chip G-string."

24. R. Hundt and N. Minow, "A Cure for Kids' TV."

25. L. Mufflin, "F.C.C. Urged to Strengthen Children's TV."

26. Leo Bogart, *Commercial Culture: The Media System and the Public Interest*.

27. Pat Aufderheide, "What Makes Public TV Public?"

28. Doreen Carvajal, "Triumph of the Bottom Line."

29. See Virginia Held, *The Public Interest and Individual Interests;* and Michael J. Copps, "The Price of Free Airwaves."

30. James Brooke, "Lawsuit Tests Lethal Power of Words."

31. Diana T. Meyers, "Rights in Collision: A Non-punitive, Compensatory Remedy for Abusive Speech."

32. See Virginia Held, "Access, Enablement, and the First Amendment."

33. See Virginia Held, "Media Culture and Democracy."

34. Gustav Niebuhr, "Number of Religious Broadcasters Continues to Grow."

35. Hubert Buchstein, "Bytes That Bite: The Internet and Deliberative Democracy."

36. Katha Pollitt, "For Whom the Ball Rolls," 9.

37. Michael Kimmelman, "Does It Really Matter Who Sponsors a Show?"

38. Douglas Kellner, *Media Culture: Cultural Studies, Identity and Politics between the Modern and the Postmodern*, 1. On the ever continuing commercialization of the culture and infantilization of the public see Benjamin R. Barber, *Consumed: How Markets Corrupt Children, Infantilize Adults, and Swallow Citizens Whole*.

CHAPTER 7

1. For further discussion of moral inquiry see Held, *Rights and Goods*.

2. The discussions of more complex and refined definitions in Jerome A. Shaffer, ed., *Violence*, are helpful. See also Francis C. Wade, "On Violence," and Joseph Betz, "Violence, Garver's Definition, and a Deweyan Correction." In this chapter I concentrate on questions of justification rather than those of definition.

3. For arguments concerning what our moral rights to property should and should not include see Virginia Held, ed., *Property, Profits, and Economic Justice.* What, from a moral point of view, our "property" is taken to include may affect whether we are "harmed" by its destruction. In this chapter I do not explore the meaning of "harm."

4. See John Harris, "The Marxist Conception of Violence." Harris shows why "the moment we realize that harm to human beings could be prevented, we are

entitled to see the failure to prevent it as a cause of harm" (204–205). He also defends Engels's view that violence "has been committed if thousands of workers have been deprived of the necessities of life or if they have been forced into a situation in which it is impossible for them to survive" (Frederick Engels, *The Condition of the Working Class in England,* 108).

5. Are hockey, football, and boxing, then, when voluntarily engaged in, not violent sports? I find this a difficult question. Player A does not commit an act of violence in tripping, tackling, or punching player B if both are voluntarily playing the game by the rules. However, since the outcomes of such acts may be very similar to what they would have been had the acts been ones of violence, it may be appropriate to call such sports violent. Additionally, players performing such acts against the rules are acting coercively and hence, here, violently.

6. See Virginia Held, "Coercion and Coercive Offers."

7. See, for instance, Morton Kaplan, *System and Process in International Politics,* 14.

8. Charles Tilly, "Collective Violence in European Perspective," 4–10, my italics.

9. Ibid., 37.

10. Ibid., 42.

11. Coser, "Some Social Functions of Violence," 14.

12. Georges Sorel, *Reflections on Violence,* 58–59.

13. Hannah Arendt, "Civil Disobedience."

14. Sorel, *Reflections on Violence,* 82. Sorel's note here is: "Syndicalism has no head with which it would be possible to carry on diplomatic relations usefully."

15. Ibid., 82.

16. Philip Taft and Philip Ross, "American Labor Violence: Its Causes, Character, and Outcome," 382–383.

17. See, for example, Addison Gayle Jr., *The Black Situation.* See also Stokely Carmichael and Charles V. Hamilton, *Black Power: The Politics of Liberation in America.*

18. Coser, "Some Social Functions of Violence," 15.

19. Arendt, "Civil Disobedience," 19.

20. For further discussion see Held, *Rights and Goods,* and Held, "Justification: Legal and Political."

21. Joan Bondurant, *Conquest of Violence,* viii.

22. Walter Laqueur, "The Anatomy of Terrorism," 20.

23. Bondurant, *Conquest of Violence,* 227.

24. See Sorel, *Reflections on Violence;* and Franz Fanon, *The Wretched of the Earth,* 22, 85.

25. For further discussion see Held, *Rights and Goods,* and Held, "Justification: Legal and Political."

26. Immanuel Kant, *The Metaphysical Elements of Justice,* 76–77.

27. Jean-Paul Sartre, Preface to Fanon, *Wretched of the Earth,* 17–21.

28. See Held, *Rights and Goods.*

29. Plato, *The Republic*, 328.

30. See Held, *Rights and Goods.*

31. Sartre, Preface to Fanon, *Wretched of the Earth*, 21.

32. Paul Wilkinson, "The Laws of War and Terrorism," 310–311. See also Walzer, *Just and Unjust Wars*, especially chapter 12.

33. Wilkinson, *Political Terrorism*, 17.

34. Dugard, "International Terrorism," 77.

35. Robert Young, "Revolutionary Terrorism, Crime, and Morality," 288.

36. Ibid., 289.

37. Wardlaw, *Political Terrorism* (1982), 13.

38. Ibid., 41–42.

39. Amar Ouzegane, *Le meilleur combat*, 257, quoted in Wardlaw, *Political Terrorism* (1982), 41.

40. Dugard, "International Terrorism," 77.

41. Ibid., 91.

42. Ibid.

43. See Bondurant, *Conquest of Violence*, chapter 6.

CHAPTER 8

1. Emotivism is the metaethical theory that moral judgments merely express our feelings or attitudes and cannot make assertions such as that certain moral judgments are true or moral principles valid.

2. See especially Held, *Rights and Goods.*

3. See especially Held, *Ethics of Care.*

4. See Held, *Rights and Goods;* and Held, *Feminist Morality*, chapter 2.

5. For further discussion see Virginia Held, "The Political 'Testing' of Moral Theories," and Held, *Rights and Goods*, chapters 3 and 15. For a different view of moral principles, but one that supports the claim that we can make judgments about particular cases independently of our moral principles, see Jonathan Dancy, "Ethical Particularism and Morally Relevant Properties."

6. See Virginia Held, "The Normative Import of Action."

7. See Alan Gewirth, *Reason and Morality;* see also Alan Gewirth, *Human Rights: Essays on Justification and Applications;* and Alan Gewirth, *The Community of Rights.*

8. Gewirth, *Reason and Morality*, 135.

9. Karl-Otto Apel, *Towards a Transformation of Philosophy;* Seyla Benhabib, *Situating the Self;* and Jürgen Habermas, *Moral Consciousness and Communicative Action.*

10. Rawls, *Theory of Justice;* and Norman Daniels, "Wide Reflective Equilibrium and Theory Acceptance in Ethics."

11. See, for example, Gilbert Harman, *The Nature of Morality.*

12. This problem was raised by Sidney Morgenbesser.

13. See Held, *Feminist Morality*.

14. See Held, "Moral Subjects."

15. Hilary Bok, "Acting without Choosing"; quote at 192–193.

16. Ronald Dworkin et al., "Assisted Suicide: The Philosophers' Brief."

17. Harman, *Nature of Morality*.

18. For instance, *The Reluctant Fundamentalist*, a short novel by Mohsin Hamid, makes understandable the growing anti-Americanism of a young Pakistani despite his success as a student and professional in the United States.

19. Richardson, *What Terrorists Want*.

20. Ruddick, *Maternal Thinking*, 172.

21. Ibid., 148.

22. Ibid., 183.

BIBLIOGRAPHY

Alali, A. O., and K. K. Eke, eds. 1991. *Media Coverage of Terrorism: Methods of Diffusion*. Newbury Park, Calif.: Sage.

Anaya, S. James. 1995. "The Capacity of International Law to Advance Ethnic or Nationality Rights Claims." In *The Rights of Minority Cultures*, ed. Will Kymlicka, 321–330. New York: Oxford University Press.

Annan, Kofi A. 1999. "Two Concepts of Sovereignty." *Economist* (September 18): 49–50.

————. 2002. "Kofi Annan's Blunt Words Criticizing Israeli Tactics," Text of Letter. *New York Times* (March 19): A12.

Apel, Karl-Otto. 1980. *Towards a Transformation of Philosophy*, trans. G. Adey and D. Frisby. London: Routledge and Kegan Paul.

Arendt, Hannah. 1970. "Civil Disobedience." *New Yorker* (September 12): 7–105.

Aufderheide, P. 1988. "What Makes Public TV Public?" *Progressive* (January): 35–38.

Azmeh, Aziz al-. 1988. "The Middle East and Islam: A Ventriloqual Terrorism." *Third World Affairs*: 23–34.

Baier, Annette. 1991. "A Naturalist View of Persons." Presidential address. *Proceedings and Addresses of the American Philosophical Association* 65(3) (November): 5–17.

Bar On, Bat-Ami. 2005. "Just (Decent? Mere?) War." In *Feminist Interventions in Ethics and Politics*, ed. Barbara S. Andrew, Jean Keller, and Lisa H. Schwartzman, 201–211. Lanham, Md.: Rowman and Littlefield.

————, Claudia Card, Drucilla Cornell, Alison Jaggar, Maria Pia Lara, Constance Mui, Julian S. Murphy, Sherene Razack, Sara Ruddick, and Iris Marion Young. 2003. "Forum on the War on Terrorism." *Hypatia* 18(1): 157–231.

Barber, Benjamin R. 2002. "Beyond Jihad vs. McWorld." *Nation* (January 21): 11–18.

Barber, Benjamin R. 2003. "The War of All against All." In *War after September 11,* ed. Verna V. Gehring. Lanham, Md.: Rowman and Littlefield.

———. 2004. *Fear's Empire: War, Terrorism, and Democracy.* New York: Norton.

———. 2007. *Consumed: How Markets Corrupt Children, Infantilize Adults, and Swallow Citizens Whole.* New York: Norton.

Bayefsky, Anne F., ed. 2000. *Self-determination in International Law: Quebec and Lessons Learned.* The Hague: Kluwer.

Benhabib, Seyla. 1992. *Situating the Self.* New York: Routledge.

Benjamin, Daniel, and Gabriel Weimann. 2004. "What the Terrorists Have in Mind." *New York Times* (October 27), op-ed page.

Bennet, James. 2003. "Israeli Voters Hand Sharon Strong Victory." *New York Times* (January 29), A1, A8.

———. 2003. "Israelis Storm a Gaza Camp; 11 Palestinians Are Killed." *New York Times* (March 7), A10.

———. 2004. "On the West Bank, a Hint of Resistance without Blood." *New York Times* (February 29), Week in Review, 1, 4.

Betz, Joseph. 1977. "Violence, Garver's Definition, and a Deweyan Correction." *Ethics* 87(4) (July): 339–351.

Bica, Camillo. 1995. "Just War and Practical Pacifism." PhD diss., City University of New York.

Blake, Michael. 2003. "Reciprocity, Stability, and Intervention: The Ethics of Disequilibrium." In *Ethics and Foreign Intervention,* ed. Deen K. Chatterjee and Don E. Scheid, 53–71. New York: Cambridge University Press.

Blumenfeld, Laura. 2002. *Revenge: A Story of Hope.* New York: Simon and Schuster.

Bogart, Leo. 1995. *Commercial Culture: The Media System and the Public Interest.* New York: Oxford University Press.

Bok, Hilary. 1996. "Acting without Choosing." *Noûs* 30(2): 174–196.

Bondurant, Joan. 1965. *Conquest of Violence.* Berkeley: University of California Press.

Borman, William. 1986. *Gandhi and Non-violence.* Albany: State University of New York Press.

Boynton, Graham. 1997. *Last Days in Cloud Cuckooland: Dispatches from White South Africa.* New York: Random House.

Brooke, James. 1996. "Lawsuit Tests Lethal Power of Words." *New York Times* (February 14), A12.

Brooks, David. 2004. "Al Qaeda's Wish List." *New York Times* (March 16): op-ed page.

Brown, Chris. 2003. "Selective Humanitarianism: In Defense of Inconsistency." In *Ethics and Foreign Intervention,* ed. Deen K. Chatterjee and Don E. Scheid, 31–50. New York: Cambridge University Press.

Brown, David. 2006. "Study Claims Iraq's 'Excess' Death Toll Has Reached 655,000." *Washington Post* (October 11), A12.

Buchanan, Allen. 2002. "Political Legitimacy and Democracy." *Ethics* 112(4) (July): 689–719.

———. 2003. "Reforming the International Law of Humanitarian Intervention." In *Humanitarian Intervention: Ethical, Legal, and Political Dilemmas,* ed. J. L. Holzgrefe and Robert O. Keohane, 130–173. New York: Cambridge University Press.

Buchstein, H. 1997. "Bytes That Bite: The Internet and Deliberative Democracy." *Constellations* 4(2) (October): 248–263.

Bukovansky, Mlada. 2002. *Legitimacy and Power Politics: The American and French Revolutions in International Political Culture.* Princeton, N.J.: Princeton University Press.

Bull, Hedley, ed. 1984. *Intervention in World Politics.* New York: Oxford University Press.

Butterfield, Fox. 1988. "8-Year Gulf War: Victims but No Victors." *New York Times* (July 25), A1.

Byers, Michael, and Simon Chesterman. 2003. "Changing the Rules about Rules? Unilateral Humanitarian Intervention and the Future of International Law." In *Humanitarian Intervention: Ethical, Legal, and Political Dilemmas,* ed. J. L. Holzgrefe and Robert O. Keohane, 177–203. New York: Cambridge University Press.

Card, Claudia. 1996. "Rape as a Weapon of War." *Hypatia* 11(4) (Fall): 5–18.

———. 2003. "Questions Regarding a War on Terrorism." *Hypatia* 18(1) (Winter): 264–269.

Carmichael, Stokely, and Charles V. Hamilton. 1967. *Black Power: The Politics of Liberation in America.* New York: Random House.

Carter, Bill. 1996. "A New Report Becomes a Weapon in Debate on Censoring TV Violence." *New York Times* (February 7), C11, C16.

Carvajal, Doreen. 1996. "Triumph of the Bottom Line." *New York Times* (April 1).

Chatterjee, Deen K., and Don E. Scheid. 2003. *Ethics and Foreign Intervention.* New York: Cambridge University Press.

Chesterman, Simon. 2001. *Just War or Just Peace? Humanitarian Intervention and International Law.* New York: Oxford University Press.

Chomsky, Noam. 2003. *Power and Terror.* New York: Seven Stories Press.

———. 2003. "Terror and Just Response." In *Terrorism and International Justice,* ed. James P. Sterba, 69–87. New York: Oxford University Press.

———. 2006. *Failed States: The Abuse of Power and the Assault on Democracy.* New York: Metropolitan Books.

Coady, C. A. J. 1985. "The Morality of Terrorism." *Philosophy* 60 (January): 47–69.

———. 2004. "Terrorism and Innocence." *Journal of Ethics* 8: 37–58.

Cobban, Helena. 2007. *Amnesty after Atrocity: Healing Nations after Genocide and War.* Boulder, Colo.: Paradigm.

Cohan, John Alan. 2001. "Formulation of a State's Response to Terrorism and State-sponsored Terrorism." *Pace International Law Review* 14 (Spring): 77–119.

Cohen, Philip J. 1996. "The Complicity of Serbian Intellectuals in Genocide in the 1990s." In *This Time We Knew: Western Responses to Genocide in Bosnia*, ed. Thomas Cushman and Stjepan G. Mestrovic, 39–64. New York: New York University Press.

Cohen, Roger. 2000. "Who Really Brought Down Milosevic?" *New York Times Magazine* (November 26): 43–148.

Committee on Foreign Affairs, comp. 1983. *Human Rights Documents*. Washington, D.C.: Government Printing Office.

Cooper, David E. 1991. "Collective Responsibility." In *Collective Responsibility*, ed. Larry May and Stacey Hoffman, 35–46. Lanham, Md.: Rowman and Littlefield.

Copp, David. 1998. "International Law and Morality in the Theory of Secession." *Journal of Ethics* 2(3): 219–245.

Copps, Michael J. 2007. "The Price of Free Airwaves." *New York Times* (June 2), op-ed page.

Corlett, J. Angelo. 2001. "Collective Moral Responsibility." In *Essays in Honor of Burleigh Wilkins: From History to Justice*, ed. Aleksandar Jokić. New York: Peter Lang.

———. 2003. *Terrorism: A Philosophical Analysis.* Boston: Kluwer.

Coser, Lewis A. 1966. "Some Social Functions of Violence." *Annals of the American Academy of Political and Social Science* 364 (March): 8–18.

Crawford, Neta C. 1993. "Decolonization as an International Norm: The Evolution of Practices, Arguments, and Beliefs." In *Emerging Norms of Justified Intervention: A Collection of Essays from a Project of the American Academy of Arts and Sciences*, ed. Laura W. Reed and Carl Kaysen, 37–61. Cambridge, Mass.: Committee on International Security Studies, American Academy of Arts and Sciences.

Crenshaw, Martha. 2007. "The Debate over 'New' vs. 'Old' Terrorism." Paper presented at the annual meeting of the American Political Science Association. Chicago, September 1.

Cushman, Thomas, and Stjepan G. Mestrovic, ed. 1996. *This Time We Knew: Western Responses to Genocide in Bosnia.* New York: New York University Press.

Dahbour, Omar. 2003. *Illusion of the Peoples: A Critique of National Self-determination.* Lanham, Md.: Lexington Books.

———. 2005. "The Response to Terrorism." *Philosophical Forum* 36(1): 87–95.

Damrosch, Lori Fisler. 1993. "Changing Conceptions of Intervention in International Law." In *Emerging Norms of Justified Intervention: A Collection of Essays from a Project of the American Academy of Arts and Sciences*, ed. Laura W. Reed and Carl Kaysen, 91–110. Cambridge, Mass.: Committee on International Security Studies, American Academy of Arts and Sciences.

Dancy, Jonathan. 1983. "Ethical Particularism and Morally Relevant Properties." *Mind* 92: 530–547.

Daniels, Norman. 1979. "Wide Reflective Equilibrium and Theory Acceptance in Ethics." *Journal of Philosophy* 76 (May): 256–282.

Danner, Mark. 1998. "Operation Storm." *New York Review of Books* (October 22): 73–79.

Dillon, Sam. 2003. "Reflections on War, Peace, and How to Live Vitally and Act Globally." *New York Times* (June 1), A28.

Donnerstein, E., R. Slaby, and L. Eron. 1994. "The Mass Media and Youth Aggression." In *Reason to Hope: A Psychosocial Perspective on Violence and Youth,* ed. L. Eron, J. Gentry, and P. Schlegel, 219–250. Washington, D.C.: American Psychological Association.

Dowd, Maureen. 2006. "Who's Hormonal? Hillary or Dick?" *New York Times* (February 8), op-ed page.

Dugard, John. 1976. "International Terrorism and the Just War." *Stanford Journal of International Studies* 12: 21–37.

Dumas, Lloyd J. 2003. "Is Development an Effective Way to Fight Terrorism?" In *War after September 11,* ed. Verna V. Gehring, 65–74. Lanham, Md.: Rowman and Littlefield.

Dworkin, Ronald, Thomas Nagel, Robert Nozick, John Rawls, Thomas Scanlon, and Judith Jarvis Thomson. 1997. "Assisted Suicide: The Philosophers' Brief." *New York Review* (March 27): 41–47.

Engels, Frederick. 1958. *The Condition of the Working Class in England,* trans. and ed. W. O. Henderson and W. H. Chaloner. New York: Oxford University Press.

Erlanger, Steven. 2000. "Did U.S. Bombs Help or Hinder?" *New York Times* (December 25), 16.

———. 2004. "Palestinian Politicians Try to Head Off a Power Struggle." *New York Times* (November 6), 3.

Evangelista, Matthew. 2002. *The Chechen Wars: Will Russia Go the Way of the Soviet Union?* Washington, D.C.: Brookings Institution Press.

Falk, Richard A. 1988. *Revolutionaries and Functionaries: The Dual Face of Terrorism.* New York: Dutton.

———. 2002. "Ending the Death Dance." *Nation* (April 29): 11–13.

———. 2003. "What Future for the UN Charter System of War Prevention?" *American Journal of International Law* 97 (July): 590–598.

———. 2004. *The Declining World Order: America's Imperial Geopolitics.* New York: Routledge.

Fallows, James. 1996. *Breaking the News: How the Media Undermine American Democracy.* New York: Pantheon.

Fanon, Franz. 1968. *The Wretched of the Earth.* Preface by Jean-Paul Sartre. New York: Grove Press.

Farer, Tom J. 2003. "Humanitarian Intervention before and after 9/11: Legality and Legitimacy." In *Humanitarian Intervention: Ethical, Legal, and Political Dilemmas,* ed. J. L. Holzgrefe and Robert O. Keohane, 53–89. New York: Cambridge University Press.

Farer, Tom J. 2003. "The Prospect for International Law and Order in the Wake of Iraq." *American Journal of International Law* 97 (July): 621–628.

Feinberg, Joel. 1970. *Doing and Deserving: Essays in the Theory of Responsibility.* Princeton, N.J.: Princeton University Press.

Felice, William F. 1996. "The Case for Collective Human Rights: The Reality of Group Suffering." *Ethics and International Affairs* 10: 47–61.

Franck, Thomas M. 2003. "Interpretation and Change in the Law of Humanitarian Intervention." In *Humanitarian Intervention: Ethical, Legal, and Political Dilemmas,* ed. J. L. Holzgrefe and Robert O. Keohane, 204–231. New York: Cambridge University Press.

———. 2003. "What Happens Now? The United Nations after Iraq." *American Journal of International Law* 97: 607–620.

———. 2006. "The Power of Legitimacy and the Legitimacy of Power: International Law in an Age of Power Disequilibrium." *American Journal of International Law* 100: 88–106.

Frankel, Max. 1995. "The Murder Broadcasting System." *New York Times Magazine* (December 17), 46–47.

Frankena, William K. 1973. *Ethics,* 2d ed. Englewood Cliffs, N.J.: Prentice-Hall.

French, Peter A. 1984. *Collective and Corporate Responsibility.* New York: Columbia University Press.

French, Shannon E. 2003. "Murderers, Not Warriors: The Moral Distinction between Terrorists and Legitimate Fighters in Asymmetric Conflicts." In *Terrorism and International Justice,* ed. James P. Sterba, 31–46. New York: Oxford University Press.

French, Stanley G. 1994. *Interpersonal Violence, Health, and Gender Politics,* 2d ed. Dubuque, Iowa: Brown and Benchmark.

Friedman, Thomas L. 1996. "At God's Elbow." *New York Times* (April 10), op-ed page.

———. 2004. "Footprints in the Sand." *New York Times* (November 7), op-ed page.

———. 2006. "No More Mr. Tough Guy." *New York Times* (February 8), op-ed page.

Fullinwider, Robert K. 1988. "Understanding Terrorism." In *Problems of International Justice: Philosophical Essays,* ed. Steven Luper-Foy, 248–259. Boulder, Colo.: Westview Press.

———. 2003. "Terrorism, Innocence, and War." In *War after September 11,* ed. Verna V. Gehring, 21–33. Lanham, Md.: Rowman and Littlefield.

Gayle, Addison, Jr. 1970. *The Black Situation.* New York: Horizon.

Gettleman, Jeffrey. 2004. "For Some Iraqis in Harm's Way, $5,000 from U.S. and 'I'm Sorry.'" *New York Times* (March 17), 1, 9.

———. 2007. "The Perfect Weapon for the Meanest Wars." *New York Times* (April 29), Week in Review, 1, 4.

Gewirth, Alan. 1978. *Reason and Morality*. Chicago: University of Chicago Press.

———. 1982. *Human Rights: Essays on Justification and Applications*. Chicago: University of Chicago Press.

———. 1996. *The Community of Rights*. Chicago: University of Chicago Press.

Gilbert, Margaret. 1989. *On Social Facts*. Princeton, N.J.: Princeton University Press.

Goodin, Robert E. 2006. *What's Wrong with Terrorism?* Malden, Mass.: Polity.

Gordon, Neve, and George A. López. 2000. "Terrorism in the Arab-Israeli Conflict." In *Ethics in International Affairs,* ed. Andrew Valls, 99–113. Lanham, Md.: Rowman and Littlefield.

Gould, Carol C. 2004. *Globalizing Democracy and Human Rights*. New York: Cambridge University Press.

Grimes, W. 2005. "Does Life Imitate Violent Films?" *New York Times* (November 30), BI, B3.

Habermas, Jürgen. 1995. *Moral Consciousness and Communicative Action,* trans. Christian Lenhardt and Shierry W. Nicholsen. Cambridge, Mass.: MIT Press.

Halwani, Raja. 2006. "Terrorism: Definition, Justification, and Applications," Review essay. *Social Theory and Practice* 32(2) (April): 289–310.

Hamid, Mohsin. 2007. *The Reluctant Fundamentalist*. New York: Harcourt.

Hammond, John L. 2005. "The Bush Doctrine, Preventive War, and International Law." *Philosophical Forum* 36 (Spring): 97–111.

Harden, Blaine. 1999. "The Milosevic Generation." *New York Times Magazine* (August 29): 30.

Hare, R. M. 1979. "On Terrorism." *Journal of Value Inquiry* 13(4) (Winter): 241–249.

Harman, Gilbert. 1977. *The Nature of Morality*. New York: Oxford University Press.

Harris, Adrienne, and Ynestra King, eds. 1989. *Rocking the Ship of State*. Boulder, Colo.: Westview Press.

Harris, John. 1974. "The Marxist Conception of Violence." *Philosophy and Public Affairs* 3(4) (Winter): 192–220.

Hedges, Chris. 2003. *What Every Person Should Know about War*. New York: Free Press.

Held, Virginia. 1970. "Can a Random Collection of Individuals Be Morally Responsible?" *Journal of Philosophy* 68(14): 471–482.

———. 1970. *The Public Interest and Individual Interests*. New York: Basic Books.

———. 1972. "Coercion and Coercive Offers." In *Coercion.* Nomos, vol. 14, ed. J. Roland Pennock and John W. Chapman, 49–62. Chicago: Aldine Atherton.

———. 1975. "Justification: Legal and Political." *Ethics* 86(1) (October): 1–16.

———, ed. 1980. *Property, Profits, and Economic Justice*. Belmont, Calif.: Wadsworth.

———. 1982. "The Political 'Testing' of Moral Theories." *Midwest Studies in Philosophy* 7: 343–363.

Held, Virginia. 1984. *Rights and Goods: Justifying Social Action.* New York: Free Press; Chicago: University of Chicago Press, 1989.

————. 1984. "Violence, Terrorism, and Moral Inquiry." *Monist* 67(4) (October): 605–626.

————. 1986. "Corporations, Persons, and Responsibility." In *Shame, Responsibility, and the Corporation,* ed. Hugh Curtler, 159–181. New York: Haven.

————. 1988. "Access, Enablement, and the First Amendment." In *Philosophical Dimensions of the Constitution,* ed. Diana T. Meyers and Ken Kipnis, 158–179. Boulder, Colo.: Westview Press.

————. 1993. *Feminist Morality: Transforming Culture, Society, and Politics.* Chicago: University of Chicago Press.

————. 1998. "Media Culture and Democracy" (in German). In *Demokratischer Experimentalismus,* ed. Hauke Brunkhorst, 67–91. Frankfurt am Main: Suhrkamp.

————. 1999. "The Normative Import of Action." In *Gewirth: Critical Essays on Action, Rationality, and Community,* ed. Michael Boylan, 13–27. Lanham, Md.: Rowman and Littlefield.

————. 2002. "Moral Subjects: The Natural and the Normative." Presidential address. *Proceedings and Addresses of the American Philosophical Association* 76(2) (November): 7–24.

————. 2006. *The Ethics of Care: Personal, Political, and Global.* New York: Oxford University Press.

————. 2008. "Gender Identity and the Ethics of Care." In *Global Feminist Ethics,* ed. Rebecca Whisnant and Peggy DesAutels. Lanham, Md.: Rowman and Littlefield.

————, Sidney Morgenbesser, and Thomas Nagel, eds. 1974. *Philosophy, Morality, and International Affairs.* New York: Oxford University Press.

Helsinki Watch. 1992. *War Crimes in Bosnia-Hercegovina.* New York: Human Rights Watch.

Higgins, Rosalyn. 1984. "Intervention and International Law." In *Intervention in World Politics,* ed. Hedley Bull, 29–44. New York: Oxford University Press.

Hoffman, Bruce. 1998. *Inside Terrorism.* New York: Columbia University Press.

Hoffmann, Stanley. 1993. "Commentary on 'Beware the Slippery Slope.'" In *Emerging Norms of Justified Intervention: A Collection of Essays from a Project of the American Academy of Arts and Sciences,* ed. Laura W. Reed and Carl Kaysen, 88–89. Cambridge, Mass.: Committee on International Security Studies, American Academy of Arts and Sciences.

————. 1996. *The Ethics and Politics of Humanitarian Intervention.* Notre Dame, Ind.: University of Notre Dame Press.

Holmes, Robert L. 1987. "Terrorism and Other Forms of Violence: A Moral Perspective." Paper presented at the meeting of Concerned Philosophers for Peace, Dayton, Ohio, October 16.

Holmes, Steven A. 1993. "Choice for National Security Advisor Has a Long-awaited Chance to Lead." *New York Times* (January 3): 16.

Holzgrefe, J. L., and Robert O. Keohane, eds. 2003. *Humanitarian Intervention: Ethical, Legal, and Political Dilemmas.* New York: Cambridge University Press.

Honderich, Ted. 2002. *After the Terror.* Edinburgh: Edinburgh University Press.

———. 2006. *Right and Wrong, and Palestine, 9/11, Iraq, 7/7.* New York: Seven Stories Press.

Hundt, R., and Newton Minow. 1995. "A Cure for Kids' TV." *New York Times* (October 19), op-ed page.

Independent International Commission on Kosovo. 2000. *The Kosovo Report: Conflict, International Response, Lessons Learned.* New York: Oxford University Press.

International Commission on Intervention and State Sovereignty. 2001. *The Responsibility to Protect.* Ottawa, Ontario, Canada: International Development Research Center.

Jaggar, Alison M. 2005. "What Is Terrorism, Why Is It Wrong, and Could It Ever Be Morally Permissible?" *Journal of Social Philosophy* 36 (Summer): 202–217.

Jenkins, Brian. 1983. "Research in Terrorism: Areas of Consensus, Areas of Ignorance." In *Terrorism: Interdisciplinary Perspectives,* ed. B. Eichelman, D. Soskis, and W. Reid. Washington, D.C.: American Psychiatric Association.

Johnson, James Turner. 1981. *Just War Tradition and the Restraint of War.* Princeton, N.J.: Princeton University Press.

Kahn, Paul W. 2003. "The Paradox of Riskless Warfare." In *War after September 11,* ed. Verna V. Gehring, 37–49. Lanham, Md.: Rowman and Littlefield.

Kamm, F. M. 2004. "Failures of Just War Theory: Terror, Harm, and Justice." *Ethics* 114(4) (July): 650–692.

Kant, Immanuel. 1965. *The Metaphysical Elements of Justice,* trans. John Ladd. New York: Liberal Arts.

Kapitan, Tomis. 2003. "The Terrorism of 'Terrorism.'" In *Terrorism and International Justice,* ed. James P. Sterba, 47–66. New York: Oxford University Press.

Kaplan, Morton. 1957. *System and Process in International Politics.* New York: Wiley.

Keane, John. 2003. *Global Civil Society?* New York: Cambridge University Press.

Kellner, Douglas. 1990. *Television and the Crisis of Democracy.* Boulder, Colo.: Westview Press.

———. 1995. *Media Culture: Cultural Studies, Identity, and Politics between the Modern and the Postmodern.* New York: Routledge.

Kifner, John. 1999. "Inquiry Estimates Serb Drive Killed 10,000 in Kosovo." *New York Times* (July 18), 1, 6.

Kimmelman, Michael. 1996. "Does It Really Matter Who Sponsors a Show?" *New York Times* (May 19), H33.

Koh, Harold Hongju. 1997–1998. "Commentary: Is International Law Really State Law?" *Harvard Law Review* 111: 1824–1861.

Kovach, Karen. 2001. "Ethnic Groups and Moral Agency." Typescript.

———. 2001. "Who We Are and What We Do: Ethnicity and Moral Agency." PhD diss., City University of New York.

Kristof, Nicholas D. 2002. "A Toast to Moral Clarity." *New York Times* (December 27), op-ed page.

Kymlicka, Will, ed. 1995. *The Rights of Minority Cultures*. New York: Oxford University Press.

Lackey, Douglas. 1989. *The Ethics of War and Peace*. Englewood Cliffs, N.J.: Prentice-Hall.

Ladd, John. 1970. "Morality and the Ideal of Rationality in Formal Organizations." *Monist* 54(4) (October): 488–516.

LaFraniere, Sharon. 2004. "A South African Journey: Bomb Maker to Police Chief." *New York Times* (February 28), A4.

Langewiesche, William. 2007. *The Atomic Bazaar*. New York: Farrar, Straus, and Giroux.

Lango, John. 2005. "Preventive Wars, Just War Principles, and the United Nations." *Journal of Ethics* 9(1–2): 247–268.

Laqueur, Walter. 1979. "The Anatomy of Terrorism." In *Ten Years of Terrorism: Collected Views,* ed. Jennifer Shaw, E. F. Guerin, and A. E. Younger, 7–21. Royal United Services for Defense Studies. London: Crane, Russak.

———. 1987. *The Age of Terrorism,* rev. and exp. Boston: Little, Brown.

———. 2003. *No End to War: Terrorism in the Twenty-first Century*. New York: Continuum.

Lee, Steven, ed. 2006. *Intervention, Terrorism, and Torture: Challenges to Just War Theory in the 21st Century*. New York: Springer.

Leiser, Burton. 1979. *Liberty, Justice, and Morality*. New York: Macmillan.

Lewis, H. D. "Collective Responsibility." In *Collective Responsibility,* ed. Larry May and Stacey Hoffman, 17–33. Lanham, Md.: Rowman and Littlefield.

Lieven, Anatol, and John Hulsman. 2006. *Ethical Realism: A Vision for America's Role in the World*. New York: Pantheon.

Liptak, Adam. "Suspected Leader of Attacks on 9/11 Is Said to Confess." *New York Times* (March 15, 2007), 1, 23.

Luttwak, Edward N. 2004. "Rewarding Terror in Spain." *New York Times* (March 16), op-ed page.

Margalit, Avishai. 1996. *The Decent Society*. Cambridge, Mass.: Harvard University Press.

———. 2002. *The Ethics of Memory*. Cambridge, Mass.: Harvard University Press.

Marighela, Carlos. 1971. "Handbook of Urban Guerrilla Warfare." In Carlos Marighela, *For the Liberation of Brazil,* trans. John Butt and Rosemary Sheed. Harmondsworth, UK: Penguin.

Martin, Rex. 2005. "Just Wars and Humanitarian Interventions." *Journal of Social Philosophy* 36(4) (Winter): 439–456.

May, Larry. 1992. *Sharing Responsibility*. Chicago: University of Chicago Press.

————. 1998. *The Morality of Groups: Collective Responsibility, Group-based Harm, and Corporate Rights*. Notre Dame, Ind.: University of Notre Dame Press.

————, and Stacey Hoffman, eds. 1991. *Collective Responsibility*. Lanham, Md.: Rowman and Littlefield.

McAllister, Pam. 1982. "Introduction." In *Reweaving the Web of Life: Feminism and Nonviolence,* ed. Pam McAllister. Philadelphia: New Society.

McGary, Howard. 1986. "Morality and Collective Liability." *Journal of Value Inquiry* 20: 157–165.

McMahan, Jeff. 2004. "The Ethics of Killing in War." *Ethics* 114(4) (July): 693–733.

McPherson, Lionel K. 2007. "Is Terrorism Distinctively Wrong?" *Ethics* 117 (April): 524–546.

Means, Angelia. 2003. "The Idea of the Enemy." Typescript, 4. Quoted with permission.

Mellema, Gregory. 1988. *Individuals, Groups, and Shared Moral Responsibility*. New York: Peter Lang.

Merkl, P. H., ed. 1986. *Political Violence and Terror*. Berkeley: University of California Press.

Meyers, Diana T. 1995. "Rights in Collision: A Non-punitive, Compensatory Remedy for Abusive Speech." *Law and Philosophy* 14: 203–243.

Miller, Richard W. 2003. "Respectable Oppressors, Hypocritical Liberators: Morality, Intervention, and Reality." In *Ethics and Foreign Intervention,* ed. Deen K. Chatterjee and Don E. Scheid, 215–250. New York: Cambridge University Press.

Mitchell, Alison. 2002. "Israel Winning Broad Support from U.S. Right." *New York Times* (April 21), A1, 13.

Morgan, Robin. 2001. *The Demon Lover: The Roots of Terrorism*. New York: Washington Square Press.

Mueller, John. 2006. *Overblown: How Politicians and the Terrorism Industry Inflate National Security Threats and Why We Believe Them*. New York: Free Press.

Mufflin, L. 1996. "F.C.C. Urged to Strengthen Children's TV." *New York Times* (April 2).

Myre, Greg. 2004. "A Palestinian Asks, Who Made My Son a Suicide Bomber?" *New York Times* (January 14), A3.

Nasr, Kamel B. 1997. *Arab and Israeli Terrorism*. Jefferson, N.C.: McFarland.

Nathanson, Stephen. 2006. "Terrorism, Supreme Emergency, and Noncombatant Immunity." *Iyyun: The Jerusalem Philosophical Quarterly* 55 (January): 3–25.

Netanyahu, Benjamin, ed. 1986. *Terrorism: How the West Can Win*. New York: Farrar, Straus, and Giroux.

New York Times (AP). 1988. "200,000 Youths Said to Be in World's Armies." *New York Times* (August 7), A8.

Nickel, James W. 1987. *Making Sense of Human Rights*. Berkeley: University of California Press.

——. 1995. "What's Wrong with Ethnic Cleansing?" *Journal of Social Philosophy* 25(1) (Spring): 5–15.

Niebuhr, Gustav. 1996. "Number of Religious Broadcasters Continues to Grow." *New York Times* (February 12), D9.

Ouzegane, Amar. 1962. *Le meilleir combat*. Paris: Julliard.

Packer, George. 2006. "Comment: Unrealistic." *New Yorker* (November 27): 83, 86.

Pape, Robert A. 2003. "The Strategic Logic of Suicide Terrorism." *American Political Science Review* 97(3) (August 2003): 343–361.

——. 2005. *Dying to Win: The Strategic Logic of Suicide Terrorism*. New York: Random House.

Pavković, Aleksandar. 1997. *The Fragmentation of Yugoslavia: Nationalism in a Multinational State*. New York: St. Martin's Press.

Pellet, Alain. 2000. "Legal Opinion on Certain Questions of International Law Raised by the Reference." In *Self-determination in International Law: Quebec and Lessons Learned*, ed. Anne Bayefsky, 85–123. Boston: Kluwer.

Philipose, Liz. 1996. "The Laws of War and Women's Human Rights." *Hypatia* 11(4) (Fall): 46–62.

Philosopher's Index, The. 2006. Vols. 1–40. Bowling Green, Ohio: Philosophy Documentation Center.

Picard, Robert G. 1991. "News Coverage as the Contagion of Terrorism." In *Media Coverage of Terrorism: Methods of Diffusion*, ed. A. O. Alali and K. K. Eke, 49–62. Newbury Park, Calif.: Sage.

Plous, Scott L., and Philip G. Zimbardo. 2004. "How Social Science Can Reduce Terrorism." *Chronicle of Higher Education* (September 10), B9.

Pogge, Thomas W. 1997. "Group Rights and Ethnicity." In *Ethnicity and Group Rights*, ed. Ian Shapiro and Will Kymlicka, 187–221. New York: New York University Press.

Pollitt, Katha. 1996. "For Whom the Ball Rolls." *Nation* (April 15): 9.

Poole, Ross. 1999. *Nation and Identity*. New York: Routledge.

Primoratz, Igor. 1997. "The Morality of Terrorism." *Journal of Applied Philosophy* 14: 221–233.

——. 2004. "State Terrorism and Counter-terrorism." In *Terrorism: The Philosophical Issues*, ed. Igor Primoratz, 113–127. New York: Palgrave/Macmillan.

——, ed. 2004. *Terrorism: The Philosophical Issues*. New York: Palgrave/Macmillan.

——. 2004. "What Is Terrorism?" In *Terrorism: The Philosophical Issues*, ed. Igor Primoratz, 15–27. New York: Palgrave/Macmillan.

QQ: Report from the Institute for Philosophy and Public Policy. 1987. University of Maryland 7(4) (Fall).

Quinton, Anthony. 1975–1976. "Social Objects." *Proceedings of the Aristotelian Society* 76: 1–27.

Raika, Juha. 1997. "On Disassociating Oneself from Collective Responsibility." *Social Theory and Practice* 23(1) (Spring): 93–108.

Rawls, John. 1971. *A Theory of Justice.* Cambridge, Mass.: Harvard University Press.

———. 1999. *The Law of Peoples.* Cambridge, Mass.: Harvard University Press.

Reed, Laura W., and Carl Kaysen, eds. 1993. *Emerging Norms of Justified Intervention: A Collection of Essays from a Project of the American Academy of Arts and Sciences.* Cambridge, Mass.: Committee on International Security Studies, American Academy of Arts and Sciences.

Reisman, W. Michael. 2004. "Why Regime Change Is (Almost Always) a Bad Idea." *American Journal of International Law* 98: 516–525.

Resnik, Judith. 2006. "Law's Migration: American Exceptionalism, Silent Dialogues, and Federalism's Multiple Ports of Entry." *Yale Law Journal* 115: 1564–1670.

Rich, Frank. 1996. "The V-chip G-string." *New York Times* (February 28), op-ed page.

Richardson, Louise. 2006. *What Terrorists Want: Understanding the Enemy, Containing the Threat.* New York: Random House.

Rieff, David. 1995. *Slaughterhouse: Bosnia and the Failure of the West.* New York: Simon and Schuster.

Robinson, Fiona. 1999. *Globalizing Care: Ethics, Feminist Theory, and International Affairs.* Boulder, Colo.: Westview Press.

Rodin, David. 2004. "Terrorism without Intention." *Ethics* 114(4) (July): 752–771.

Rosenthal, Elisabeth. 2004. "Study Puts Iraqi Deaths of Civilians at 100,000." *New York Times* (October 29): A8.

Ruddick, Sara. 1989. *Maternal Thinking: Toward a Politics of Peace.* Boston: Beacon.

Sachs, Susan. 2004. "Poll Finds Hostility Hardening toward U.S. Policies." *New York Times* (March 17), A3.

Satris, S., ed. 1994. *Taking Sides: Clashing Views on Controversial Moral Issues,* 4th ed. Guilford, Conn.: Dushkin Group.

Schell, Jonathan. 2006. "Too Late for Empire." *Nation* (August 14–21): 13–14, 17–18, 20, 22, 24.

Schelling, Thomas C. 1991. "What Purposes Can 'International Terrorism' Serve?" In *Violence, Terrorism, and Justice,* ed. R. G. Frey and C. Morris, 18–32. New York: Cambridge University Press.

Schlesinger, P., G. Murdock, and P. Elliott. 1983. *Televising "Terrorism": Political Violence and Popular Culture.* London: Comeda.

Schmemann, Serge. 2002. "Not Quite an Arab-Israeli War, but a Long Descent into Hatred." *New York Times* (April 22), A1, A11.

Schreiber, Jan. 1978. *The Ultimate Weapon: Terrorists and World Order*. New York: Morrow.

Sciolino, Elaine. 2002. "Don't Weaken Arafat, Saudi Warns Bush." *New York Times* (January 27), A8.

————. 2003. "Self-appointed Israeli and Palestinian Negotiators Offer a Plan for Middle East Peace." *New York Times* (December 2), 8.

Seppa, N. 1996. "News Shows Exaggerate Prevalence of Violence." *American Psychological Association Monitor* (4) (April): 9.

Shaffer, Jerome A., ed. 1971. *Violence*. New York: McKay.

Slaughter, Anne-Marie. 2004. *A New World Order*. Princeton N.J.: Princeton University Press.

Smith, Craig S., and Don Van Natta Jr. 2004. "Officials Fear Iraq's Lure for Muslims in Europe." *New York Times* (October 23), A9.

Smith, Patricia. 1998. *Liberalism and Affirmative Obligation*. New York: Oxford University Press.

Sorel, Georges. 1961. *Reflections on Violence*, trans. T. E. Hulme and J. Roth. London: Collier-Macmillan.

Soyinka, Wole. 1998. "Hearts of Darkness." *New York Times Book Review* (October 4), 11.

Stahn, Carsten. 2003. "Enforcement of the Collective Will after Iraq." *American Journal of International Law* 97 (October): 804–823.

Sterba, James P. 2003. "Introduction." In *Terrorism and International Justice*, ed. James P. Sterba, 1–27. New York: Oxford University Press.

Stern, J. 1996. "Preventing Portable Nukes." *New York Times* (April 10), op-ed page.

Stromseth, Jane. 2003. "Rethinking Humanitarian Intervention: Gradations in Sovereignty." In *Humanitarian Intervention: Ethical, Legal, and Political Dilemmas*, ed. J. L. Holzgrefe and Robert O. Keohane, 232–272. New York: Cambridge University Press.

Sullivan, Stacy. 1999. "Milosevic Is One Problem; National Denial Is the Other." *New York Times* (August 21), op-ed page.

Taft, Philip, and Philip Ross. 1969. "American Labor Violence: Its Causes, Character, and Outcome." In *Violence in America: Historical and Comparative Perspectives*, ed. Hugh Davis Graham and Ted Robert Gurr, 281–395. New York: Bantam.

Taft, William H., IV. 2006. "A View from the Top: American Perspectives on International Law after the Cold War." *Yale Journal of International Law* 31: 503–512.

Teichman, Jenny. 1986. *Pacifism and the Just War: A Study in Applied Philosophy*. New York: Blackwell.

Tilly, Charles. 1969. "Collective Violence in European Perspective." In *Violence in America: Historical and Comparative Perspectives*, ed. Hugh Davis Graham and Ted Robert Gurr, 4–45. New York: Bantam.

Trainor, Bernard. 1988. "Turning Point: Failed Attack on Basra." *New York Times* (July 19), A9.

Traub, James. 2006. "Old World Order." *New York Times Book Review* (November 12), 50.

Tronto, Joan C. 2008. "Is Peace Keeping Care Work?" In *Global Feminist Ethics,* ed. Rebecca Whisnant and Peggy DesAutels. Lanham, Md.: Rowman and Littlefield.

Urquhart, Brian. 2006. "The Outlaw World." *New York Review* (May 11): 25–28.

U.S. Department of State. 1985. "Patterns of Global Terrorism: 1984." Washington, D.C.: Author.

———. 1998. "Patterns of Global Terrorism: 1997." Department of State Publication 10321. Washington, D.C.: Author.

———. 2001. "Patterns of Global Terrorism, 1983–2001." Office of the Coordinator for Counterterrorism (April).

Valls, Andrew. 2000. "Can Terrorism Be Justified?" In *Ethics in International Affairs,* ed. Andrew Valls, 65–79. Lanham, Md.: Rowman and Littlefield.

———, ed. 2000. *Ethics in International Affairs,* ed. Andrew Valls. Lanham, Md.: Rowman and Littlefield.

Wade, Francis C. 1971. "On Violence." *Journal of Philosophy* 68(12) (June 17): 369–377.

Waldman, Amy. 2003. "Masters of Suicide Bombing: Tamil Guerrillas of Sri Lanka." *New York Times* (January 14), A1, 6.

Waldron, Jeremy. 2004. "Terrorism and the Uses of Terror." *Journal of Ethics* 8(1) (March): 5–35.

Walker, Margaret Urban. 2006. *Moral Repair: Reconstructing Moral Relations after Wrongdoing.* New York: Cambridge University Press.

Walzer, Michael. 1988. "Terrorism: A Critique of Excuses." In *Problems of International Justice: Philosophical Essays,* ed. Steven Luper-Foy, 237–247. Boulder, Colo.: Westview Press.

———. 2000. *Just and Unjust Wars,* 3d ed. New York: Basic Books.

———. 2002. "Five Questions about Terrorism." *Dissent* 49(1) (Winter).

Wardlaw, Grant. 1982. *Political Terrorism.* New York: Cambridge University Press.

———. 1989. *Political Terrorism: Theory, Tactics, and Counter-measures,* 2d ed. New York: Cambridge University Press.

Weber, Max. 1958. *From Max Weber: Essays in Sociology,* trans. and ed. H. H. Gerth and C. Wright Mills. New York: Oxford University Press.

Wellman, Carl. 1979. "On Terrorism Itself." *Journal of Value Inquiry* 13(4) (Winter): 250–258.

Wellmer, Albrecht. "Terrorism and the Critique of Society." In *Observations on "The Spiritual Situation of the Age": Contemporary German Perspectives,* ed. Jürgen Habermas, trans. A. Buchwalter, 283–307. Cambridge, Mass.: MIT Press.

Wilkins, Burleigh. 1987. "Terrorism and Consequentialism." *Journal of Value Inquiry* 21: 141–151.

———. 1992. *Terrorism and Collective Responsibility*. London: Routledge.

Wilkinson, Paul. 1974. *Political Terrorism*. London: Macmillan.

———. 1982. "The Laws of War and Terrorism." In *The Morality of Terrorism: Religious and Secular Justifications,* ed. David C. Rapoport and Yonah Alexander, 308–324. New York: Pergamon.

———. 1986. *Terrorism and the Liberal State*. New York: New York University Press.

Wilson, Heather A. 1988. *International Law and the Use of Force by National Liberation Movements*. New York: Oxford University Press.

Wines, Michael. 2002. "Mourners at Israeli Boys' Funeral Lament a Conflict with No Bounds." *New York Times* (December 2), A9.

Winston, Morton E. 2003. "The Right of Rescue." In *Policymaking and Democracy: A Multinational Anthology,* ed. Stuart S. Nagel, 1–14. Lanham, Md.: Lexington Books.

Woodward, Susan L. 1995. *Balkan Tragedy: Chaos and Dissolution after the Cold War*. Washington, D.C.: Brookings Institution Press.

Young, Iris Marion. 2003. "Violence against Power: Critical Thoughts on Military Intervention." In *Ethics and Foreign Intervention,* ed. Deen K. Chatterjee and Don E. Scheid, 251–273. New York: Cambridge University Press.

———. 2006. "Responsibility and Global Justice: A Social Connection Model." *Social Philosophy and Policy* 23(1): 102–130.

Young, Robert. 1977. "Revolutionary Terrorism, Crime, and Morality." *Social Theory and Practice* 4(3) (Fall): 287–302.

———. 2004. "Political Terrorism as a Weapon of the Politically Powerless." In *Terrorism: The Philosophical Issues,* ed. Igor Primoratz, 55–64. New York: Palgrave/Macmillan.

Zimmerman, Michael J. 1985. "Sharing Responsibility." *American Philosophical Quarterly* 22 (April): 115–122.

Zimmerman, Warren. 1996. *Origins of a Catastrophe*. New York: Random House.

INDEX